Majority Voting as a Catalyst of Populism

Peter Emerson

Majority Voting as a Catalyst of Populism

Preferential Decision-making for an Inclusive Democracy

 Springer

Peter Emerson
The de Borda Institute
Belfast, UK

ISBN 978-3-030-20218-7   ISBN 978-3-030-20219-4   (eBook)
https://doi.org/10.1007/978-3-030-20219-4

This Springer imprint is published by the registered company Springer Nature Switzerland AG.
The registered company address is: Gewerbestrasse 11, 6330 Cham, Switzerland

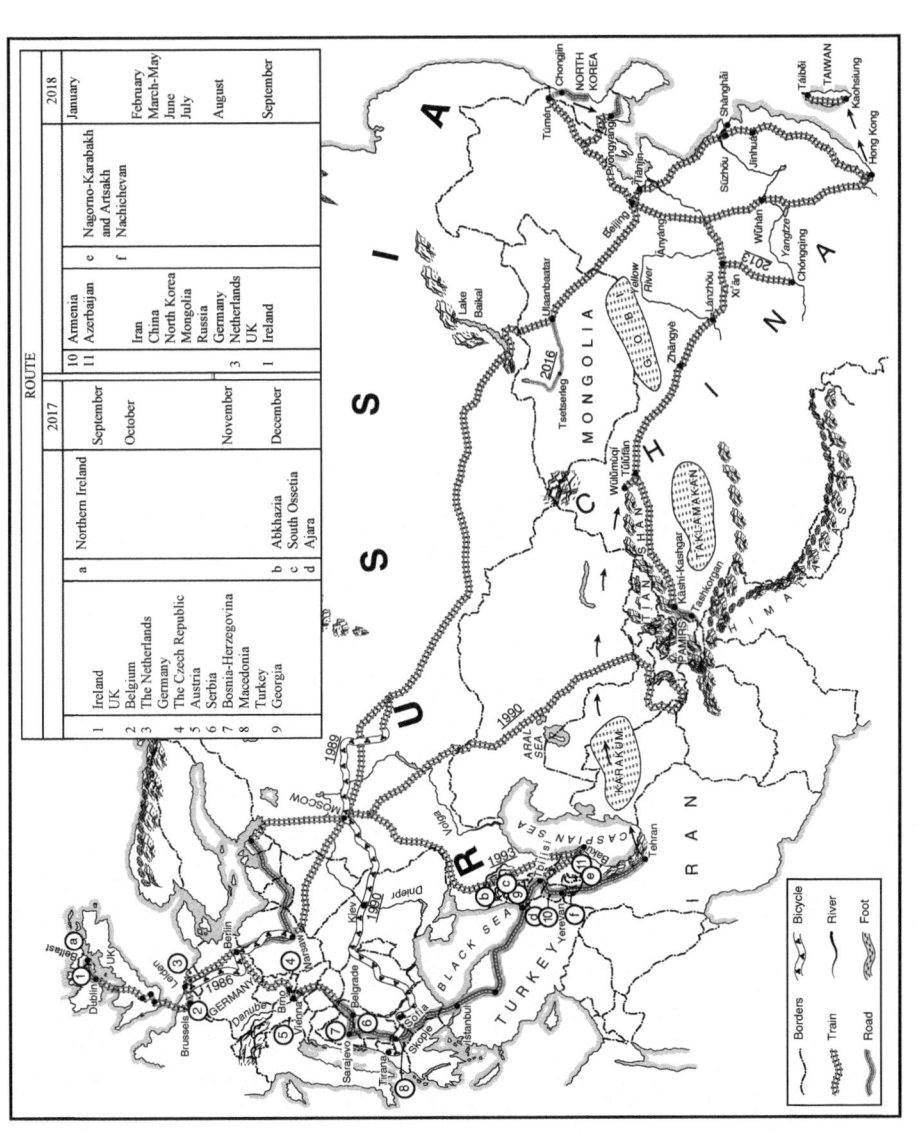

In praise of the complexity of the human mind, in admiration of the diversity of homo sapiens, *and in a plea for a more suitably sophisticated polity.*

Foreword

Theory versus experiment; they can differ. Can the East meet the West?

I am a theoretical mathematician where one of my goals is to discover and explain what can go wrong with voting and decision systems. Peter Emerson is an activist who, dealing with groups facing actual conflict, has experimented with decision approaches to determine which ones can successfully culminate in a group consensus. We have common objectives, but we explore them from very different perspectives.

These viewpoints should unify. Poorly paraphrasing Robert Frost's line "my goal in life is to unite my avocation with my vocation, As two eyes make one in sight,"[1] an objective of voting theory, of social choice, must be to combine theory, practice and experience into a common advisory theme. Society must be informed about what voting methods and what group decision approaches can cause significant harm, and which ones are most reliable.

As manifested by this book, Peter is doing his part. Armed with his foldable bike, curiosity, an interest in people, a thirst for adventure and a missionary zeal to pass on what he has learned, Emerson travels the world to then describe the realities of what he has discovered: Namely, poor choices of voting rules, of decision methods, can cause disastrous outcomes across the world! Be warned: Emerson attacks decision methods so commonly embraced that some readers might equate them with "motherhood": This includes majority voting and the plurality vote. Emerson's arguments derive primarily from observations, experiments and experience, so let me offer some supporting theoretical comments. (Most of what follows is based on results in my book Saari 2018.)

Consider a hypothetical setting where you are to cook a gourmet dinner for an important party. To your dismay, while standing in the kitchen on the morning of the event, you discover that the complicated recipe is missing *many crucial pages!* Moving ahead with the limited, available information could result in a perfectly fine dinner, but a more likely scenario, reflecting the lost information, is a disaster.

---

[1] From Frost's poem "Two Tramps in Mud Time".

The same "lost critical information" phenomenon plagues most voting rules by dismissing information identifying who the voters truly want! To indicate how this can be so, suppose 30 surgeons are ranked based on their performance over several criteria; the ranking method only counts how many times a surgeon placed first in a category. Thus, surgeons in 2nd, or 3rd, ..., or 30th place in an event are treated the same—as losers. This means that a surgeon who finishes 1st in only one category, and 30th in all others, will be ranked over a surgeon who is second ranked over all criteria. I doubt whether the reader, when facing surgery, would accept this ranking approach; I would not!

But, in fact, we do embrace this method! Consider, for instance, the plurality vote (or first-past-the-post). Only a voter's first place choice is registered; the plurality vote lumps the voter's remaining candidates—from second to last place—into the same "loser" category. Sound familiar? The plurality vote is that discredited process to rank the surgeons (where criteria become the voters). Knowing what causes difficulties makes it easy to create disturbing examples. Suppose, for instance, that 27 voters have Bob ranked first, David second, Ann third and Carol fourth, as given in the first line of the array

Number	Firstplace	Secondplace	Thirdplace	Fourthplace
27	Bob	David	Ann	Carol
26	David	Carol	Ann	Bob
24	Ann	David	Carol	Bob
23	Carol	David	Ann	Bob

David is highly popular: Each voter ranks him either first or second. But David loses! Bob is the plurality winner even though 73% of the voters rank him at the bottom! It is arguable that this distortion explains why Buchanan (here, Bob) beat a very popular candidate Dole (here, David) in the 1996 New Hampshire US Presidential primary election.

The message: As with the gourmet dinner story, it is possible to have sensible plurality outcomes, but, realistically, expect problems. In fact, the form of this lost information, which equates the second to the bottom ranked candidates, makes it easy to prove that in closely contested multi-candidate elections, it is reasonably likely for a favoured candidate *not* to be the plurality winner, or for a disliked candidate to win! One must wonder: does this partly explain Trump's election?

Emerson goes on to discredit a variety of rules such as approval voting and plurality run-offs. To provide intuition, suppose that bricks from a particular foundry are, well, crumbly and defective. Should they be the building blocks for an edifice? While a fortuitous arrangement may compensate for their deficiencies, it is realistic to anticipate disaster. To connect this story to Emerson's complaints, the plurality vote is the building block for his disparaged methods, so expect them to inherit difficulties. For instance, sites for Olympic Games are selected with a plurality run-off: After ranking the sites with a plurality vote, the last place alternative is dropped. This process, of re-ranking remaining sites with a plurality vote and then dropping the loser, continues until a single site emerges. Now, in the competition for the 2016 Summer Games, the strong favorite, Chicago, was dropped at the very first stage! Blame the voting rule! Plausible explanations follow from the surgeon story. Suppose, for instance, that the four candidates are A, B, C, D, where

Number	Firstplace	Secondplace	Thirdplace	Fourthplace
4	C	A	B	D
5	A	C	B	D
6	B	C	D	A
7	D	C	B	A

everyone has C either first or second ranked; C is a favored choice. But because the crumbly plurality vote treats the second to the last ranked candidates the same (losers), C is bottom ranked at the first stage to become the first site to be eliminated. (D wins.)

Moving to other procedures, Emerson makes it clear in this book that he worries about the dangers associated with the pairwise majority vote. His arguments about the need to avoid "either-or" settings of selecting between two extremes (remedy: include intermediate options) are solid, so let's consider other problems. As Emerson points out (in the book), opponents to his views may invoke something called Arrow's impossibility theorem. This widely cited result is often described as "with three or more alternatives, no voting rule is fair." Presumably, opponents could try to minimize the impact of Emerson's complaints about the majority rule by arguing "Arrow proved all rules have faults." This application of Arrow's result is wrong.

To explain with another story, suppose a careful study seeks to discover the traits authors need in order to compose sweet romantic novels; for undisclosed reasons, it is required that the authors must sport a full beard. Suppose the discovered result is that all writers have serious faults. Wait! Such a sweeping assertion does not follow! The study only exposes the limitations of heavily bearded men; nothing applies to the excluded beardless authors. A similar restriction is embedded in Arrow's Theorem; rather than considering only bearded voting methods, one of Arrow's conditions (with the unwieldily name of "independence of irrelevant alternatives") admits *only paired comparison voting rules*, such as the majority vote! All other rules are excluded, so they are not subject to Arrow's conclusion. (This effect is made explicit in my paper Saari 2019.) Thus, a correct interpretation of Arrow's result is that "with three or more alternatives, no rule based on paired comparisons, such as the majority vote, is fair." This is precisely what Emerson asserts!

It is known what causes all possible majority vote problems (e.g. see Saari 2018, 2019), and Emerson captures the source with examples. To expand upon Emerson's thoughts, suppose in majority votes, Ann beats Barbara and Barbara beats Connie. Will Ann beat Connie? We can't know; similar to the gourmet dinner, the culprit is "lost information". When the majority vote considers, say, how Ann fares with Barbara, it ignores all information about Connie. Stated otherwise, the {Ann-Barbara} information is shuttled off to a silo that is totally separated from the {Ann-Connie} silo. To explain this phenomenon to students in her voting theory courses, Katri Sieberg (University of Tampere, Finland) imaginatively captures the complexity of trying to combine the separated majority vote parts into a general meaning with the exercise: "How many sentences can be constructed from the components 'that man,' 'his wife,' 'an apple,' 'smiled at,' 'and,' 'took a bite out of'? What does this tell us about voting mechanisms?" She is correct; just as wild sentences (such as "His wife smiled at an apple and took a bite out of that man") can be constructed from these isolated pieces, majority votes over pairs are missing the connecting information required to make sense of the voting outcomes.

It is possible to go on and on and on—particularly to discuss Emerson's (and my) favorite topic, the Borda count. But this is an appropriate place to recommend that the reader turn to Emerson's story. Rather than the traditional "Enjoy", my hope is that you will reflect upon Emerson's message and, yes, become upset when you discover how widely used but defective voting rules can cause serious damage. Hopefully you will fight for reform!

Irvine, CA   Donald G. Saari

References

Saari, D. G. (2018). *Mathematics motivated by the social and behavioral sciences.* Pittsburg, PA: SIAM.

Saari, D. G. (2019). Arrow, and unexpected consequences of his theorem. *Public Choice, 179*(1), 133–144.

Preface

Whoever truly creates is alone.

(Czeslaw Milosz 1985: 217).

P.1   The Journey

With my laptop, a fold-up bicycle and a toothbrush, I left Belfast in September 2017 to go overland to China. The purpose was simple: to change the world. In particular, I wanted to re-examine, firstly, the ubiquitous nature of the belief in majority voting and the practice of binary majority rule, and secondly, in each country visited, to compare the consequences of this mindset which have often been problematic if not indeed, as in Belfast, disastrous. And why September? Because I had been invited to give a TEDx talk[2] in Vienna on all of this majoritarianism: *So What is Democracy, Anyway?*

As everyone knows, majority rule as practised was a huge factor in the Northern Ireland, NI, conflict. But this ancient form of decision-making was also a part of the reason why the Brexit vote in Britain was so inept; the political establishment said the referendum identified "the will of the people" but, as all the arguments since have shown, it did not do that at all.

Continental Europe has also had some difficulties: as my journey unfolded, the Netherlands spent over 200 days trying to sort out a majority coalition government; Germany, which has seen the rise of the extreme right, also took quite a long time; the Czechs gave up and opted for a minority administration; and the elections in Austria were soon to lead to an extremist party being in government, again.

---

[2]https://www.youtube.com/watch?v=UiCJhSuLdok

From there I went to the Balkans and the Caucasus, two regions of the world which I have frequently visited since my first trips to both in 1990—I speak some Serbo-Croat and quite a lot of Russian. Yet again, binary majority rule was a provocation if not a cause of much of the violence, and the similarities with NI are numerous. Next, after a brief sojourn in Iran, I spent five months in China—where my linguistic talents are rather more limited—travelling from Xīnjiāng via Běijīng to Hong Kong and Taiwan, pausing on occasion to deliver a university lecture on the way; after all, majoritarianism, which has been so harmful in Europe, was even worse in Máo Zédōng's China. I then managed to get into North Korea at the very time that Kim Jong-un was in Singapore meeting Donald Trump.

The journey home started with a couple of weeks in Mongolia prior to spending a fortnight with old friends in Moscow. Here too, majoritarianism has been. . . well, the Russian translation of this word was "bolshevism".

P.2   The Book

The book is divided into two parts. The first three chapters look at the theory of voting under the headings of decision-making, elections and governance. Chapter 1 evaluates majority voting, confirms that it can be hopelessly inaccurate and suggests that a more democratic decision-making procedure could be a preferential points system. In many situations, a change in the voting methodology can mean a different result, so the decision as to how decisions are to be taken can be fundamental to the workings of any democracy. . . yet for some reason, the topic is seldom discussed.

Next, Chap. 2 is devoted to electoral systems which, in stark contrast to decision-making systems, are often debated. But, as with binary voting in decision-making, plurality voting—or first-past-the-post, FPTP—can also be very unfair. Other systems, especially those which are proportional, can be more accurate, and for the election of both parliaments and presidents, the best of all systems, it is argued, are both preferential and proportional. A more inclusive electoral system can lead to a more accurate representation of what can be, on topics of controversy, the public's wide spectrum of opinions. If the chosen few adopt the better decision-making of Chap. 1, the public can then enjoy a more wholesome polity and politics can indeed be "the art of compromise".

The third topic is governance, and if majority voting is not very good, then maybe the ubiquitous form of simple majority rule which is based thereon is also inadequate. Time and time again, however, politicians of all hues appear to believe in a binary form of majority rule which relies on decisions being taken by majority vote, hence the almost universal practice of power-dividing, and only when it all goes horribly and violently wrong is resort made to its opposite, all-party power-sharing. Perhaps, however, the latter should be the norm, and if the conclusions of the first two chapters were implemented, such an inclusive structure could indeed be common practice. Just one problem would remain: the question of how a parliament could (not *select* but rather) *elect* an all-party coalition—choosing who was to serve and in which portfolio. But the answer now follows: a description of the appropriate voting system, the matrix vote.

From time to time in Part I, I refer to examples from the various countries visited, but I also mention a few other jurisdictions as and when necessary.

Part II embarks on the journey itself, to see what happens in practice, and, from West to East and back again, political establishments everywhere are all very majoritarian. Chapter 4 looks at three parts of my home archipelago: Northern Ireland, the Republic of Ireland and Britain, and in all three, majority rule and/or majority voting have been at least problematic. Chapter 5 is devoted to the countries I visited on the continent of Europe: two of the Low Countries, Germany, the Czech Republic, Austria, three republics in the Balkans, Turkey, two nations in the Caucasus and, a little out of sequence, Russia. The belief in, or at least the practice of majority voting, is common to all. . . and is still common to all, despite what has often been terrible consequences—bloody revolution and in many instances, war. The journey concludes in Chap. 6 in Asia, and the largest section is devoted to China, a country which has suffered more than any other from binary politics.

I should point out that some of the sections in these three chapters of Part II are very small; only in regard to those lands which I know a little more do I go into rather more detail, but always on the theme of voting and governance.

Finally, Chap. 7 questions the rise of populism and suggests it is exacerbated by the use of simplistic and inaccurate voting procedures. One possible source of redress could lie with the more widespread use of electronic voting in our debating chambers, so as to make preferential decision-making more practicable; another might be facilitated by more precise definitions of democratic structures in Charters on Human Rights and so forth.

There are also five annexes of a more mathematical bent. Annex A analyses a five-option voters' profile, so as to discuss the Condorcet rule. Annex B is a detailed description of partial voting, which it is felt is or should be a vital element of any Borda analysis; indeed, it is a matter of huge regret that the original Borda count, BC, has long since been corrupted into a methodology which, in any bitterly divided electorate, is little better than a plurality vote—so hence the term, the modified Borda count, MBC. The rules for the conduct of an MBC debate are summarised in Annex C and experience suggests that, if these rules are followed closely, many of those voting will indeed submit full votes. Next comes an analysis of range voting, so as to show that it is not as easy as some of its advocates suggest. And finally, Annex E explains what can happen in a real-life matrix vote—it can become quite complex but, as long as the user understands what's going on, our computers can deal with all the calculations.

Now the journey certainly had its wonderful moments—as when, for example, I visited the Buddhist caves in Turpan or Tŭlŭfān, as the oasis is called. There were also the usual bureaucratic problems, as when Azerbaijan refused to issue a visa because, on an earlier journey to the Caucasus, I had been to the enclave of Nagorno-

Karabakh. These fascinating or infuriating details are all to be found on my blog: https://debordaabroad.wordpress.com/2017/09/07/de-borda-abroad/.

The book, however, is devoted only to the subject of voting: to the theory, its history and then the use or abuse to which certain voting procedures have been and are still used both in decision-making and in elections, with an occasional word on some of my efforts to try and persuade societies to adopt a non-majoritarian polity. The hope is that, one day, soon, our democratic institutions will adopt voting procedures which are suitable for the sophisticated creatures we all are. Simple majoritarian structures have caused too much suffering; consensus voting could allow democracy to flourish. If the so-called democracies do not adapt, the Chinese model could well come to dominate the world... though it too might adapt.

P.3   Notes on the Text

As and when appropriate, if and when I can, foreign words are spelt with their accents; or, when the words are Russian, in transliteration; or, when they are Iranian, Korean or Mongolian, as best I may; or, if they are Chinese, with their tones. The sound "ba", for example, can be pronounced as bā 八, bá 拔, bǎ 把 or bà 爸, with tones "high", "going up", "going down-up" or "going down", and each, depending on the character, signifying a different meaning: the four shown here mean "eight", "to pull", "to hold" or "father", respectively. So a word like "beijing", if it is spelt without its tones, could be Běijīng 北京, the northern capital; or bèijǐng 背景, background context; or bēijìng 杯静, a cup of stillness, or, in theory, any one of a number of things depending on which of four 'bei's is combined with which of four 'jing's. What a fascinating language. Accordingly, on first use, this text gives the word in pinyin, or rather pīnyīn, 拼音, as well as in (the simplified characters of) Mandarin Chinese, and it will sometimes repeat the pīnyīn version of those words with which the Western reader may not be too familiar.

Persons in the text are not so complicated, but in China and Korea, the surname comes first: so just as Donald Trump is referred to as just "Trump" in any second or subsequent mention, the Chinese President, Xi Jinping, or rather Xí Jìnpíng, 习近平, may later be referred to as Mr. Xí or Xí or even just Xi. Meanwhile, any anonymous persons—the voter, the chair, Mr./Ms. Speaker and so on—will have alternate genders, and rather cumbersome expressions like he/she and his/her will be used sparingly.

When talking of voting theory, options and candidates are lettered from the beginning of the alphabet, A, B, C and so on, in bold, italicised capitals; individuals, again of alternate gender, are i, j, k, etc., usually italicised in small letters; parties are named **W**, **X**, **Y** and **Z**, in bold capitals; and candidates in parties are named **W**i, **W**j, **W**k, **X**i, **X**j, etc.

Now there are many social choice scientists who base their writings on elections rather than on decision-making, not least because while it might be difficult to imagine options which are totally opposite to each other, candidates being human are always mutually exclusive, even when their policies are fairly similar: John Major and Tony Blair in the UK, for example, or Leon Trotsky and Josef Stalin in the USSR. Even with the biggest questions of all, however—"Are you communist or capitalist?" for instance—there is a huge amount of overlap. This tends to mean that many theorists fall into the same trap as journalists and politicians: they question electoral systems at length, but decision-making not very much. In the pages which follow, therefore, if I am writing about decision-making and quoting some established writer who is talking about elections but in a way which might just as easily apply to decision-making, I might well insert "[option]" in place of "candidate". In a similar style, I will sometimes bring a citation up to date by replacing the word "men" by "[people]".

Some books spell out any numbers less than ten, and only larger figures are written in the appropriate digits. This book complies with this custom unless, for the sake of clarity, an infringement is considered appropriate. In like manner, rather than repeating the words "percent" *ad nauseam*, I sometimes use just the symbol, %. Preferences are referred to as ordinals—1st, 2nd, etc.—while other phenomena are described in full—first, second and so on. Furthermore, when talking about calculations in the matrix vote, any quantity of points written in the main matrix is called a "sum"; the addition of two or more "sums" is described as a "score"; and the summation of two or more "scores" is referred to as a "total".

Finally, may I add two very important notes. In this book, the term "power-sharing" refers to all the (main) parties in the said parliament, from right across the political spectrum. Secondly, many people refer to majority rule as if it is a given, a human right even. But it's not that easy. Accordingly, I refer to binary or simple majority rule, if and when it is based on binary voting; the phrase pluralist majority rule or pluralism implies a more sophisticated form of rule based on multi-option and, at best, preferential decision-making.

Belfast   Peter Emerson
30 November 2018

Reference

Milosz, C. (1985). *The captive mind.* London: Penguin Books.

Acknowledgements

Great journeys do not merely consist in passing over vast
spaces, but owe their greatness far more to the human
[exchange] and knowledge of fellow-men which they involve.
Mildred Cable in the Gobi Desert in the 1930s (Cable 1984: 172).

I was so lucky. It is sometimes quite difficult to get visas and things, yet everything seemed to fall into place, as if by forces unknown. So there are lots of people to thank, which I will do in geographical sequence.

The first ones are in Belfast. Jess and Will were my fantastic tenants, for without someone(s) to look after Rhubarb Cottage—my home and garden—I would not have been able to go anywhere. By way of a sort of contract, just a verbal agreement really, we agreed to give each other three months notice: and we both gave it to each other, nine months after my departure. Perfect. What's more, not only did they do a magnificent job, they actually paid me for it; the world is upside down—the landlord should pay the tenant for looking after the house, not the other way round.

Also in Belfast are Wes and Helen, he of the New Ireland Group and the occasional whiskey, she definitely of neither but of much good food. They gave me great support throughout the journey; it started with a farewell dinner, a little glass or two and a farewell card stuffed full of cash!

My first stop was Dublin to see Audrey and David—she is my Irish sister who often gave me relief from the trials and tribulations of the Troubles in Belfast. Indeed, on one occasion, a friend of hers, a member of an endangered species called the Irish Lords, wanted someone to look after his quaint country cottage in Co Monaghan, for free! And she thought I'd be much safer, out of Northern Ireland. Well, it certainly looked like a good idea but, after much careful thought, I decided my own bijou residence was fine, so I declined. One week later, a headline in the *Irish Times* read, "Cottage, Co. Monaghan, blown up".

Also in Dublin are Phil and Sien. He and I go back a long way; indeed, we first met in 1982, at the first convention of the Irish Green Party, at which I gave a seminar on consensus politics. Since then, we have worked assiduously together, first in the Greens and later in that which we set up together—indeed, it was his idea—the de Borda Institute.

By ferry I went to England and Oxford, where Blanka from Slovakia gave me a walk with the dog in the evening, and cause for its hair in the morning. Next came Carol and Paddy, old pals from Co. Down whose kids decided they would not want to raise their own children in such a backwater as Northern Ireland, so the grand-parents have now moved to be near them all in another backwater called England.

My cousin Tim is an academic in the university in Cambridge. Oh God, he voted for Brexit! So did my British brother—what crazy relatives I have. We nevertheless shared a pleasant bottle of wine and, as on other visits, I was thus able to go to the library in the Joseph Needham Institute, of which there's more in Chap. 6.

In London I met Rosemary for the first time—she has often put articles of mine onto her openDemocracy website—and then I spent the night with Celia and family who, like myself, are Anglo-Irish; the only time they feel at home, they say, is when they're on the ferry.

The Eurostar on the morrow took me to Brussels where I made full use of my little fold-up bicycle to call on some of the many NGOs which abound in that city and where I stayed with Jeremy, another colleague from the first gathering of the Irish Greens. He entertained me to some nice Belgian beers—if nothing else (and sadly, it was/is not always nothing else), celibate clergy make damned good alcohol.

Whenever I'm in Leiden, I stay with Leo and Marjanne, who had fallen in love with Belfast and each other, in that order, back in the 1970s. At the time, we were all involved in a summer play-scheme, giving kids the opportunity to meet their peers of the other religion, and our best achievement was taking a bunch of 10–12 year-olds on a seven-day cycling holiday to Donegal: three adults with all the tents, eight kids with only themselves. Since then, of course, we have both moved on, by bicycle of course, and Leo arranged for me to give a talk in Leiden on consensus voting.

Berlin was my third bicycle-friendly city where Angela and Helmut—not quite a couple—have often entertained me on my journeys eastwards—the first was in 1986, when I cycled across the Iron Curtain on my way to Moscow. In more recent years, Angela has hosted four workshops on consensus voting in the old campus of Potsdam University, which has now been demolished. . . but not, they tell me, as a direct result of my seminars.

In Brno, and again, not for the first time, I stayed with Věra and her family, plus another bigger dog. We first met in Konjic in Bosnia, just after the 1992–1995 war, and as a result, jointly edited *Party Politics in the Western Balkans*. A second consequence was my second lecture in Brno University, in March 2017. . .

. . .a short train journey from Vienna. So while I was there, I invited TEDx to invite me to give a TEDx talk at their event scheduled for October. They said "yes" and so did I. The event was only fantastic. Albert, my mentor, gave me some wonderful advice, while all of the TEDx folk were so friendly before and after the talk—my first in front of an audience of a thousand, so even for one as old as I, it was all a bit nerve-racking. A drink was definitely needed after all that, and Patricia with her two girls were my fine hosts.

At the same meeting in Konjic where I first met Věra, I also met Valery, now my host in Belgrade as on many other visits to Sarajevo. A true "Balkanista" who knows all the ropes and has many good contacts, especially in Bosnia, she also has a fine political brain and, unusually for an American, a sound fluency of a second language—Serbo-Croat. My most emotional contact in the Balkans was with Nada, in Sarajevo. We had met during the war, in December 1992. Three of us journalists had arrived on a UN flight from Zagreb, only on the condition that, once in Sarajevo, we were on our own, with no guarantee of a flight back or any other sort of help. None of us had been here before but one of our company, Nicola—a Croat pretending to be a Czech; linguistically that was quite easy but politically very brave—had a friend in Prague whose parents lived in the Bosnian capital, the Blažević family. We managed to get a lift to the Holiday Inn where—no food, no lighting, no heat—it was $70 a night. OK, we said, we'll share. $70 a head, they replied. So we said bye-bye. Nicola had the address of his friends' parents; we had no idea where it was, but off we went to find it. The streets were cold, dark and empty. Candles flickered behind polythene "windows" and the sound of gunfire was pretty well constant. One hour later, we knocked on the Blažević's door. An elderly man opened. . . "Yes?" "Excuse me, but I am a friend of your son and. . ." "Oh come in come in," he cried emotionally, having heard nothing from him since the beginning of the war. Three elderly couples shared this flat by day—the Blaževićs had a wood-burning stove, their neighbours had nothing; the hosts were Catholic, this couple was Orthodox, the other two were Moslem. As always.

They looked after me for a week, sharing what little there was of the UN rations. I had brought some foods with me—cheeses, coffee and other non-perishables—which I offered to share. They refused. But I wasn't going to take them back to Zagreb, so I hid them under the mattress. On my return to Sarajevo some ten weeks later—I spent three months in the Balkans on my bicycle—I again, unannounced, knocked on their door. Of course, I had not been able to give them advance notice. In war, there is nothing. So I just knocked. Nada opened. . . paused. . . smiled. . . and exclaimed, *"O, ti moi!"* Like a mother to her own son. And all this we recalled together—Martin had died a few years ago, so she now had a student lodger—before one final hug. On the morrow, she was going to Prague to see her Martina; how lucky it was that I had chosen that day!

My first visit to Skopje in 1990, before any of the Yugoslav wars, was brief, so now I stayed with new contacts: Kurt was another kind American, while Slavica and Jane were local (if he, a Greek, may be so described)—all great hosts.

Istanbul was just for a day or two, and then it was an overnight bus to Tbilisi, where Nato looked after me for a whole month! She had met me on the platform on my first visit in 1990 and took me to see some friends whose little ten-year-old was learning French. They were all at least bilingual: Georgian of course, so that was one script; Russian was obligatory, so that was another; and for many children in the city, a West European language was also desirable, and that meant a third script! So we were all chatting in French—mine is not very good—until the dog walked in. *"Idi syuda,"* said mum. Why do you talk to your dog in Russian, I asked. "It's a dog's language." Which was a bit naughty.

By my next visit three years later, a newly independent Georgia had two ethnic wars and one civil war. That's careless, Oscar Wilde might have said. But again, Nato looked after me. On my return in 1999, she introduced me to Dito, who was another host. On this occasion, though, while I struggled with visas for both Iran and China, Nato had to look after me for longer than she had wanted or I had anticipated: her patience was fantastic, her coffee the best, her cat lovingly terrible! The visa problem was eventually solved by getting a (Georgian) residency permit to stay to thus get a (Chinese) permit to go—another bit of luck.

Yerevan was my second hotel, but Tatev and Anush, two mediators whom Angela had trained, both pretty young and pretty-pretty, were my companions on several evenings. Then it was another overnight bus to Tehran where my hosts were only fantastic. I had been a little apprehensive of visiting Iran which, after all, does not always get a good press, but my reception, all from persons whom I had not met beforehand, was just amazing—Hossein and Nino, Mehran and Puneh, Ali and Nazein. These Iranians are a highly sophisticated and very hospitable people— would that the world's politicians were on a similar plane.

And then China. Xīnjiāng was also new for me. Press reports talk of repression and ethnic conflict, but I was "arrested" only once when two police officers decided I was far too old to cycle all the way to the railway station, so they bunged the bike in the back and gave me a lift. Admittedly, some Chinese officials were very official, but the multi-ethnic locals—Huí and Hàn (both Chinese Chinese), Kazakh, Tajik and Uighur (all Chinese but not quite)—were all lovely, especially those Tajik and Uighur families who invited me into their homes. In Gānsù province, where I stayed on an organic farm with Bóbǔ and his grandparents for over a week, the hospitality was all Hàn, as it was from Xiǎojūn in Ānyáng, Yīng in Běijīng, Tián and Dōngkè in Sūzhōu and Péi and Bó in Jīnhuá, while the two main professional contacts were Professors Yáng Lóng, 杨龙, in Nánkāi University in Tiānjīn and Wàng Lěi, 王磊, in the Beijing International Studies University. I lectured in both institutions, yet again, on decision-making, not so much as it could be in Congress, more on the theory of it all for the village council or the local collective.

Other academics in Hong Kong and Taiwan—especially Professors Benny Tai, Dài Yàotíng 戴耀廷 and Dáchí Liào, 廖達琪 who also hosted de Borda presentations—were equally receptive, and while I was there, Alf and Candy in Kaohsiung, Gāoxióng, were great hosts, both on this occasion and on my 2014 lecture tour.

Then came North Korea and my luck was still in for not only did I manage to get in; more importantly, I also managed to get out. This was the first country on this tour where for some reason I was not asked to give a talk on power-sharing. So I asked the questions instead, and some of the guides—a necessary requirement of any visit to the DPRK—were pleasant though not always informative. That said, like their counterparts everywhere, some of the younger ones first wanted to travel!

Mongolia was a lovely contrast, and I was so lucky to have been sent here for six weeks as an election observer in June 2017. Granted, not every vegetarian would enjoy the traditional meal with which granny and granddad entertained their son,

Batsaikhan Dorj, possibly the future Governor in *Arkhangai Aimag*, one of the most beautiful provinces in Mongolia. We were out on the steppe, in his parents' *ger* or *yurt*, and in she came with a great bowl of... well, there were no vegetables and no meat, but it was all from a sheep: the stomach, intestines, blood and that sort of stuff. Umm... well, it tasted better than it looked.

My last port of call was Moscow, where my colleagues of over 30 years, Irina and Sergei, were there to meet me after my five days of lovely slow travel on the Trans-Siberian Railway. In 1986 when my Russian was terrible and so was my bicycle, Sergei, a keen cyclist, had shown me what was then Moscow's one and only bicycle shop—(a dusty old shed full of old cranks and illegal booze, "*samogon*", literally, home-made fire)—and then at home, another keen cyclist, his wife Irina. On many evenings, everything was in Russian, so if I wanted a piece of bread, I had to use the appropriate Russian words; it was that or no bread. On my return to Moscow in 1988, I needed a translator for an article on cycling, and only then did she tell me she was fluent in English and French. Thus, she became my co-author, and as Chap. 5 relates, we wrote articles on consensus politics for some of Russia's leading publications: *Moscow News* and *Novy Mir* (New World).

* * *

To all of the above, I owe my thanks, not only for much good food and, even in Iran, the occasional drink, but also for much encouragement from either one or the other and sometimes both of my hosts (not every male/female partner is equally enthusiastic about talking politics). In addition, the keener of the two has often helped me with my research material. Thanks too are due to my publishers in Heidelberg—Judith Kripp and Johannes Glaeser—for some excellent editorial advice. By sheer good fortune, my nephew lives in this charming old city—ah, at last, a relative who voted "remain". I must also thank Rob, my proofreader, who doubtless can now repeat the advice which was first said by my teacher at school: your English is lousy my boy, stick to the maths; Abdus Salam Mazumder, my cartographer for his great help in map-reading; Audrey, Phil and Wes again, who supported me on this sojourn and sometimes worried about my welfare, as when I was out of e-mail contact first in Iran due to the sanctions and then initially in China because of the firewall; my friends in the de Borda Institute who continue to help in whatever ways they can, and all for no financial reward; and finally those few select colleagues in political science who have given me such encouragement over the years, not least Don Saari in California, the gentle professor who has long since encouraged me to keep going, talking and cycling, and who now writes such a positive foreword.

Reference

Cable, M. (1984). *The Gobi Desert*. London: Virago.

Contents

List of Abbreviations

AEI	American Enterprise Institute
AfD	Alternative for Germany, *Alternative für Deutschland* (Germany)
ANO	Action of Dissatisfied Citizens, *Akce nespokojených občanů* (Czech)
AKP	Justice and Development Party, *Adalet ve Kalkınma Partisi* (Turkey)
ApV	Approval Voting
AV	Alternative vote (= IRV, PV or STV)
BBC	British Broadcasting Corporation
BC	Borda count
BCE	Before the Common Era
BDI	Albanian Democratic Union for Integration, *Bashkimi Demokratik për Integrim* (Macedonia)
BiH	Bosnia and Herzegovina
CC	Consensus coefficient
CCP	Chinese Communist Party, *Zhōngguó Gòngchǎndǎng* 中国共产党 (China)
CDU	Christian Democratic Union, *Christlich Demokratische Union Deutschlands* (Germany)
CE	Common Era
CIA	Central Intelligence Agency (USA)
CiviQ	"Quality consultation and opinion insights"
CPSU	Communist Party of the Soviet Union *Коммунистическая Партия Советского Союза* (USSR)
CQ	Congressional Quarterly
CR	Condorcet rule
ČSSD	Czech Social Democratic Party, *Česká strana sociálně demokratická* (Czech)
CSU	Christian Social Union, *Christlich-Soziale Union in Bayern* (Germany)

CUP	Cambridge University Press
DC	District of Columbia
DMZ	De-militarised Zone (Korea)
DOS	Democratic Opposition of Serbia,
	Демократска опозиција Србије, ДОС (Serbia)
DP	Democratic Party (Mongolia)
DPP	Democratic Progressive Party (Taiwan)
DPRK	Democratic People's Republic of Korea (Korea)
DUP	Democratic Unionist Party (NI)
EEA	European Economic Area
EC/EU	European Community/Union
EUMM	EU Monitoring Mission
FDP	Free Democratic Party,
	Freie Demokratische Partei (Germany)
FF	*Fianna Fáil* (Ireland)
FG	*Fine Gael* (Ireland)
FPÖ	Freedom Party of Austria,
	Freiheitliche Partei Österreichs (Austria)
FPTP	First-past-the-post (or fake post-truth polling)
FRG	Federal Republic of Germany,
	Bundesrepublik Deutschland (Germany)
GDP	Gross domestic product
GDR	German Democratic Republic,
	Deutsche Demokratische Republik (Germany)
GNU	Government of National Unity
GP	Green Party (England, Ireland, Georgia, Germany)
HDP	The Peoples' Democratic Party,
	Halkların Demokratik Partisi (Turkey)
HDZ BiH	Croatian Democratic Union,
	*Hrvatska demokratska zajednic*a, BiH (Bosnia)
ID	Identification
IDEA	Institute for Democracy and Electoral Assistance
IMF	International Monetary Fund
IRA	Irish Republican Army (Ireland)
IRV	Instant run-off voting (= AV, PV and STV)
ISIL	Islamic State of Iraq and the Levant (Iraq)
KDU-ČSL	Christian Democrats,
	Křesťanská a demokratická unie—Československá strana lidová. (Czech)
KGB	Комитет Государственной Безопасности,
	Committee of State Security (USSR)
KLA	Kosovo Liberation Army
KMT	Kuomintang or Guómíndǎng, 国民党, (China)
	Chinese Nationalist Party (Taiwan)

KPD	Communist Party of Germany, *Kommunistische Partei Deutschlands* (Germany)
MBC	Modified Borda count
MEP	Member of the European parliament
MLA	Member of Legislative Assembly (NI)
MMP	Multi-member proportional
MP	Member of parliament
MPP	Mongolian People's Party (Mongolia)
MPRP	Mongolian People's Revolutionary Party (Mongolia)
NATO	North Atlantic Treaty Organization
NGO	Non-governmental organization
NI	Northern Ireland
NIG	New Ireland Group
NI GP	NI Green Party (NI)
NSDAP	National Socialist German Workers' Party, Nazis, *Nationalsozialistische Deutsche Arbeiterpartei* (Germany)
NZ	New Zealand
OHR	Office of the High Representative (Bosnia)
OSCE	Organization for Security and Co-operation in Europe
OUP	Oxford University Press
ÖVP	Austrian People's Party, *Österreichische Volkspartei* (Austria)
PD	Progressive Democrats (Ireland)
PKK	Kurdistan Workers' Party, *Partiya Karkerên Kurdistanê* (Turkey)
PM	Prime minister
PNG	Papua New Guinea
PR	Proportional representation
PSNI	Police Service of NI (NI)
PV	Plurality voting or Preference voting (= AV, IRV and STV)
PVV	Party of Freedom, *Partij voor de Vrijheid* (Netherlands)
QBS	Quota Borda system
RoI	Republic of Ireland
RS	*Republika Srpska* (Bosnia)
RUC	Royal Ulster Constabulary (NI)
RV	Range Voting
SAR	Special Administrative Region (China)
SDA	Party of Democratic Action, *Stranka demokratske akcije* (Bosnia)
SDLP	Social Democratic and Labour Party (NI)
SDP	Social Democratic Party (Bosnia)
SDS	Serbian Democratic Party,

	Srpska demokratska stranka (Bosnia)
SDSM	Social Democratic Union of Macedonia (Macedonia),
	Социјалдемократски сојуз на Македонија, СДСМ
SF	*Sinn Féin* (RoI, NI)
SNP	Scottish National Party (Scotland)
SNS	Serbian Progressive party,
	Српска напредна странка, СНС (Serbia)
SNSD	Alliance of Independent Social Democrats
	Савез независних социјалдемократа (Bosnia)
SNTV	Single non-transferable vote
SPD	Social Democratic Party,
	Sozialdemokratische Partei Deutschlands (Germany)
SPÖ	Social Democratic Party of Austria
	Sozialdemokratische Partei Österreichs (Austria)
SPS	Socialist Party of Serbia,
	Социјалистичка партија србије, СПС (Serbia)
SR	Socialist Revolutionary (Russia)
SRS	Serbian Radical Party,
	Српска радикална странка, СРС (Serbia)
SS	*Schutzstaffel*—Protection Squadron (Germany)
STV	Single transferable vote (= AV, PV and IRV)
TD	*Teachta Dála* (member of the Irish parliament) (Ireland)
TRS	Two-round system
UK	United Kingdom
UKIP	UK Independence Party (UK)
UN	United Nations
USA	United States of America
USSR	Union of Soviet Socialist Republics,
	Союз Советских Социалистических Республик, СССР
UUP	Ulster Unionist Party (NI)
VMRO-DPMNU	Internal Macedonian Revolutionary Organization—Democratic
	Party for Macedonian National Unity
	Внатрешна македонска револуционерна организација—
	Демократска партија за македонско национално единство,
	вмро дпмне (Macedonia)
WTO	World Trade Organization
WWI/II	World War I/II

List of Figures

List of Tables

List of Graphs

Part I
Voting Theory

Chapter 1
Decision-making in Parliaments and Referendums

The truth of an Assembly's decisions depends as much on the form by which they are reached as on the enlightenment of its members.
Le Marquis de Condorcet, quoted in McLean and Urken
(1995: 113)
(Citations from this work are reprinted courtesy of the
University of Michigan Press).

Abstract For some extraordinary reason, many people in the world place their faith in a voting procedure which is ancient, primitive and, in a word, blunt: majority voting. It is usually divisive, often imprecise and, at worst, a provocation to violence. Accordingly, this chapter looks at voting theory and proves that this binary voting can indeed be hopelessly inaccurate if not, on occasions, plain wrong (while Chaps. 4–6 show that in many instances in practice, it is also at best inappropriate); the text then talks of various forms of multi-option voting; and finally, it describes a preferential points system which can be not only more accurate but actually, in certain circumstances, a very exact measure of the general will.

1.1 Democracy, a Definition

Democracy, says the dictionary, "is synonymous with majority rule" (McLean and McMillan 2003: 139). But read on, it tells us.

Alas, many do not. Instead, they believe or just assume that a majority opinion is that which emerges from a majority vote, and that, *ergo*, this sort of decision is democratic. So (nearly) everything political is binary. So (nearly) always, politics is adversarial.

Therefore, sure enough, there are rules by which political disputes may be resolved—or not, as the case may be—by majority voting. Take a simple example: if there is a debate on motion *A*, with two possible amendments, the procedure laid down (Cannell and Citrine 1982: 45–6), is straight forward.

© Springer Nature Switzerland AG 2020
P. Emerson, *Majority Voting as a Catalyst of Populism*,
https://doi.org/10.1007/978-3-030-20219-4_1

3

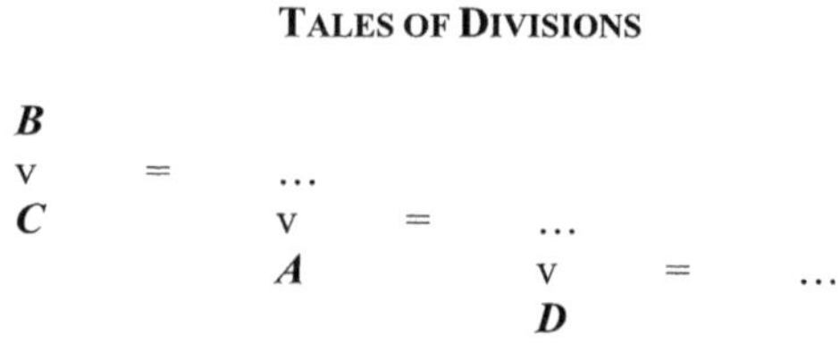

Fig. 1.1 Tales of divisions

TALES OF DIVISIONS

$$
\begin{array}{ccccccc}
B & & & & & & \\
\text{v} & = & \ldots & & & & \\
C & & \text{v} & = & \ldots & & \\
& & A & & \text{v} & = & \ldots \\
& & & & D & &
\end{array}
$$

Table 1.1 A three-person voters' profile

	The voters		
Preferences	Ms. i	Mr. j	Ms. k
1st	A	B	C
2nd	B	C	D
3rd	C	D	A
4th	D	A	B

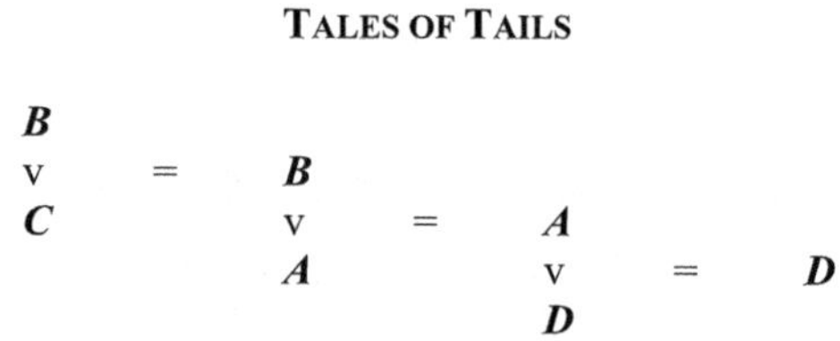

Fig. 1.2 Tales of tails

TALES OF TAILS

$$
\begin{array}{ccccccc}
B & & & & & & \\
\text{v} & = & B & & & & \\
C & & \text{v} & = & A & & \\
& & A & & \text{v} & = & D \\
& & & & D & &
\end{array}
$$

Let A be the motion, B the motion if it is amended by the first amendment, C the motion if subject to the second, and D the *status quo ante*. OK, first things first, the rules tell the users to choose the better (or best) amendment; so the two of them, B and C, are formally moved, seconded, debated, and then voted on, which is B v C. Next comes the question of whether or not to amend the original motion by the more popular amendment, so the motion itself is now proposed and debated, and then there is another majority vote, B/C v A; the outcome of this ballot is called the substantive. Finally there's the denouement: the last binary vote, the substantive versus the status quo. The order of voting is as shown in Fig. 1.1.

It is all very fair and logical, or so it would seem. So now, to take a practical example based on an argument used by Professor William H. Riker of the University of Rochester (Riker 1988: 74), let it be assumed that a committee of just three people, Ms. i, Mr. j and Ms. k, have preferences on these four options, A, B, C and D, as shown in Table 1.1.

In the first ballot, B v C, the winner is B by 2–1—both Ms. i and Mr. j prefer B. So the next vote is B v A, and now A comes out on top, again by 2–1—Ms. i and Ms. k both prefer A to B. Finally, there is the vote on this substantive, A v D, and it's a victory for D, again by 2–1, a majority of 67%. All very democratic, as shown in Fig. 1.2, and this margin of 67% presumably puts the outcome, D, beyond any dispute.

But hang on: have another look at Table 1.1: all three voters prefer C to D. So the answer is wrong. In such a scenario—and sometimes too in real life—majority voting produces the wrong answer. On some occasions, therefore, binary voting can be hopelessly inaccurate. And yet, for some extraordinary reason, people still use it.

In fact, in the above profile, we have the (not so) extraordinary situation in which *A* is more popular than *B*, and this we can write as $A > B$; that $B > C$; that $C > D$; and that $D > A$. In total, therefore:

$$A > B > C > D > A \ldots$$

... and it goes on and on, *ad nauseam*, for ever! It is called 'a cycle' or 'the paradox of [binary] voting', which was first noted back in the Eighteenth Century by Le Marquis de Condorcet. Taking two options at a time, by the way—$A:B, A:C$ etc.—is called a pairing, a term used in a Condorcet vote; and there's more about all this in Annex A.

The point could be demonstrated with a sporting parallel: in the 2018 six-nations' rugby championship, England beat Wales, Wales beat Scotland and Scotland beat England, so nobody knew which team was the champion (except the Irish of course, because we beat them all).

1.1.1 Majoritarianism

But back to voting: this Chapter first takes a more detailed look at that which many regard as democratic decision-making—binary voting—before then considering decision-making procedures which might be more democratic—multi-option or even preferential voting.

For some extraordinary reason, people who do not read the full dictionary definition believe, not only that, "democracy is synonymous with majority rule," but also that, as it were by implication, decisions should be subject to a majority vote. "Democracy," we are told, "is premised ... on majority rule," (Huntington 1991: 66), and it "works on the basis of a decision by the majority," (Whitaker 1996: 398) ... just as it did in the old days, 2000 years or so ago, when the citizens of Athens—well, the male slave-owners—decided "all the great issues of state: the making of war or peace, the passing of laws, and the political exile or death of individual leaders ... by simple majority vote"[1] (Dunn 2008: 241).

Similarly, in the Imperial Court of the Former Han Dynasty in China, decisions were taken by using the same voting procedure (Sect. 6.3.2), and what's more, the outcomes of these ballots were normally accepted by the Emperor. So binary voting is ancient, and while much else has changed in the intervening centuries, when it comes to decision-making, society in general is still using this primitive and divisive methodology, one of the most inaccurate measures of collective opinion ever

---

[1]Reproduced with permission of the Licensor through PLSclear.

invented. It is everywhere, in local councils and parliaments[2] and even in top decision-making bodies like the UN Security Council. But it cannot measure the degree of *consensus* because, with so many votes 'for' and so many others 'against', it quantifies the very opposite—the degree of *dissent*.

It is time to return to that dictionary definition. Democracy is indeed majority rule, but it goes on to say, "In votes between two options . . . this [majority voting] poses no difficulty; in votes among three or more it does" (McLean and McMillan 2003: 139). So while "majority rule seems to be the most natural, or commonsensical way of voting . . . when there are three or more alternatives there can be problems . . ." (Mackie 2003: 5). This was first recognized in CE 105 by Pliny the Younger: it was in a Roman court of law where a servant of the Consul, Afranius Dexter, was accused of his master's murder (McLean and Urken 1995: 15), and there were three options 'on the table'—*A*, acquittal; *B* banishment, and *C* capital punishment. In any majority vote on *A*, those who thought the accused was guilty would vote 'no'; on *C*, those opposed to the death penalty would vote 'no'; and so on. As in the British House of Commons when debating Brexit (Sect. 4.4.3.3), there might be no majority for anything.

The inadequacies of majority voting have often been recognised, not only by numerous social choice scientists but also by other great writers, like Lev Nikolaevich Tolstoy. "If one man . . . rules over all, it is unjust, and in all likelihood such rule will be harmful to the people. The same will be the case when the minority rules over the majority. But the power of the majority over the minority also fails to secure a just rule," (Tolstoy 1966: 328). For the politician, however, it is easier to control things when everything is reduced to a choice of only two alternatives—"*A* or *B*?"—so nearly all of them like to use (simple or weighted) majority voting. Indeed, as was pointed out by Condorcet, many assemblies have the custom "of reducing the subject for debate to the most widely supported opinions about it and, if possible, to just two of them" (McLean and Urken 1995: 131). It suits them. It definitely suits those who are in charge. Some political leaders, like David Cameron on Brexit, use an even more simplistic formula—"*A*, yes or no?"—and not only the supposedly democratic ones, but also the likes of Adolf Hitler (Sect. 5.3.1).

Admittedly, in courts of law, questions may indeed be dichotomous: guilty or not guilty? In politics, however, when discussing budgets, economic policies, planning proposals and/or constitutional arrangements, there is often no reason at all why debates in which 'everything is on the table' should be resolved in questions reduced to dichotomies or, as in Fig. 1.1, series of dichotomies. Alas, politics has evolved into an adversarial sport, so sometimes those who pose the question ask, "should a certain action be taken, yes or no? [and] unless there is . . . unanimity . . . the use of either majority rule or minority veto cannot be avoided," (Lijphart 1977: 39). Oh yes it can: change the question.

Instead of asking, "Capital punishment, yes or no?" would it not be more sensible to debate, "How should a convicted murderer best be dealt with?" Instead of, "The

---

[2]The Scandinavian parliaments use multi-option voting procedures, sometimes; (Sect. 3.3.1).

atomic bomb, yes or no?" a more nuanced debate could be based on the question, "How best could we defend ourselves?" Or in place of "Brexit, yes or no?" why not a short list: "Would you like the UK to be in the EU, the EEA or the WTO?"[3] (Sect. 4.4.3.3). In a nutshell, as sometimes in the work-place, as usually in the home, and as always in mediation work, questions should be more *open*; unfortunately, in politics, they are all too often *closed*.

Now in parliaments of hundreds let alone societies of millions, it's a bit impractical to have questions which are totally open. So maybe a short list is the way to proceed, and ideally, this could be formulated in a process which is itself open; more of that later. This text now considers a selection of decision-making voting procedures, some binary, some multi-optional, and some preferential.

1.1.2 Binary Voting

Majority voting may be conducted in a number of ways. A few countries insist on a minimum turnout—the Dutch, for example, have used a 30% threshold (Sect. 5.2.4), while Macedonia opted for 50% (Sect. 5.6.7.1). Quite a few parliaments rely on a weighted majority, the South Korean parliament requires a 60% majority on much legislation, while its neighbour North Korea lays down a two-thirds threshold for constitutional amendments; (Sects. 6.6.3 and 6.6.4)—there are not too many of those, of course. Switzerland sometimes makes use of a twin vote in referendums, and this requires two majorities: one of the general population, the other of the cantons. Lastly, in plural societies like Belgium or conflict zones like Northern Ireland, NI (Sect. 4.2.4.2), Bosnia (Sect. 5.6.5), and even in the former Warsaw Pact country of Czechoslovakia (Sect. 5.4.1), reliance is or was sometimes placed on a consociational vote—the Belgians call it a special vote—by which a policy shall be approved only if it gains majority support in both or all the relevant constituencies.

All of that said, there are basically two types of binary questions, either, as hinted earlier,

A?   an "option *A*, yes-or-no?" type question,

or the slightly more sophisticated,

AB?   "option *A* or option *B*?"

and either ballot may be subject to a simple or weighted majority.

---

[3]The United Kingdom in the European Union, the European Economic Area, or the World Trade Organisation.

As noted, not least in some referendums, complex questions are often reduced to simple dichotomies, and the outcome is then assumed to be "the will of the people" even when it is only by the slimmest of margins,[4] or, as in NI's border poll of 1973 (Sect. 4.2.2), it is of Stalinist proportions. In both instances, however, there may be much cause for doubt.

Consider a debate on what should be the tax rate for high-income earners.[5] In theory, it could be anything between 0 and 100%, but doubtless any rational discussion would reduce the range of possibilities to practical levels. So the politician who wants it to be 50% could ask the **A?** type of question, "50%, yes-or-no?" In such a setting, those who want 40% might vote 'no', but so too might others who prefer 60%. Indeed, there is the likelihood that such a ballot could easily be lost by those of very disparate views joining forces against the one in the middle. Such was the fate of Ireland's 1992 referendum on abortion, which "aligned liberals and ultra-conservatives against moderate conservatives," (Gallagher 1996: 97) (Sect. 4.3.5.1). Little wonder, then, that Hippodamus of Milketus, 498–408 BCE, had "a not unreasonable dissatisfaction with the simple 'yes or no' verdicts demanded in Athenian courts" (Aristotle 1992: 132). Others today are equally unhappy (Obama 2006: 130).

So, the vote is held, and maybe there is a majority in favour of 50% plus. But nobody can know for sure whether that is a true statement of fact. Or there might be a majority against, in which case no one is any the wiser.

In a nutshell, one cannot identify the *collective* will if lots of respondents do not express their *individual* wills, if, in other words, lots of people vote only 'no'. A question of the **A?** variety is just totally unsuitable. Logically, when trying to find an average opinion, only positive data is needed. Information as to what certain individuals do not want—"I would not like a 50% tax rate,"—is not required, and nor for that matter are any embellishments—"nor would I like a 51% tax rate." By asking every member of parliament, MP, to state their preference, however—and for the moment, to the nearest 5% should suffice—could be a more successful way of identifying the most acceptable option.

The other format is the **AB?** type of question: "45 or 50%?" In this instance, those who would have preferred to vote for a 60% rate could vote for 50%, that or abstain; while in like manner, those who campaigned for 40% might settle for 45. As a methodology, however, if and when the debate in question is multi-optional—which in politics, as noted above, is or should be (nearly) always—to reduce everything to a dichotomy is at least unfair and at worst a distortion; furthermore, it might well mean that the outcome is inaccurate. Who is to know, for example, in the above "45 or

---

[4]For a list of some of those parliamentary votes and referendums which have been won or lost by one vote or by less than one per cent respectively, see *Won by One* on http://www.deborda.org/won-by-one/

[5]In the budget debate of 20.3.2012, the British Chancellor of the Exchequer, (Tory), proposed to reduce the previous (Labour) tax band of 50–45%. The vote was on only these two options.

50?" question, if a majority does support 50%, whether or not the most popular level is not actually 55%?

Despite its weaknesses, many politicians do indeed like majority voting, especially those who operate within political structures which allow these leaders to choose the question. Sadly, undemocratic and democratic alike, many of these structures often do, and many rulers take advantage of this monopoly power. As shall be seen in Part II, Napoléon took a fancy to majority voting and lots of other dictators followed suit (Emerson P 2012: 143 et seq.); they chose the question and, with but one exception—in his third referendum in 1988, the Chilean dictator, Augusto Pinochet, got only 43.0%—the question was the answer.[6] Democratic leaders have enjoyed rather more modest levels of success: nevertheless, "The vast majority of referendums have been sponsored by governments and have produced the voting outcomes desired by those governments" (Butler and Ranney 1994: 261). The point was demonstrated magnificently in Iran: in three separate referendums under three very different rulers, the people voted with 99% levels of enthusiasm to be socialist, capitalist, and then neither (Sect. 6.2.1).

The conclusion, therefore, is this: in a modern plural society, in a modern pluralist democracy, a debate on any contentious question must, by definition, allow not only for every relevant option to be 'on the table', but also a summary of everything, a (short) list of options—usually from four to six—on any subsequent ballot paper. In other words, in so far as it is possible, the question should indeed be *open*.

1.1.3 Multi-option, Single-preference Voting

As shall be seen later on (Sect. 1.6.1), and as Condorcet implied at the beginning of this chapter, the nature of the voting procedure to be used at the end of any debate will in large measure determine the milieu in which that debate is conducted. If the question is contentious then, in all probability, any debate which is scheduled to conclude with a divisive majority voting will itself be divisive. Majority voting may be not only inaccurate, it can also be inappropriate. If, in contrast, the final vote is to be multi-optional or, better still, preferential, the preceding debate will almost certainly be more rational, the behaviour of the protagonists more civilised, and the eventual outcome more accurate.

Sadly, to put it at its mildest, many in the West continue to believe in majority rule—which may be OK—and continue to use majority voting—which in many instances is definitely not OK. "Democracy as commonly conceived ... is the government of the whole people by a mere majority of the people," (Dunn 2008: 131). Indeed, "many people are [captivated] by what may be called the mystique of the majority; it is often thought to be the foundation of democracy that the will of a

---

[6]One other dictator 'lost'—Zimbabwe's Robert Mugabe in 2000, 45.3–54.7%—but he had taken the precaution of making the vote non-binding.

Table 1.2 A dozen voters' profile on three options		The 12 voters		
	Preferences	5	3	4
	1st	*A*	*B*	*C*
	2nd	*B*	*C*	*B*
	3rd	*C*	*A*	*A*

majority should be paramount. [But] it is *not* the foundation of democracy ..."
(Dummett 1997: 71), neither in the West nor abroad where this "assumption of the
majority's right to overrule a dissident minority ... does violence to conceptions
basic to non-Western peoples" (Emerson R 1966: 284).

In days which should be but alas are not long gone, the word 'democracy' was
imprecisely understood. Either it meant "that the will of the majority must prevail,"
or that "all who are affected by a decision should have the chance to participate in
making that decision, either directly or through their chosen representatives" (Lewis
1965: 64). If, however, representatives are grouped into a government and an
opposition, the former definition contradicts the latter. A better definition is indeed
required, and is coming up shortly.

It is time to consider a more pluralist approach to decision-making, so what might
happen in a multi-option vote? There are, after all, quite a few ways in which such
ballots may be analysed: is the outcome to be the option with the most 1st preferences, or the one with the least last preferences, or the one with the highest average
popularity, or whatever? Take, then, a dozen voters, casting their preferences on just
three options, *A*, *B* and *C*, as shown in Table 1.2.

On the face of it, option *A* is fairly divisive, while opinions on option *C* are a bit
mixed, so maybe option *B*, the 1st or 2nd preference of literally *every* voter, best
represents the said voters' collective will. Furthermore, this common sense thinking
would suggest the correct social ranking is *B-C-A*. Well, what happens when these
preferences are analysed according to three different methodologies? The first lets
the voters use only a single preference, so is still rather Orwellian[7]; the second caters
for a more pluralist approach, and the third is even more inclusive.

PV Plurality Voting

Yes, this methodology allows the voters to cast only their 1st preferences, so only
the 1st preferences from Table 1.2 are taken into account. Hence the result is *A*-5, *C*-
4 and *B*-3, and the winner is *A*. As happens quite often with this sort of voting, the
plurality vote winner may not enjoy majority support, but only that of the largest
minority. Such is the case in this instance: indeed, while 5 think *A* is the best, a
majority of 7 think it is the worst option! Like binary voting, plurality voting can be
hopelessly inaccurate.

---

[7]This 'good', that or those 'bad'—from George Orwell's *Animal Farm*.

TRS Two-round System

A TRS vote is based on a plurality count but, if no one option gets 50% in the first round plurality vote, a second round majority vote is held between the two leading options from the first round; so the ballot consists of one single preference Orwellian vote followed perhaps by another. In Table 1.2, with a first round result of A-5, C-4 and B-3, so A and C go into the second round and, if everyone's preferences stay the same, the winner is now C with a score of 7.

1.1.4 Non-Orwellian Preference Voting

If the chosen democratic process of decision-making is to be fair to all, it must, as an absolute minimum, be accurate. Accordingly, to identify the *collective* will accurately, those voting must be able to express their own individual opinions, not only positively but with a reasonable degree of precision as well. At the very least, therefore, any ballot on a contentious topic should allow for a short list of options, in the given example of tax-rates, something like five options of 40, 45, 50, 55 and 60%, and obviously, the range of options listed on the ballot should reflect the debate; (the appropriate rules are shown in Annex C).

Having such a list would allow every MP to choose something that was close to what they wanted. Furthermore, if the vote were preferential, they could express their opinion with a considerable degree of accuracy; he who wanted 53%, for example, might give a 1st preference to 55 and a 2nd to 50; while she who preferred 52 could vote 50–55 (see below), if, that is, the pluralist voting procedure catered for such subtlety.

AV The Alternative Vote

AV allows the voters to cast as many preferences as they wish, which is good. Unfortunately, however, the way the count works means that, in some instances, not every preference cast shall be counted. This is because, like TRS, AV is based on a plurality count or rather, perhaps quite a few of them. At each stage of the count, the supposedly least popular option is eliminated and its votes are transferred in accordance with the relevant voters' 2nd or subsequent preferences, until one of the options gains at least 50% support (that or the option with the biggest minority is chosen by default).

In Table 1.2, stage (i) of the count gives the same result as did the above plurality vote: A-5, C-4 and B-3, so that is the end of B. Accordingly, its three votes are transferred to the three B voters' 2nd preference, C, so the stage (ii) count is A-5, C-7, and thus the AV social choice is C. AV and TRS often give the same social choice.

Table 1.3 Three different options and three different outcomes

Voting procedure	Social choice	Social ranking and scores		
Plurality voting	*A*	*A*-5	*C*-4	*B*-3
TRS	*C*	*C*-7	*A*-5	–
AV	*C*	*C*-7	*A*-5	–
BC	*B*	*B*-27	*C*-23	*A*-22

It must be pointed out, however, that in getting this result, the nine 2nd preferences cast for *B* are not even counted!

BC   A Borda Count

In a BC, as in AV, voters may cast as many preferences as they want to, and in a BC although as maybe not in AV, every preference cast is counted in the analysis. In this three-option example of a points system of voting, with everyone casting a full ballot, a 1st preference gets 3 points, a 2nd gets 2 and a 3rd 1. So the BC social ranking is *B*-27, *C*-23, *A*-22. And the winner is now *B*. Which is what had been anticipated as a fair outcome.

* * *

The results, then, the four analyses of Table 1.2, are as shown in Table 1.3: so if the choice of voting system is not considered to be too important, the supposedly *democratic* choice of these voters is either *A* or *B* or *C*. So it could be anything? That cannot be right! The outcome depends on the voting procedure? In this particular profile, and in many others for that matter, plurality voting can be inaccurate and, unsurprisingly, systems which are based on plurality voting, TRS and AV, can also be erroneous.

We could go further, for the plurality voting social ranking—*A-C-B*—is the very opposite of the BC ranking, *B-C-A*. In other words, again in this particular instance, if as common sense suggests and this book argues, the BC outcome is indeed correct, then the plurality vote is wrong and couldn't be more wrong! Yet people still believe in it. What's more, they use it, not least in elections where it is called first-past-the-post, FPTP, and often described as "fair" (Sect. 2.1.3).

Now consider a four-option scenario and 14 voters: the same dozen with the same preferences as shown above in Table 1.2, are joined by two more voters, who add option *D* to the debate. Umm, that's not a bad idea it seems, in the opinion of the dozen; indeed, as seen in Table 1.4, they all give it their 2nd preference. So a cursory glance at this voter's profile would suggest that option *D*, the new 1st or 2nd preference of again everyone, should be the new social choice; and *D-B-C-A* is likely to be the true social ranking.

With plurality voting, the outcome is now *A*-5, *C*-4, *B*-3 and *D*-2, so the winner is still *A*.

Table 1.4 Fourteen voters' profile on four options

Preferences	Number of voters			
	5	3	2	4
1st	*A*	*B*	*D*	*C*
2nd	*D*	*D*	*B*	*D*
3rd	*B*	*C*	*C*	*B*
4th	*C*	*A*	*A*	*A*

Table 1.5 Four different options and four different outcomes

Voting procedure	Social choice	Social ranking and scores			
Plurality voting	*A*	*A*-5	*C*-4	*B*-3	*D*-2
TRS	*C*	*C*-9	*A*-5	–	–
AV	*B*	*B*-9	*A*-5	–	–
BC	*D*	*D*-44	*B*-36	*C*-31	*A*-29

Next is TRS. In this example, the two top scorers are still *A* and *C* with scores of 5 and 4, so, in the second round between these two, *A* and *C*, again assuming that everyone's preferences stay the same, the score is now *A*-5, *C*-9, so *C* is again the TRS winner.

With AV, the stage (i) score line is the above plurality vote social ranking: *A*-5, *C*-4, *B*-3, *D*-2, and the least popular is option *D*; so it's out, and its 2 votes are transferred to option *B*, and the stage (ii) score line is *A*-5, *B*-5 and *C*-4. This spells the end of option *C*, and its 4 votes are transferred (not to their 2nd preference, *D*, which has been eliminated but) to *B*, for a final score line of *A*-5, *B*-9, so the AV winner is *B*.

Finally, in a BC, where in this instance a 1st preference gets 4 points, a 2nd gets 3, a 3rd 2 and a 4th 1, the scores are *D*-44, *B*-36, *C*-31and *A*-29, so the winner, as was suspected it should be, is option *D*.

Yet again, for those who think that a democratic decision is that which emerges from a vote, regardless of which voting procedure is used, the *totally democratic* outcome could be anything at all—Table 1.5. So if a political leader knows the preferences of all the MPs, he can use the voting procedure that produces the social choice that he wants; choosing a voting procedure can be—and often is—an act of manipulation.

Furthermore, for a second time, plurality voting produces the completely incorrect answer: the plurality voting social ranking—*A*-*C*-*B*-*D*—is the absolute opposite of the correct one, as in the BC, *D*-*B*-*C*-*A*. Here too, plurality voting is wrong and couldn't be more wrong!

CR   Condorcet Rule

That's enough mathematics for the moment, but there is another very accurate methodology which deserves a mention: the Condorcet rule. It is another preferential methodology, and a full explanation is shown in Annex A.

1.1.5 A Comparison

These various voting procedures can be compared to a sports competition. A straight knock-out event, as in a tennis tournament, is like a series of **AB?** majority votes. If it were to be completely at random, if everything depended upon the draw, then in theory, the two finalists could include only one of the two best players, and the second finalist might be the best of only half the players, namely, all the not-so-good ones. Accordingly, in Wimbledon and elsewhere, the organisers rely on a process of seeding. But you couldn't have that in politics, could you?

So maybe a league system would be the fairer way of deciding which option is the most popular (*and which team is the best*). (*Let every team play every other team and*) let the voters cast their preferences. The analysis could consider (*which team wins the most matches or*) which option wins the most pairings—and this is called (*the champion or*) the Condorcet winner. A different procedure could count up (*all the goals scored or*) all the points, to see which (*team has the best goal difference or*) which option is the Borda social choice. In many (*seasons or*) voters' profiles, the (*champion or*) Condorcet winner is the same as (*the team with the best goal difference or*) the Borda winner. But not quite always. (*In the English Premier League, if Chelsea were to win more of their matches but Liverpool were to beat Chelsea 9-0, Liverpool might have the best goal difference but the Londoners might still win the championship. In most seasons, however, and*) "in most practical circumstances, the Condorcet winner and the Borda winner coincide" (Mackie 2003: 7).

1.1.6 Democracy Defined

It is time to go back to the dictionary definition: democracy is indeed majority rule, and "when there are more than two [options]," which, it is worth repeating, whenever the subject under discussion is complex and/or contentious, should be (nearly) always, "[the Borda and Condorcet rules] are the two best interpretations of majority rule" (McLean and McMillan 2003: 139).

For some crazy reason, however, not only this definition but also "... the theory of voting [in general] appears to be wholly unknown to anyone concerned with its practical applications. It is certainly quite unknown to the politicians ... [and] it appears to be largely unknown to experts in political institutions ..." (Dummett 1984: 5). So it is that, in parliamentary divisions and referendums, votes take place and the results are declared as often as not as if they are accurate, as if the relevant voting procedure, the measure of collective opinion, was an instrument of some precision. Yet as the reader (now) knows, many of these procedures can be hopelessly inaccurate, and many outcomes are, to use a contemporary term, fake. "In blunt words, by not publicising what can go wrong, by not informing the general public how to avoid these problems … [we must] expect to experience societal consequences that are significant and serious" (Saari 2008: 217). Hence in decision-making, Brexit, of which more anon, and many other horrible decisions. It is all so damned dangerous. Majority voting is the catalyst of populism.

1.2   Variations on Another Theme

There are two other voting systems which are sometimes suggested as a solution to the malaise which is brought about by majority voting. They are both multi-optional but neither is preferential.

ApV   Approval Voting

In this methodology, voters just 'approve' of those options which they consider to be brilliant, good, or maybe just OK; and the option which gets the most 'approvals' is the winner. In an analysis of a three-option ballot, consideration could be given to all 1st and 2nd preferences; while in a four-option poll, maybe the 3rd preferences could also be considered. In Table 1.2, the corresponding results would be A 5, B 12 and C 7, so the outcome would be B. In Table 1.4, the results could be, respectively, for 1st and 2nd preferences A 5, B 5, C 4 and D 14, or maybe, for the top three preferences, A 5, B 14, C 9 and D 14; so the outcome could be D, or maybe a B/D tie. For debates involving more than four options, the rules become even more arbitrary.

RV   Range Voting

In range voting, voters are given, say, 10 points, which they can distribute as they choose. In a four-option scenario, an individual could give 5 to his favourite, 3 to his next choice, and 2 to a 3rd preference; while another person could give all 10 points to her favourite, and zero to the other options.

Obviously, it is a system which gives the advantage to and thus encourages the intransigent, the one who just 'plonks' all ten points onto her 1st preference—and is therefore referred to as a 'plonker'. To a lesser extent, the same criticism applies to approval voting (see also Annex D).

1.3 Decision-making Methodologies

All the different decision-making voting procedures discussed above may be summarised in Table 1.6. Preferential methodologies are shown in tint.

In some voters' profiles, and especially in those debates in which nearly everybody is almost unanimous, the outcome of a plurality vote might well be the same as those of TRS, AV, the Borda winner and/or the Condorcet winner. Indeed, if there is unanimity, the outcome of all the **A?**—CR voting procedures will be the same; but in such circumstances, it might not be necessary to take a vote anyway.

Furthermore, if the **A?** option is the correct one, or if the two alternatives in the **AB?** question include the correct one, even a majority vote outcome might be correct. Indeed, in instances of near unanimity, no matter which voting procedure is used, the outcome will represent the majority opinion and could properly be called democratic. With majority voting, however, one cannot be sure (unless, of course, the procedure includes a lot of other majority votes on all the other options or pairings, which would be like a Condorcet count).

The conclusion is stark: in nearly all political circumstances, whenever the problem concerned is complicated and/or controversial, majority voting can be inappropriate, inadequate, inaccurate or even wrong.

Plurality voting can also be problematic because in practice, in any multi-option contest (as in many a multi-candidate election—see Chap. 2), the list of options tends to boil down, or to be boiled down by the media, to a choice of just a few or at worst only two 'favourites', so plurality voting can be almost as bad as majority voting—as in a US presidential election (Sect. 2.1.3). Secondly, the former can be even more unfair when the outcome wins not a majority but only a plurality, the largest minority.

The same is true when plurality voting is used as an FPTP, first-past-the-post, electoral system, not least because, "There is no post," (Dummett 1997: 39), that is, there is no fixed proportion of votes which an option has to attain in order to be chosen (Sect. 2.1.3). Thirdly, this system "effectively disenfranchises every voter whose vote does not go to the winner" (Grayling 2017: 83).

Table 1.6 Some decision-making systems

Decision-making		
Binary	A?	Majority vote – '*A*, yes-or-no?'
	AB?	Majority vote – '*A* or *B*?'
Multi-option Single preference	PV	Plurality voting
	TRS	Two-round system
Multi-option Preferential	AV	Alternative vote
	BC	Borda count
	CR	Condorcet rule
Multi-option non-preferential	ApV	Approval voting
	RV	Range voting

As noted, because TRS and AV are both based on plurality voting, they too can be capricious. Either can be used as an electoral system—TRS most famously in France, but it has also been used in the Balkans for example (Sect. 5.6.2); AV is the Australian electoral system while, in its proportional representation, single transferable vote format, PR-STV, it is used in both jurisdictions in Ireland (Sects. 4.2.1 and 4.3.3).

As implied above, approval voting and range voting *allow* the voter to be consensual; but they both give the advantage to and thereby encourage the intransigent extremist and would, therefore, be quite inappropriate for use in any conflict zone, or for that matter in any so-called stable democracy whenever the subject concerned is contentious. Therefore, at least in the opinion of this author, they are both inadequate in politics, anywhere.

Returning to the above-mentioned dictionary definition, the Borda and Condorcet rules are "the two best interpretations of majority rule." Secondly, as noted, in many instances the Borda winner is the same as the Condorcet social choice, and sometimes too even their social rankings coincide. If a parliament wanted to be really sure that the outcome of a ballot was indeed accurate, both counts could be conducted; and if both the Borda and the Condorcet social choices were one and the same, then all concerned could have total confidence that this outcome did indeed represent the will of parliament or at the very least, the will of those who had voted. This idea has long since been mooted by others, for example, Charles Dodgson, Duncan Black and Arthur Copeland; (Emerson P 2007: 17). It is time, therefore, to examine the Borda rule; but first, there is one further aspect of majority voting which has had and still has huge implications in countless conflict zones—the right of self-determination.

1.4 Self-determination

When President Woodrow Wilson introduced the concept of self-determination in 1918, during WWI, he proposed a principle by which small countries like Belgium could regain their sovereignty, and colonies (or at least those not affected by the Monroe Doctrine) could become independent. In later years, he confessed, "I never knew there were a million Germans in Bohemia" (Eban 1998: 38).

Furthermore, it must be pointed out that this right was meant to be the means by which a society could solve the *external* problems of colonialism, not the *internal* difficulties of separatism. Sadly, it is now used in this latter capacity. Secondly, the declaration did not specify the voting methodology by which such a choice was to be made; it is just assumed to imply a majority vote. So take Iraq and the mixed town of Kirkuk. If a line were drawn to put Kirkuk into a northern part of Iraq, such a northern zone would have a Kurdish majority; if the city were to be in a south-easterly area, the population would be mainly Shi'a; and if it were in a westerly district, the area would be predominantly Sunni.[8] If, therefore, the right of self-determination is indeed to be exercised by a majority vote, the right itself may well be a source of conflict: in Scotland's referendum in 2014 (Sect. 4.4.3.2) nobody died; but in the Balkans and the Caucasus (Chap. 5) and elsewhere, binary referendums were indeed a cause of war.

The declaration states that nations can "freely choose" their constitutional status.[9] So the theory is as follows. If a majority wants a big country to stay big, then that's fine; that is democracy. If a minority in a small part of that land wants to opt out, however, and if a majority of that minority vote for it, then that's fine too; that also is democracy. But if a minority in that minority, in a tiny corner of that small part of that land, want to opt out of opting out and to opt back in again, or whatever, and if a majority of that second minority of that first minority vote for it, then that is absolutely fine as well, apparently; that too is democracy. The right is indeed a source of conflict.

The right first went wrong in the UK. In 1920, what later became the Republic of Ireland, RoI, opted out of the UK; so NI opted out of the RoI and back into the UK. Why West Belfast did not opt out of opting back in again is not clear. Then came the Balkans: Croatia opted out of Yugoslavia, so some of the Serb areas tried to opt back in; Bosnia-Herzegovina[10] opted out, so *Republika Srpska, RS*, tried to rejoin Belgrade, while Herzeg-Bosna wanted to unite with Zagreb (Sect. 5.6.2). And so on. Similarly, in the Caucasus, Georgia opted out of the USSR whereupon Abkhazia opted out of Georgia and so too did South Ossetia (Sects. 5.8.2.1 and 5.8.2.2). What a mess.

For as long as the right of self-determination is based on a majority vote, this principle will only bring peace and stability to the world when every couple is an independent nation-state, each with its own seat at the UN and so on; the law is an ass.

1.5   Multi-option Referendums

In contrast to what has often been a tale of bitterness and division if not war, some countries have legislated for multi-option plebiscites. One of the first was Britain, surprise surprise! In 1948, Westminster suggested Newfoundland should have a binary choice, but the people of Halifax protested and demanded a third option. This

---

[8]In Kirkuk, the vote was duly held on 25.9.2017. It was indeed a source of conflict. On 15th October, Iraqi forces chose to retake the disputed region by force; thankfully, two weeks later, Masoud Barzani, the President of Iraqi Kurdistan, stepped down, and the problem was defused.

[9]"All peoples have the right of self-determination. By virtue of that right they freely determine their political status and freely pursue their economic, social and cultural development..." *Article 1.1. The International Covenant on Civil and Political Rights*. The UN General Assembly, 1996.

[10]Hereinafter, this book refers to this beautiful sad country as just Bosnia.

was duly included . . . and in a TRS ballot, with a turnout of over 80% in both rounds, this last addition was the winner.

Puerto Rico followed suit in 1967, again with three options, with the winning option gaining 60% in the first round. Maybe the best multi-option ballot of all was the TRS poll used in Guam in 1982, when the electorate was offered six possible constitutional arrangements . . . and just in case that was not enough, a further space was left blank, so any one(s) who wanted to (campaign and) vote for a seventh option could do exactly that (Emerson P 2012: 164).

As it stands at the moment, then, majority vote constitutional plebiscites have been a provocation if not indeed a cause of violence, not only in the Balkans and Caucasus as will be discussed later on, but also in East Timor where the violence was relatively minor, and in South Sudan which then imploded. Despite these horrors, people still talk of referendums for independence in Kashmir[11] for example, where doubtless it would provoke dreadful levels of violence, and more recently in Hong Kong and Taiwan (Sects. 6.4.2 and 6.5.2), even though the consequences of any vote in Tibet or Xīnjiāng, could also be terrible (Sect. 6.3.11).

1.6   A More Inclusive Polity

Having dismissed binary voting as being totally inappropriate for contemporary society, and having decided that a preferential procedure would be better, consideration shall now be given to a preferential points system of voting.[12]

The first principle is as follows. If the process of decision-making is to be as open as possible, a society which aspires to be a participatory democracy should allow (the people or) their elected representatives to participate, not only by voting in any ballot which takes place at the end of the (national or) parliamentary debate, but also by being involved in choosing the options which are to be included on that ballot during the course of that debate. Given, then, that many politicians like to control debates, one essential element of any inclusive polity is that the choice of options must be decided impartially. Accordingly, a team of 'consensors' (see Annex C), or maybe just the Speaker—for the moment, what follows is confined to a parliamentary setting—should listen to the debate in order to draw up a list of all relevant options, everything that is 'on the table'. This may be displayed in summary on a computer screen and/or in full on a dedicated web-page.

If as is likely on any point of policy, the MPs fail to come to a verbal consensus, the Speaker may call for a multi-option preferential ballot. On subjects of any complexity, as was implied earlier, this shall normally be limited to about five options.

---

[11]UN Resolution 47 of August 1948.

[12]As noted, the Condorcet rule is also very good; of the two, this author prefers the Borda rule because, as will be discussed later on, (Sect. 3.3.1), the latter is non-majoritarian.

The count shall be conducted according to the following rules. In a ballot of n options, the voter may cast up to m preferences, where obviously $n \geq m \geq 1$, and points shall be awarded to (1st, 2nd ... last) preferences cast according to the rule:

$$(m, m - 1 \ldots 1) \ldots \text{rule (a)}.$$

This rule was originally put forward by Jean-Charles de Borda in 1770 (Saari 2008: 197). Unfortunately, it was soon corrupted to:

$$(n, n - 1 \ldots 1) \ldots \text{rule (b)}.$$

if not indeed

$$(n - 1, n - 2 \ldots 0) \ldots \text{rule (c)}.$$

Now if all the voters submit full ballots—that is, if $m = n$—there is no mathematical difference in the outcome. If, however, some people truncate their votes, if someone casts only a 1st preference and that option then gets n points as in rule (b) or $(n - 1)$ points in rule (c), the BC can deteriorate into something little better than a plurality vote ... which de Borda criticised at length (Emerson P 2013: 353–8). He wanted everyone to submit full ballots; he wanted those concerned to participate fully in the decision-making process, and not to manipulate the ballot by casting a low preference to their 2nd preference, in order to increase the chances of their favourite 1st preference: "My [voting] method," he said, "is only for honest [people]" (McLean and Urken 1995: 40). To see how partial voting can have what might be a huge impact, see Annex B.

1.6.1   The Original Borda Count

If, then, the count is in accordance with rule (a)—and to distinguish this procedure from that which applies if rule (b) or (c) is used, this voting procedure is called the modified Borda count, MBC—the effect is as follows:

- he who votes for only one option gives his favourite just 1 point;
- she who casts two preferences gives her favourite 2 points (and her 2nd choice 1 point); while
- he who casts all n preferences gives his favourite n points (his 2nd choice $n - 1$ points, his next preference $n - 2$ points, etc.).

In the count, preferences cast are translated into points according to rule (a), and the option with the most points is the winner. The protagonist, therefore, will hope not only that her own supporters will submit full ballots and give her favourite their 1st preference; she will also want other voters to give her option a relatively high preference, and she will have much to gain, therefore, by campaigning positively amongst her erstwhile (majoritarian) opponents. Meanwhile, the voters will be incentivised to cast all of their preferences, each to state their favourite, but also to note their best compromise option(s). In so doing, they will thus recognise the validity of these other options, the aspirations of their neighbours.

In summary, while majority voting promotes division, the MBC can be the catalyst of a much more sophisticated campaign, and the basis of a much more inclusive polity. Furthermore, if every voter states their compromise option, then, in theory at least, it should be possible to identify the collective compromise ... which is supposedly what politics is all about: the art of compromise. The MBC is its science. It is robust, inclusive, and very accurate.

1.6.2 A Little History

The MBC was 'invented' by the author in the 1970s, in Belfast, at the height of the Troubles (as the NI violence is euphemistically called), and he wrote about it in *That Sons May Bury Their Fathers* (Emerson P 1978). At the time, he did not know that this voting procedure had already been invented by the Rev. Charles Dodgson, who in 1784 did not write a book to describe it, in part because he wrote *Alice in Wonderland* instead—he was, of course, Lewis Carroll. He, in turn, did not know of Jean-Charles de Borda, whose work dated from one century earlier. The latter was equally unaware of the ideas of Nicholas Cusanus, who promulgated his thoughts on preferential points voting in 1435 (Sigmund 1963: 212). And only Nicholas of Cusa knew of the first inventor, Ramón Llull, a Spanish Catalan, whose work dates from 1199 (McLean and Urken 1995: 18).

Little was known about most of this in our contemporary world until, during WWII, Duncan Black decided to write about the science of social choice. There again, when he first put pen to paper, he "was unacquainted with the earlier history of the theory, and, indeed, did not know that it had a history" (Black 1987: xi). But not only is the MBC very accurate—and therefore very democratic; in certain circumstances, it can actually be a scientific measure of extreme precision.

1.6.3 Single-peaked Curves

Returning to the example of tax-rates and the five-option choice mentioned above—*A* 40, *B* 45, *C* 50, *D* 55 and *E* 60%—in those instances where the voters cast all of their preferences (of which more in a moment), it could be assumed that he, Mr. *j*, who wanted 58, 59 or 60% would have (1st, 2nd ... last) preferences of *E-D-C-B-A*, which translates into (5, 4 ... 1) points. This can be represented as in Graph 1.1.

Meanwhile, she—Ms. *k* or Ms. *l*—whose favourite is 45% might have preferences *B-A-C-D-E* or *B-C-A-D-E* as shown in Graph 1.2, or maybe *B-C-D-A-E* or *B-*

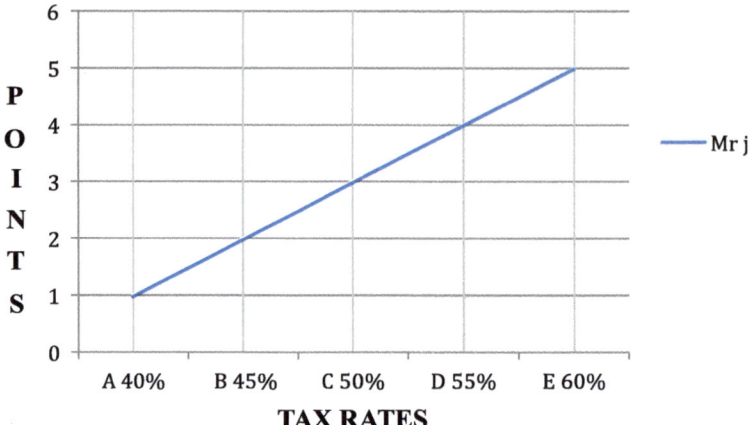

Graph 1.1 The points cast by Mr. *j*

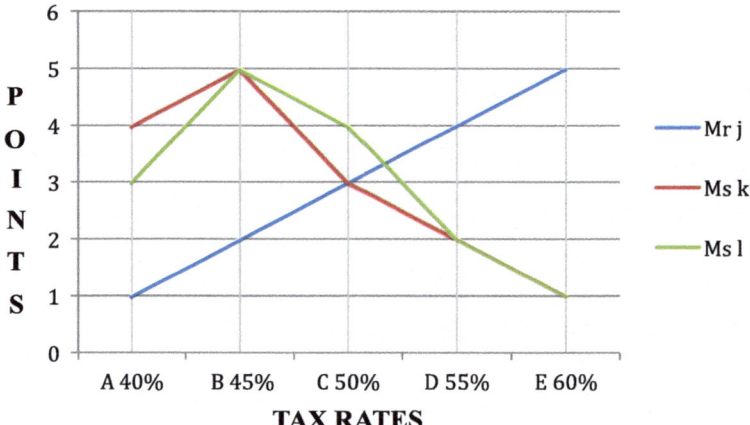

Graph 1.2 The points cast by Mr. *j*, Ms. *k* and Ms. *l*

C-D-E-A. All of these 'curves' have what is called a single peak: his is at ***E***, 60%, while that of the two women is at ***B***, 45%.

Two other MPs, Mr. *m* and Ms. *n*, might have a more varied set of preferences. Mr. *m*, for instance, might have chosen ***B-D-A-E-C***, and the depiction of his preferences—the red curve in Graph 1.3—therefore has two peaks. Opting for ***C-A-E-B-D***, Ms. *n* has three peaks, the blue curve. In such a setting, any journalists in the press box or, more importantly, voters in the MPs' respective constituencies, should have some questions to ask. Indeed, such illogical sets of preferences might well prompt some voters to think that their MP is drunk, drugged or just plain dumb.

Examining for the moment only the theory of voting, this text continues with just the single-peaked curves of the first three MPs—Mr. *j*, Ms. *k* and Ms. *l*. And in order to establish their *collective* will, the points cast are simply *collected*, collated, added

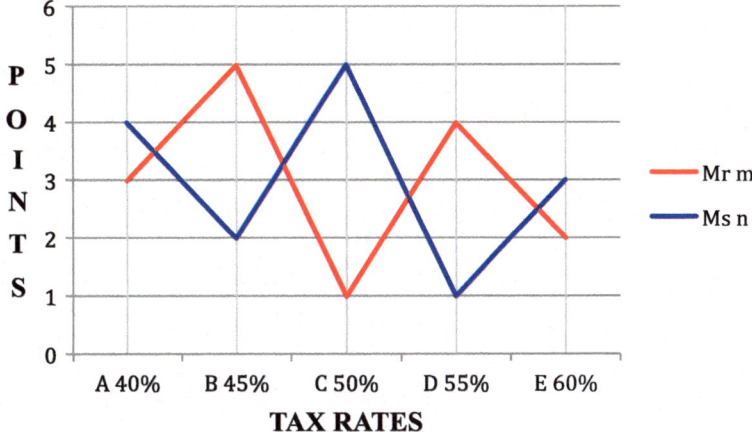

Graph 1.3 The points cast by Mr. *m* and Ms. *n*

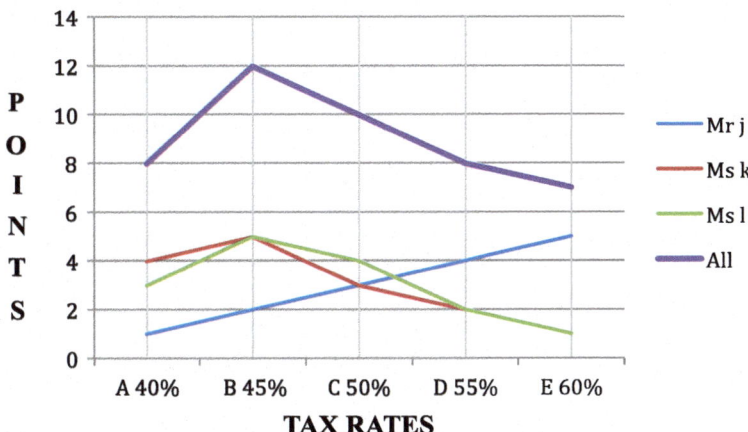

Graph 1.4 The collective will

up, as shown in Graph 1.4. If all the voters have submitted single-peaked sets of preferences, then the collective will, the collation or addition of all their points, will also be single-peaked. Always.

So, as in Graph 1.4, the collective will is 45%. Or is it? Well, not exactly. After all, this 'All' curve is a little bit biased to the right. So maybe the actual answer is 46 or 47%.

1.6.4   Precision

Before trying to lay down the rules for an exact interpretation of a collective will, consider what happens if a fourth member joins in the debate, not a drunk and disorderly Mr. *m* or Ms. *n*, but a wise and wily Mr. *o*, whose preferences are *C-D-B-A-E*, all very logical and again single-peaked. The collective will, as shown in Graph 1.5, is then a plateau between *B* and *C*. So this outcome, presumably, is 47.5%. Or is it? may be asked again. It might be possible to be even more exact.

A similar analysis can be done mathematically. Going back to the three voters— Mr. *j*, Ms. *k* and Ms. *l*—their preferences cast, or rather their points, may be displayed and totalled as in Table 1.7.

If the points cast by Mr. *o* are now added as well, the totals are as shown in Table 1.8, whence the outcome is a *B/C* tie—the plateau. So maybe there is indeed more to a 'curve' than first meets the eye.

It was noted above that she who gave a 1st preference to option *B*, like Ms. *k*, could have preferences *B-A-C-D-E*. Another, Ms. *l*, might choose *B-C-A-D-E*. Other *B* supporters may prefer even *B-C-D-A-E* or *B-C-D-E-A*. So all of them opt for option *B* but leaning either one side, towards *A*, or in varying degrees leaning the other way.

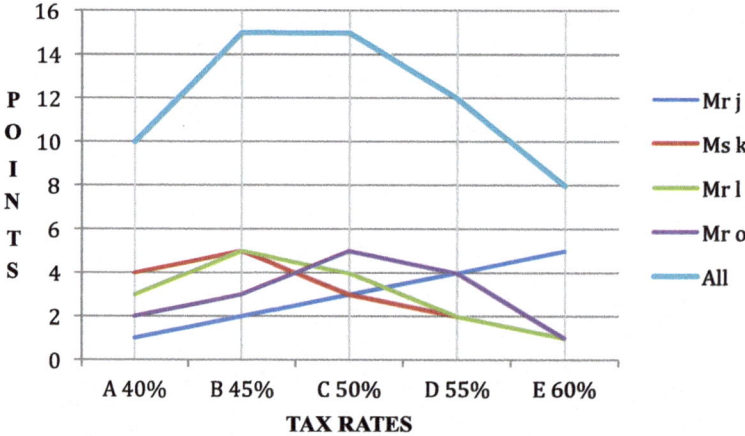

Graph 1.5 The plateau

Table 1.7 The three voters' points

Options	Voters' points			
	Mr. *j*	Ms. *k*	Ms. *l*	Totals
A	1	4	3	8
B	2	5	5	12
C	3	3	4	10
D	4	2	2	8
E	5	1	1	7

Table 1.8 The four voters'
points

| Options | Voters' points | | | | |
	Mr. j	Ms. k	Ms. l	Mr. o	Totals
A	1	4	3	2	10
B	2	5	5	3	15
C	3	3	4	5	15
D	4	2	2	4	12
E	5	1	1	1	8

To be more exact, consider those who vote as follows:

- she who wants 46 or 47% should vote **B-C-D-B-A**,
- he who wants 48 or 49% should vote **C-B-A-D-E**, and
- she who wants 50% exactly should vote **C-B-D-E-A** or **C-D-B-A-E**.

Before any vote is taken, therefore, the consensors should specify which particular tax level should correspond to which set of preferences. Furthermore, the participants should be told of the importance of submitting full ballots: it is not just to show respect for those colleagues and/or neighbours who have different aspirations, it can also influence the count (see Annex B and Annex C, C.3).

There is another possible problem which is often raised in discussions on this methodology, but it is actually tiny. It concerns the choice of options. What would happen, some people ask, if when choosing the options, the consensors decided to have, instead of the above five, the following six options: 40, 44, 48, 52, 56 and 60%, **A-B-C-D-E-F**? In this circumstance:

- she who wanted 50% would now vote **C-D-B-A-E-F** or **D-C-E-F-B-A**.

In majority voting, as noted above, the choice of just two options **AB?**—or worse, the choice of only a single option **A?**—is crucial, and such a choice has often been made by either a dictator or the democratic leader who likes to dictate. With the MBC, however, it matters less whether the consensors' final choice of options is four, five or six, as long as the list is balanced and covers the full debate. Suffice to say that the outcome, the collective will, can be interpreted graphically or mathematically with a high degree of accuracy ... although when discussing tax rates, it might well be agreed by all concerned that the nearest whole number should be sufficient. Nevertheless, given that the plateau in Graph 1.5 is as it were leaning to the right a little, the exact collective will might not be 47.5 but rather 48%. Unfortunately, the structure of an actual formula for interpreting the final graph's (Graph 1.5) or the final table's (Table 1.8) collective will, is beyond the mathematical capabilities of this author.

With other topics, when choosing a nation's constitutional status or whatever, or choosing the next venue for the Olympics, say, it might not be so easy for the consensors to lay out the options in a linear and logical sequence (but see below). That said, when debating five constitutional varieties, it is highly unlikely that every option will be totally mutually exclusive of all four of the other options. If, therefore, one option, the winner, is only just ahead of the next, the runner-up, then the consensors may still decide to form a composite (Annex C).

1.6.5 Manipulation

Manipulation is still possible, perhaps. If the choice of questions is the responsibility of the consensors, however, at least the decision-making process cannot be manipulated by the politician who dictates the option(s) to be put on the ballot paper. In theory, of course, manipulation is still possible in the vote. With an MBC, however, while the risk of truncations may still exist, the chances that this might have an adverse effect on the outcome will be minimal. Furthermore, if the consensors have managed to list the options in sequence, any MP's constituents may suspect an attempt at manipulation if his preferences reveal more than a single peak. Finally, to manipulate successfully, the perpetrator of such a misdemeanour should first be able to estimate the ballots of all the other MPs. To do this in a majority vote setting, especially in a parliament where the whip is used, is relatively easy. If the ballot is multi-optional, however, it becomes more difficult. If the vote is free, it becomes really problematic. And if the vote is preferential, it becomes almost impossible.

Unfortunately, however, in many parliamentary votes, the outcome is manipulated by the use of the party whip. It "is illegal in every other work place . . . to secure compliance with bosses' wishes by . . . harassment and coercion" (Grayling 2017: 136). For some bizarre reason, however, whips are allowed in parliaments. Not only that: in "Ireland as in many other parliamentary democracies, the Executive effectively controls the Legislature," (FitzGerald 2003: 51), so the Executive does everything! In democratic theory, however, the Legislature should legislate, and the Executive should execute.

The MBC spells the end for the whip system. In a two-option majority vote, there are only two ways of voting, so for the party whip to tell a 'this' party MP to vote 'this' and not 'that' is probably fairly straight-forward. In a three-option MBC vote, however, there are six ways of completing a full list of preferences; in a four-option poll, there are 24; with five options, 120, and so on. Well it could be quite difficult in a five-option ballot for a party whip to convince the doubtful MP that only one way of voting was the 'correct' way and that all the other 119 ways were wrong.

Furthermore, as has just been stated, there is the possibility in an MBC of a consensors' composite. To anticipate everyone's 1st preferences may indeed be tricky. To estimate how they are going to cast their 2nd preferences might be nigh on impossible. Secondly, to attempt to manipulate the vote by casting a false 2nd preference could backfire: as the old saying goes, "Be careful of what you wish for." That 2nd preference, if it comes to be the collective 2nd preference, may perhaps be incorporated into a composite!

In taking a decision on tax-rates, it is of course quite easy to form a composite between two adjacent options. When choosing a venue for the Olympics, however, there cannot be any composites—well even that is not quite true, as in a joint bid. It might nevertheless be better for such a vote to decide on the next few venues in one ballot, so to allow for at least the possibility of compromise.

1.7   Electronic Voting

Binary voting can and is often done either by hand or in some other obvious way so that persons find it difficult to cheat. In the House of Commons, for example, the system is virtually the same as it has been since the time of Henry VIII (Sect. 4.4.1); the MPs stand and file through two doors, one marked 'aye' and the other 'nay'. It is called a division, and the whole process often takes 15 min or more.

For reasons mainly of vested interest, electronic preferential voting has rarely been used in the elected chamber. In 1989, the Russians gave every deputy in the newly elected Supreme Soviet a little console so that, with the aid of this latest technology from the Netherlands, voting could be done electronically ... but only two buttons were available: '*da*' and '*nyet*'. A few other parliaments have also introduced electronic voting, as in the Czech Republic, Serbia[13] and Armenia, for example, but not for anything more sophisticated than a binary ballot. There is, however, no reason why more cybernetics should not be used in the elected chamber in order to facilitate a more accurate identification of the collective will.[14] In which case, the vote and count could all be done in the space of a few nano-seconds, with the results and the voters' profile then displayed on the big screen. Electronic voting for the electorate, as it might be done in a referendum or an election, is described in the next chapter (Sect. 2.6).

1.8   Conclusion

In majority voting, many people have often tended to vote, as it were, for themselves. Accordingly, in some 'stable democracies', many right-wingers voted to retain their wealth, while their left-wing counterparts voted in an attempt to share it. The democratic process, however, was meant to be one by which people could come together to choose that which would benefit society as a whole. "Voting, from [Jean-Jacques Rousseau's] point of view, is not a device whereby each individual expresses [their] personal interests, but rather where each individual gives [their] opinion of the general will" (Arrow 1963: 85).

---

[13]'Yes' and 'no'... and 'undecided'.

[14]At a seminar held in Belfast City Council in 2005, the author tried to persuade the Policy and Resources Committee to suggest the Council could become the first democratically elected local council in the world to use electronic preferential voting. He was unsuccessful. At the time, while some members had their own i-pads and smart phones, there were only two electronic devices in common use in the main debating chamber: the microphone and the light bulb.

What's more, the basis of a utilitarian democracy was meant to be the identification of that which gives "the greatest good of the greatest number," to quote Jeremy Bentham's phrase (McLean and McMillan 2003: 42). The definition uses not the comparative word *greater* but the superlative *greatest*. Politics, after all, like life itself, is multi-optional. Debates should be multi-optional. So ballots should be multi-optional. Political choices should not be based on *comparative* binary but on *multi*-option ballots. As was said earlier, a collective choice can only be determined accurately if those concerned express their individual opinions accurately, so the vote should be not only multi-optional but also preferential. Hence the MBC.

In a majority vote, as often as not, it is 'left' versus 'right', and the House divides. The general will, however, Rousseau's *la volonté général*, might well be in the centre of the normal distribution curve of public and even parliamentary opinion,[15] in which case a majority vote outcome, no matter on which sides it falls, is almost bound to be wrong. Yet again, hence the MBC.

There are many who have faith in democracy, in humanity's innate moral compass. Collective decisions, it is argued, are bound to be wiser than the will or whim of just one individual politician. But that collective will can be determined accurately only if the voting procedure itself is accurate, and that in turn depends on whether or not the voters concerned are able to express their individual opinions accurately. Many bemoan the rise of populism, and hence an avalanche of books on the subject: *How Democracies Die* (Levitsky and Ziblatt 2018), *How Democracy Ends* (Runciman 2018) and *Democracy and its Crisis* (Grayling 2017), to name but three. Some writers try to advance a new democracy, as in *Out of the Wreckage* (Monbiot 2018). Yet none of these books highlight the cause of the possibly fatal problem: majoritarianism. They talk of elections. They criticise FPTP, be its use in the US or the UK, and quite right too. But these authors, it seems, are also mesmerised by "the mystique of the majority," to use Dummett's phrase again; they do not analyse majority voting and binary majority rule.

The thesis of this book, then, is as follows. People are basically nice. And people can best make nice collective decisions, if and only if they use a sensible and well-defined decision-making process. To draw an unusual parallel, if given a football and put onto a pitch, they will contest—and it's win-or-lose; if given a majority vote and put into a parliament like the House of Commons, with one side facing the other as if ready for gladiatorial combat, they will argue, there's little or no compromise, and it is again win-or-lose; but if given an MBC in which at best the outcome is the option with the highest average preference—and an average, of course, involves every voter, not just a majority of them—it's win-win; in such a setting, all concerned will be more likely to come to a consensus. And after all, democracy is, yes, for everybody, not just a majority.

As noted above and as the title of this book suggests, majority voting can be a catalyst of populism. The potential consequences have been well recognised as

---

[15]This is more likely to be true if the parliament concerned is multi-party, i.e., if it has been elected by a system of PR.

profoundly dangerous. Indeed, if societies continue to use **A?** type majority yes-or-no questions, and if as an almost direct consequence, societies continue to say 'no' to everything, then logically, they could well finish up with nothing.

The MBC, in contrast, is inclusive, robust and above all else, accurate. Others also argue that "only the [BC] offers an accurate accounting of the voters' preferences" (Saari 2001: 187). For some extraordinary reason, however, in business, in civil society, and most especially in politics, people still use majority voting. Many users don't dispute it. Most observers don't question it. And as Part II of this book relates, the world thus blunders from one ghastly mistake to the next.

References

Aristotle. (1992). *The politics*. London: Penguin.

Arrow, K. (1963). *Social choice and individual values* (2nd ed.). New Haven: Yale University Press.

Black, D. (1987). *The theory of committees and elections*. Boston: Kluwer Academic Publishers.

Butler, D., & Ranney, A. (1994). Conclusion. In D. Butler & A. Ranney (Eds.), *Referendums around the world*. Washington, DC: The AEI Press.

Cannell, M., & Citrine, M. (1982). *Citrine's ABC of chairmanship*. London: NCLC Publishing Society.

Dummett, M. (1984). *Voting procedures*. Oxford: Clarendon Press.

Dummett, M. (1997). *Principles of electoral reform*. Oxford: OUP.

Dunn, J. E. (2008). *Democracy: The unfinished journey*. Oxford: OUP.

Eban, A. (1998). *Diplomacy for the next century*. New Haven, CT: Yale University Press.

Emerson, P. (1978). *That sons may bury their fathers*. Belfast: Samizdat.

Emerson, P. (2007). *Designing an all-inclusive democracy*. Heidelberg: Springer.

Emerson, P. (2012). *Defining democracy* (2nd ed.). Heidelberg: Springer.

Emerson, P. (2013). The original Borda count and partial voting. *Social Choice and Welfare, 46*(2), 353–358.

Emerson, R. (1966). *From empire to nation*. Harvard: Beacon Press.

FitzGerald, G. (2003). *Reflections on the Irish State*. Dublin: Irish Academic Press.

Gallagher, M. (1996). Ireland: The referendum as a conservative device. In M. Gallagher & P. V. Uleri (Eds.), *The referendum experience in Europe*. Hampshire: Macmillan Press.

Grayling, A. C. (2017). *Democracy and its crisis*. London: Oneworld Publications.

Huntington, S. (1991). *The third wave*. Norman: University of Oklahoma Press.

Levitsky, S., & Ziblatt, D. (2018). *How democracies die*. New York: Crown.

Lewis, S. A. (1965). *Politics in West Africa*. London: George Allen and Unwin Ltd.

Lijphart, A. (1977). *Democracy in plural societies*. New Haven, CT: Yale University Press.

Mackie, G. (2003). *Democracy defended*. Cambridge: CUP.

McLean, I., & McMillan, A. (2003). *Oxford concise dictionary of politics*. Oxford: OUP.

McLean, I., & Urken, A. (1995). *Classics of social choice*. Ann Arbor, MI: University of Michigan Press.

Monbiot, G. (2018). *Out of the wreckage*. London: Verso.

Obama, B. (2006). *The audacity of hope*. New York: Three Rivers Press.

Riker, W. (1988). *Liberalism against populism*. Long Grove, IL: Waveland Press.

Runciman, D. (2018). *How democracy ends*. London: Profile Books.

Saari, D. (2001). *Decisions and elections*. Cambridge: CUP.

Saari, D. (2008). *Disposing dictators, demystifying voting paradoxes*. Cambridge: CUP.

Sigmund, P. (1963). *Nicholas of cusa and medieval political thought*. Cambridge, MA: Harvard University Press.

Tolstoy, L. N. (1966). The meaning of the Russian revolution. In M. Raeff (Ed.), *Russian intellectual history, an anthology*. Sussex: Harvester Press.

Whitaker, T. (1996). *Report of the constitution review group*. Dublin: The Stationery Office.

Chapter 2
Parliamentary and Presidential Elections

If a form of election is to be just, the voters must be able to rank each candidate according to [his/her] merits, compared successively to the merits of each of the others.
Jean-Charles de Borda, quoted in McLean and Urken (1995: 84).

Abstract For some inexplicable reason, while thinking that most decision-making should be based on a choice of just two options, many democrats digress from this notion and insist that elections must involve not just two but *lots* of candidates. In which case, of course, there are lots of ways of voting and lots of ways of counting the electorate's preferences. Nearly every country discussed in this book has, if not a different electoral theme, then at least a variation; (but they nearly all believe in and use only binary voting in decision-making—all very odd). The differences of these various electoral systems and their effects can be significant; yet almost without exception, all of these systems are regarded as democratic. This Chapter describes the said countries' electoral systems; compares their many effects and defects, the biggest of the former is the subsequent party structure; and then suggests a voting methodology which is both more inclusive and more accurate.

2.1 Free and Fair Elections

An election is regarded as "free and fair" if, during the campaign, every participating party has been able to campaign on an equal basis; if, on polling day, the voters were able to go to the polls without fear of intimidation; if the count was conducted in accordance with the appropriate rules; and if the results were then implemented. There are over 300 different electoral systems. In some of them, the voter is not "free" to vote as she might wish and some of them are therefore most definitely "unfair." Furthermore, as a direct result of deploying 'this' or 'that' electoral system, different countries—some democratic and some not—have different party structures: there are a couple of one-party states in this book, and a few one-party

© Springer Nature Switzerland AG 2020
P. Emerson, *Majority Voting as a Catalyst of Populism*,
https://doi.org/10.1007/978-3-030-20219-4_2

dominant states; one country is a two-party state, while several others are multi-party, with varying numbers of political parties gaining representation; and, to complete what might be a circle, there are also some all-party states.

2.1.1 Horses for Courses

Just as many decision-making methodologies are said to be democratic (Sect. 1.1.4), so too, in the opinions of many, nearly all electoral systems also qualify for this adjective—although there are of course the blatant exceptions, as in North Korea (Sect. 6.6.4)—and so too, it seems, nearly all the various party structures are also so regarded—with the same notable exception of the one-party state. Accordingly, with regard to the countries concerned, this chapter first looks at the current range of electoral systems and party structures, and then outlines that which might be better.

There are also huge variations on many related considerations. Should there be just one big constituency as in the Netherlands, or lots of smaller ones, as in Ireland? Should the outcome be proportional like Austria's, or maybe just semi-proportional as in Georgia, or maybe neither, like Britain's? Should an election involve just one ballot paper, as in Belgium, or should there be a second tier or a top-up as in Germany? Fourthly, should there be a legal threshold like Russia's, and not just an 'effective' one—(see Sect. 2.1.5.1)—and in either case, what value would be appropriate? And so on. Accordingly, this chapter first concentrates on the various electoral systems and their most immediate consequences, the various countries' different party structures, before later giving consideration to a less adversarial and more 'peace-ful' electoral system.

2.1.2 Binary Voting

An electoral system which is an **A?** type of yes-or-no question offers only one candidate. This sort of system was used in the Soviet Union and is still deployed in North Korea, and many would regard it as inadequate. Correctly so. (In decision-making, however, as noted in Chap. 1, such binary questions are considered by many to be perfectly acceptable.)

A?   a "candidate A, yes-or-no?" type question.

It is perhaps acceptable but only in some very rare instances, as in Georgia's presidential election in 1992, which was after all during their civil war (Sect. 5.8.2.1).

> **AB?**   a "candidate *A* or candidate *B*?" ballot.

More frequently, majority vote elections offer this sort of binary choice, as in the final round of a two-round system, TRS, election.

2.1.3   Multi-candidate, Single-preference Voting

As noted, many democrats regard a plurality of candidates—three or more—as a minimum criterion of a good election. There are quite a few methodologies. Some are majoritarian and are similar to what can be used in decision-making, the plurality vote and TRS, for example; others are proportional and therefore have no equivalence. After all, in decision-making, the outcome is a single decision or at most a unitary 'shopping list' or prioritisation. Admittedly, in some presidential elections, the outcome is a singleton; in parliamentary contests, however—which is what this text concentrates on—the results involve a multiplicity of successful candidates, and if the contest is conducted in one or more multi-member constituencies, proportionality may also apply.

> **FPTP**   **First-past-the-post**

Consider a multi-candidate election, with candidates from various parties of the left- and right-wing, all in open competition. Or take NI, where in a mixed constituency, the list may include candidates from every political faction, from the extreme Unionist via a more moderate one and a centre-ground candidate or two to a moderate and then a more extreme Nationalist. For any one individual to cast a single preference—as if to suggest, in Orwellian-speak, that this candidate is 'good' and that all the others are all equally 'bad' (Sect. 1.1.3, fn. 6)—is obviously an inaccurate representation of her opinion. She who votes for the extreme Nationalist would presumably think a moderate Nationalist would represent her views slightly better than an extreme Unionist, and *vice versa*. If, however, the voting system is FPTP,[1] she can cast only one preference. But (nearly) everybody does have

---

[1]One wit described FPTP as 'fake, post-truth polling.'

preferences. So in a single preference ballot, (nearly) everybody's vote is inaccurate. Therefore, in all probability, an FPTP outcome will also be inaccurate.

FPTP can also be inaccurate, as when, for example, Party **W** has just 51% support in every constituency, and thus wins 100% of the seats.[2] Maybe it's even worse: in a four-party contest, Party **W** may have only 28% support everywhere, but if all three of the other parties have only 24% support each, then again, **W** wins everything. The world record in this regard is held by Papua New Guinea, PNG, where in some elections, candidates were successful on 'success' rates of only 6.3% of the vote because, in that constituency, a score of other candidates got even less than 6.3% (IDEA 1997: 42). So who is to know: maybe 93.7% regarded the winner as the *worst* candidate? FPTP is indeed hopeless. No wonder the good people of PNG changed from FPTP to the alternative vote, AV, in time for the 2007 election.

To take another extreme example, the result of the US presidential election of 2016, Mr. Trump, was fake. It is not just the Electoral College which may distort the result; it is the fact that both the Electoral College and the US electorate in general use FPTP. In the so-called land of the free, those who supported Bernie Sanders, for example, were not free to vote for him; his name was not allowed to be on the ballot paper. The ballot still offered a list of names, so it was like a plurality vote in decision-making (Sect. 1.1.3), but because of the dominance of the two big parties, it was more like an **AB?** type of majority vote (Sect. 1.1.2). There is the added proviso that in some very tight elections, as in 2000, a Ralph Nader type of 'middle ground' candidate with 3 million votes could in effect swing the result from one candidate, Al Gore on 51 million votes, to the other contestant, George W Bush on 50.5 million.[3] Don't blame Ralph Nader—well you can actually; he should have known better— blame the electoral system. In a nutshell, FPTP is a nonsense; can anyone blame the Chinese for not wanting such an inaccurate, divisive or even masochistic form of governance?

Not only does FPTP produce fake results; it also has fake consequences: both the US and the UK, to take the two obvious examples, have two-party systems. It is widely acknowledged—it is called Duverger's Law: "the simple majority single-ballot system favours the two-party system," (Duverger 1955: 217)—that the choice of electoral system influences the party structure. In fact, of course, another huge basis of any two-party system is the majority vote decision-making process used by

---

[2]In the FPTP elections held in Ethiopia in 2015, the ruling party increased its dominance by gaining all 100% of the seats. At the previous election, they had to settle for a mere 499 of the 500 total.

Singapore was even more one-sided: in every election from its independence in 1965 to 1980, one party won all of the seats, every time. In 1980, for example, the ruling party was 100% successful on just 74.1% support.

[3]As in 2016, so too in 2000, the losing candidate actually won the popular vote.

those two parties in their parliaments but, for some odd reason, many political scientists blame only the electoral system.

TRS   Two-round system

The parallel continues for, as in decision-making so too in elections, TRS is not much better than FPTP. These 'French' and 'British' electoral systems are now used fairly extensively, not least in 'their' former colonies, but TRS was also used in 1989 in the Soviet Union as it then was (Sect. 5.9.2.1) for its first post-*perestroika* elections, and as noted earlier in the Balkans in 1990 (Sect. 5.6.2).

In effect, TRS is a single-preference system—used once or perhaps twice. It is quite inappropriate for a plural society such as was and is still in Bosnia. In 1990, the voters in Bosnia were allowed to cast only one preference; in effect, therefore, they had to take sides; as shall be seen (Sect. 5.6.5), the vote was little more than a sectarian headcount; it was indeed a cause of conflict.

2.1.4   Non-Orwellian Electoral Systems

The words used in many democratic contests suggest that candidates 'fight' elections in the hope of 'defeating' the opposition, and so on; it is all the language of war. As implied in decision-making in Sect. 1.6.1, however, an inclusive polity should be based more on a political structure by which voters come together on election-day, peacefully, to decide who best should be their society's decision-makers? and who best should represent their constituency?

Be it a small local council area, a parliamentary constituency, or the entire country, every voter should be able to propose a team of representatives to do the job; and in a plural society, that team should be representative of the whole.

Accordingly, as in decision-making, so too in elections, voters should be enabled to express their opinions accurately; therefore, the system should be preferential. It is also generally recognised, not least in plural societies, that elections should also be proportional. Even single-preference "PR systems... are praised because of the way in which they... make it more likely that women are elected." (IDEA 1997: 62–3) By the same logic, a system which is both proportional and preferential has the potential to produce an outcome which is fairer in every sense, with better gender and ethno-religious balance.

SNTV   Single non-Transferable Vote

In an SNTV election, the voter may cast just one vote, and those candidates who get the most support shall be elected. The system is sometimes used with a threshold: in Iran, for example, the candidate must get support from 25% or more of the voters to be successful. SNTV is usually referred to as semi-proportional (Lijphart 1995: 40).

AV   Alternative Vote

As an electoral system, AV is not used in any of the countries visited in this book, except in its PR format, of which more in a moment.

BC/MBC   Borda Count and/or Modified Borda Count

A BC is used in Slovenian elections, for the election of its ethnic minority representatives. This electoral system, however, is not proportional.

CR   Condorcet Rule

In the countries covered in these pages, the Condorcet rule is not used as a parliamentary electoral system.

2.1.5 Proportional Representation (PR)

Many modern democracies have chosen a system of PR and in some plural societies, in one form or another, it is often regarded as an essential ingredient of any post-conflict polity. Nevertheless, by a similar logic to that which applies to FPTP and TRS, any single preference PR-list system is likely to be inaccurate.

PR-l(c)   PR-list, closed

If a PR-list system is 'closed', the voter is able to choose only one of several parties. Every party submits a 'list' of candidates—hence the system's name—and depending on the success of the party, these candidates will then be elected in descending order as listed.

PR-l(o)   PR-list, open

In most 'open' systems, the voter may choose either one particular party in general, or from its list of candidates, one particular candidate of that party. With PR, as long as the constituency is large enough, the outcome will be multi-party. In the Netherlands, for example, which has a parliament of 150 members, the entire country as was said earlier is just the one constituency; so the effective threshold (Sect. 2.1.5.1) required for a party to gain representation in that parliament is quite small—0.67% is the Dutch figure (*Ibid*: 29). As a direct result, the Netherlands has a multi-party structure, and the *Tweede Kamer* currently has 13 parties represented.

Belgium, where voting is compulsory, has a slightly different open PR-list system: the voter may cast more than one preference, but only among the candidates of one party.[4] Here too, 13 parties are currently represented in parliament.

A further disadvantage of any PR-list election is that each party is incentivised to produce a long *list* of candidates, if only to try and show how strong it is... even when it is not.[5]

2.1.5.1   Proportional Representation (PR) with Preferential Voting

PR-STV   PR-Single Transferable Vote

Proportional Representation—single transferable vote, PR-STV, is the PR version of AV, and Ireland's PR-STV is indeed pluralist. To be fair, it's not Irish at all; it was invented in Britain in 1821 by a certain Thomas Hill, and again in Denmark in 1855 by Carl Andrae. But its main advocate came a couple of years later when an English Tory MP, one Thomas Hare, believing the voters should have freedom of choice, campaigned for its introduction in the UK. Unfortunately, some of his party colleagues disagreed and criticised his 'hare-brained scheme'. He lost.

The advantages of this preferential system were nevertheless recognised, so in 1920, when Britain 'gave' the two new jurisdictions in Ireland their new administrations, PR-STV was part of the package both North and South (Sect. 4.2.1). In fact, the British have been quite good at imposing good electoral systems on other

---

[4]The PR-list system in Switzerland is even more pluralist, for Swiss voters may cast their votes, not only across the gender gap, but also across the party divide.

[5]The author was an election observer in the 1997 elections in Bosnia, and spent lots of time on election night recording the zero totals of literally countless candidates.

peoples: they were also behind the mixed-member proportional, MMP, system adopted in Germany in 1949; (see below). Sadly, they managed to give themselves only FPTP which, as seen above, is one of the very worst systems.

PR-STV, then, is like AV, but with one big difference: the vote takes place in *multi*-member constituencies. The voter may cast as many preferences as he wishes and, in so doing, he can vote, as in the Swiss PR-list system, across any gender, party and/or any other divides. PR-STV nowadays is usually held in multi-member constituencies of three to six elected representatives. To be successful, a candidate needs to gain a quota of votes. {Now with AV, in a single-seat constituency, the quota is of course 50% + 1, as described in (Sect. 1.1.4); but in any one constituency, an AV election elects only one person, so AV is not proportional.} With PR-STV in a two-seater constituency, the quota, as defined in (Sect. 2.3), would be 33.3% + 1; but to elect only two MPs would not be a very proportional. In practical terms, therefore, the minimum is usually a three-seater, where the quota is 25% + 1; in a four-seater, it is 20% + 1, and so on. To take this instance of a four-seater, if four candidates gets 20% + 1 votes each, then all four shall be elected, and even if all the other votes go to a fifth candidate, the latter will get only 20% – 4 votes which, of course, is less than the quota. So the 'effective threshold' as it is called, the minimum amount of support a party needs in order to *probably* get elected, decreases, as the number of seats per constituency increases.

PR-STV works quite well; it *allows* the voters to cast their preferences on a cross community basis, but it does not necessarily *encourage* them to do so. A further criticism is based on the fact that, while the voter herself may act in a cross-community way, her ballot paper may not be so regarded in the count. If her 1st preference is for a Protestant man and her 2nd for a Catholic woman, then, in the count, if her 1st preference candidate is eliminated, her vote may be transferred, in total, to the 2nd preference; so in this instance, *either* the vote goes to the former *or* it goes to the latter: it is not shared between the two. In the polling booth, she votes for one *and* the other; but in the count, it may go to one *or* the other.

Thirdly, to take an emotional example, in Bosnia's first elections in 1990 (Sect. 5.6.5), Ante Marković was probably the best hope for avoiding any war; "public opinion polls. . . showed overwhelming majorities (in the range of 70–90%) against separation from Yugoslavia and against an ethnically divided republic." (Woodward 1995: 228) He was indeed probably the 2nd preference of thousands. Unfortunately, as noted above, the system used was a single-preference procedure, TRS, so he lost. He would probably have lost in a PR-STV contest as well, gaining a small total of 1st preferences to thus be eliminated in an early stage of the count, and many of the 2nd preferences that might have been cast in his favour would probably never have been counted [like option *B* in Table 1.2 (Sect. 1.1.3)] (see also Sect. 2.5.1).

2.1.5.2   Proportional and Semi-Proportional Systems

PS   A Parallel System

This system is sometimes confused with the next one, MMP, but a parallel system is only semi-proportional. It consists of two parts: one part is non-PR, and usually consists of an FPTP election but sometimes, as in Georgia, it may be TRS; and the second part is a PR-list election. The two halves are usually 50:50 but, of course, any other ratio is also possible—the original Russian balance was 67:33, but this was changed to 50:50 in 1993.

The big difference between a parallel system and MMP is that, in the former, proportionality applies only to the PR part of the election; with MMP, however, the results are adjusted by the PR election so that the system is proportional overall.

MMP   Multi-member Proportional

The penultimate electoral system then, for this book anyway, is MMP, which as noted is used in Germany. The Weimar Republic had used PR-list so, post WWII, something new was required... but the new system was and still is a combination of an ancient procedure, FPTP, mixed with the rather more up-to-date PR-list.

The voter gets one paper but two ballots: the first is for an FPTP election in a small single-seat constituency; the second is a single-preference election but on a different ballot, and the voter now chooses one of several parties in a closed PR-list election in a much larger regional constituency, a Länder. There is also a 5% legal threshold, originally designed to keep the Communists out of parliament. For both of these reasons—the electoral system itself and the legal threshold—the German party structure consists of two large parties plus two or three small parties.

2.2   Electoral Systems

In summary, then, the electoral systems mentioned above, plus one more—the quota Borda system, QBS, another PR system which will be discussed in a moment—are shown in Table 2.1, alongside their equivalent decision-making systems from Table 1.6. Preferential methodologies are shown in tint. Approval voting and range voting can be but are not used as electoral systems in the democratic structures in the countries covered by this book, so they are not listed here on the right hand

Table 2.1 Some decision-making and electoral systems

Decision-making			Elections		
Binary	A?	Majority vote – '*A*, yes-or-no?'	A?	Binary	
	AB?	Majority vote – '*A* or *B*?'	AB?		
Multi-option	PV	Plurality voting	FPTP	Multi-candidate	
Single preference		TRS		Single preference	
			Single non-transferable vote	SNTV	Multi-candidate 'multi-preference'
Multi-option		AV^a or STV		Multi-candidate	
Preferential	BC	Borda count	BC	Preferential	
	MBC	Modified Borda count	MBC		
	CR	Condorcet	CR		
Multi-option	ApV	Approval voting			
non-preferential	RV	Range voting			
			PR-list, closed	PR-l(c)	Multi-candidate
			PR-list, open	PR-l(o)	Single preference^b
			PR single transferable vote	PR-STV	Multi-candidate Preferential
			Parallel system	PS	Single and 2nd
			Multi-member proportional	MMP	preference maybe
			Quota Borda system	QBS	Multi-candidate Preferential

^{a}In North America, AV is known as instant run-off voting, IRV, while in Australasia it is called preferential voting, PV
^{b}As noted, Belgium and Switzerland have multi-candidate versions of PR-list (open)

side, mainly because they are not considered suitable for use in plural societies (Sect. 1.3), not by this author anyway.

2.3   A Comparison

In decision-making, it is quite easy to compare and contrast different decision-making voting procedures, as was seen in the voters' profiles used earlier (Sect. 1.1.3). With electoral systems, because there are so many other variables as well, not least that of PR, life gets a little more complicated. Consider, nevertheless, an electorate of 100 persons seeking to elect a parliament of 10 MPs, whose profile in regard for their support of four parties—**W**, **X**, **Y** and **Z**—is as shown in Table 2.2. The society is assumed to be divided into two: parties **W** and **Y** sometimes work together, and on the other side, so too do parties **X** and **Z**.

If the electoral system is FPTP or TRS, the vote will take place in 10 single-member constituencies; with PR, consider either two 5-member constituencies or one 10-member constituency.

With FPTP, if all the voters are spread evenly across the country, with 4 **W**, 3 **X**, 2 **Y** and 1 **Z** supporters in each 10-voter constituency, then **W** will win every seat! The same applies to TRS and AV. If however the population is itself divided, with

Table 2.2   100 Voters' profile

Preferences	100 Voters			
	40	30	20	10
1st	W	X	Y	Z
2nd	Y	Z	W	X
3rd	Z	Y	Z	Y
4th	X	W	X	W

Table 2.3   Divisors in a 5-member constituency

Scores	Divisors and totals			
	1	2	3	4
W – 20	20	10	6.7	5
X – 15	15	7.5	5	...
Y – 10	10	5	...	-
Z - 5	5	...	-	-

Table 2.4   Divisors in a 10-member constituency

Scores	Divisors				
	1	2	3	4	5
W - 40	40	20	13	10	8
X - 30	30	15	10	7.5	...
Y - 20	20	10	6.7	-	
Z - 10	10	5	-	-	

4 constituencies full of **W** supporters, 3 of **X**, etc., then the result will be **W**-4, **X**-3, **Y**-2 and **Z**-1. In real life, most societies are probably somewhere between the two, with some cities having large working class populations, while the suburbs are more middle-class, while some countries of course have ethno-religions ghettoes. So, with FPTP, the result might be fair, but only if society itself is unfair and riddled by division; in a truly plural society, it is (almost) bound to produce an outcome which is inaccurate.

The PR-list analysis is done on the basis of d'Hondt divisors.[6] The relevant total number of votes gained by the parties, **W**, **X**, **Y** and **Z** are 20, 15, 10, 5 in each of the two 5-seater constituencies, and 40, 30, 20, 10 in the one 10-seater—and obviously, the population in a single constituency can only be regarded mathematically as mixed. Accordingly, in the analyses which follow in Tables 2.3 and 2.4, these scores are divided by divisors 1, 2, 3, 4... and on this basis, five and ten respectively of the highest totals are chosen, and these are shown in tint.

So in Table 2.3, the result is **W**-2, **X**-2, **Y**-1 in each of the two 5-member constituencies, which is **W**-4, **X**-4, **Y**-2 overall; while in Table 2.4, the outcome is **W**-4, **X**-3, **Y**-2, **Z**-1.

---

[6]Some PR systems work on quotas, others on divisors. In the latter case, party totals are divided by these 'divisors'—for example, the set of 1, 2, 3, 4 etc. are the d'Hondt divisors; 1, 3, 5, 7 etc. are those of the St. Laguë version—and seats are awarded in accordance with the resulting totals.

As noted earlier, some parallel electoral systems, like the one used in Georgia, use FPTP or sometimes TRS for some seats, and then PR for some of the others; so the overall result might not be proportional. In other systems like Germany's MMP, which is half FPTP and half PR-list, the final result is designed to represent a proportional balance overall; nevertheless, the FPTP element still favours the two big parties and so distorts the outcome in that the voter who supports a small party may vote sincerely in the PR-election, but only tactically in the FPTP part; which explains why, as already noted, Germany has a two-big-plus-a-few-small party structure (Sect. 2.1.5.2).

In many forms of PR-STV,

$$\text{the quota} \geq \frac{\{\text{the number of voters}\}}{\{\text{number of seats plus 1}\}}$$

therefore, in the 5-seater constituency, the quota is 50/6 = 8. So **W**, with 20 1st preferences, gets 2 quotas; **X** with 15 gets 1; **Y** with 10 gets 1 and **Z** with 5 gets nothing. Accordingly, **Z**'s votes are transferred to **X**, to give **X** an additional seat, so the result in each of the two constituencies is **W**-2, **X**-2, **Y**-1, **Z**-0, to give a combined total of **W**-4, **X**-4, **Y**-2, **Z**-0.

In a 10-seater PR-STV election, with a quota of 100/11 = 9, so **W**, with 40 1st preferences, gets 4 quotas; **X** gets 3; **Y** gets 2 and **Z** gets 1; so that is the result.

The full comparison of the electoral systems discussed is as shown in Table 2.5. The word 'evenly' in the second column implies that society is integrated, whereas 'separately' means that people are living in partisan or ethno-religious 'ghettoes'.

The three shaded rows in the Parallel Vote and MMP rows display an FPTP election held in five single-member constituencies, which chooses five MPs, and underneath, the PR-list election held in the one five-seater constituency, which chooses the other five; and the addition of the two gives the total result, as in the unshaded row immediately below.

So, if 4–3–2–1 is considered to be a fair result, then FPTP, TRS and AV will produce a 'fair' result, but only in those societies which are horribly unfair, that is, in those societies which have been divided into sectarian ghettoes, or where the constituencies have been gerrymandered to produce a similar effect. Accordingly, in any plural society, such systems should not be deployed.

With larger constituencies, as used in any PR-systems, gerrymandering becomes more difficult; and in the Netherlands, of course, where as was mentioned the entire country in just the one constituency, it is impossible. When the chosen system is either a PR-list system or PR-STV, if held in large constituencies, normally considered to be 5-seaters or more, then the result might indeed be fair if that is the voters have expressed their opinion accurately; as noted, with a single-preference PR-list system, this is impossible; with PR-STV, it is possible but may be unlikely; but with QBS, as shall be seen shortly, this is not only possible but actually probable.

Table 2.5 A comparison of some different electoral systems

System	Number of Constituencies	The Results			
		W	X	Y	Z
FPTP, TRS	10 'evenly'	10	-	-	-
and AV	10 'separately'	4	3	2	1
PR-list, single	2 'evenly'	4	4	2	-
preference	1	4	3	2	1
Parallel FPTP (5 seats) + PR-list (5 seats)	5 'separately'	5	-	-	-
	+ 1	2	2	1	
	= in total:	7	2	1	-
	5 'evenly'	3	2	-	-
	+ 1	2	2	1	
	= in total:	5	4	1	-
MMP	5 'evenly'	3	2	-	-
	+ 1	2	2	1	
	= in total:	4	4	2	-
	with 'overhang':[a]	5	4	2	-
PR-STV	2 'evenly'	4	4	2	-
	1	4	3	2	1

[a]See footnote to Table 2.6

2.4 Party Structures

It has already been suggested that plurality voting tends to promote a two-party structure, which is then enforced by the use of **A?** or **AB?** majority votes in parliament, and further strengthened by means of the party whip. Not least because decision-making in the relevant parliament is also majoritarian, TRS also tends to produce two main parties. In contrast, as already noted in the two Low Countries, PR-list promotes a multi-party system and, as elsewhere in continental Europe, these parliaments often have ten or more parties represented. In contrast, PR-STV usually involves lots of smaller constituencies—four- or five-seaters—so the number of parties gaining representation in Ireland is also fairly small.

Another factor which can have a huge effect is the legal threshold. In Germany, as noted above, it is 5%. In Turkey, it is ten, so the number of parties getting into the Turkish parliament is always rather small. Indeed, if the legal threshold is as high as this, the electoral system should perhaps no longer be regarded as truly proportional.

A fuller list of all the electoral systems covered by this book is shown in Table 2.6.

Table 2.6 Electoral systems encountered on the journey

JURIS-DICTION		Electoral system (o) = open (c) = closed	Single or multi-prefer-ence	No of elec-ted 'MPs'	No of constit-uencies	Effect-ive thresh-old %	Legal thres-hold %	The latest party structure
NI		FPTP	single	18	18	35[a]	-	2 + 2 +
		PR-STV	multi	90	18	14	-	a few small
Ireland		PR-STV	multi	157	48	3.75[a]	-	4 or 5
UK		FPTP	single	650	650	35[a]	-	two-party
Belgium		PR-list, (o)	multi	150	11	4.8[a]	4	multi-party
Netherlands		PR-list, (o)	single	150	1	0.67[a]	-	multi-party
Germany	MMP	FPTP	double	598[b]	299	35[a]	-	2 big +
		PR-list, (c)			c. 19	14	5	a few small
Czech		PR-list, (o)	multi	200	14	6	5	multi-party
Austria		PR-list, (o)	single	183	9	8.5	4	4/5-party
Serbia	1990	TRS	single	250	250	35	-	multi-party
	2000	PR-list, (c)	single	250	1	5	5	
Bosnia	1990	TRS	single	240	240	35[a]	-	2 + 2 + 2 +
	1996	PR-list, (c)	single	42	2	-	-	a few small
	1998	PR-list, (o)	single	42	2	-		
Mace-donia	1990	TRS	single	< 120	< 120	35[a]	-	
	1998	Parallel TRS	single	85	85	35[a]	35	2 big +
		+ PR	single	35			5	a few small
	2002	PR-list, (c)	single	120	20	5	-	
Turkey		PR-list, (c)	single	600	85	15	10	3 or 4
Georgia		Parallel TRS	single	+ 73	73	35[a]	-	two-party
		+ PR-list	single	77	1	5	5	
Armenia	1990	Parallel FPTP	single	41	41	35[a]	-	
		+ PR-list	single	90	1	1.5	5	2 big +
	2015	PR-list, (c)	single	c 50	1	2	5	2 small
		PR-list, (o)	single	c 50	13	20	5	
Iran		Parallel TRS	single	290	196	20	-	3 coalitions +
		+ SNTV	multi			15	-	a few small
China		Indirect	single	2980		90	-	1 big
Hong Kong		Indirect PR-list	single	35	5	15	-	3 big and several small
Taiwan		Parallel FPTP +	single	34	1	4	5	2 big +
		PR-list, (c)	single	73	73	35	-	a few small
North Korea		yes-or-no A?	single	675	675	100	-	1 big and 4 small parties
South Korea		Parallel FPTP +	single	253	253	35[a]	-	2 big +
		PR-list, (c)	single	47	1	3	3	a few small
Mongolia	1990	plurality	single	76	76	35[a]	-	2/3 big +
	2008	Plurality +	single	48	26	25-35	-	a few small
		PR-list, (c)	single	28	1		28	
USSR	1989	TRS	single	1068	1	35[a]	-	1 and a few independents
Russia	1993	Parallel FPTP	single	225	225	35[a]	-	1 very big + a
		+ PR-list	single	225	1	5	5	few small.

[a]Data taken from Lijphart (1995); other figures in this column are the author's best estimates
[b]There may be some additional 'overhang seats', if one or more of the larger parties has won more seats than its proportional due in the FPTP election

2.5   A More Inclusive System

As was seen in decision-making (Sect. 1.6), an MBC almost guarantees a degree of compromise because of a number of factors:

- the debate is inclusive, so all relevant options are allowed 'on the table' and included or at least represented on the final ballot paper;
- the consensors may composite some of the pairs of options;
- the voters are encouraged to cast a full ballot, and thereby to declare their own compromise option(s); and
- if the outcome is close, the consensors may composite the two leading options.

In an election, of course, candidates cannot be composited. Compromise, which should be an essential ingredient of any democratic structure, can nevertheless be achieved by ensuring that, in every presidential election, there are always two or more posts being contested—a president *and* a vice-president, for example; and in every parliamentary election, the contest should always involve three or more elected representatives in every constituency, all of which should therefore be multi-member.

The original US presidential electoral system was based on just such a pluralist system: the winner became the president, which was fair enough; and the runner-up became the vice-president, which was also pretty sensible.[7] Alas, the system did not last very long, and by the time Andrew Jackson was elected president in 1828—"the only clear parallel to Trump [in] US history," (Luce 2018: 113)—"he lost no time setting up America's spoils system in which government jobs were distributed to friends and supporters." (*Ibid*: 114) So that which might have been a no-party structure became entrenched into a two-party format. Alas, the mistakes of history. Unfortunately, while the founding fathers thought quite a lot about elections and electoral systems—in 1791, for example, Thomas Jefferson proposed a divisor system for use in PR-list elections, (and went on to become the President from 1801 to 1809)—they did not change the binary nature of decision-making to be used in Congress.

Now as implied above, if accuracy is considered to be important, the voters should be enabled to cast their preferences for more than one candidate of more than one party. So from a total of over 300 different electoral systems, this proviso reduces the choice to a list of just half-a-dozen—AV, the MBC, Condorcet, PR-list (open), and PR-STV—as well as the one which is yet to be described, QBS.

In Switzerland's form of PR-list, voters may cast a specified number of 'approvals' but no account is taken of any preferences; so that is not the best, and may discourage the moderate voter in the same way as would approval and range voting (Sect. 1.3). Australia uses AV and, like the Swiss system, this methodology encourages some cross-party co-operation, so the resulting political milieu is less adversarial than is the case with FPTP. In an AV count, however, as was seen earlier

---

[7]US Constitution 1787: Art II, Section 1, para 3.

(Sect. 1.1.4), many of the 2nd and subsequent preferences may not be taken into account at all, so AV can sometimes be capricious, inaccurate or even wrong.

The PR version of AV, PR-STV, is certainly more accurate but, as the number of seats per constituency increases, while the extent of cross-party voting might increase, the level of co-operation among some candidates, and this certainly applies in a divided society like NI, may actually decrease. In an FPTP contest, with parties 'fighting' the election, many voters cast their single preference, not so much 'for' their chosen candidate, but rather 'against' the supposed opposite. Similarly in a PR-STV election, if a candidate needs only, say, 15% support to get his quota, and if he knows he probably has that degree of support and does not need the help of any other voters, then he has little or no incentive to co-operate.

In PR-STV, parties are encouraged by the mathematics of the count to limit the number of candidates they nominate; for example, in a six-seater constituency where the quota is about 15%, if a party has an estimated 40% support, it may decide to run just two candidates in the almost certain knowledge that both will gain a quota of votes and be elected; or it may run three candidates in the hope of getting a few transfers as well, so to get a third seat; but if it runs four candidates, and if each of them gets only 10% of the 1st preferences cast, then it may find that none of them get the quota and maybe the party gets only two candidates elected—which it probably will if its supporters have filled in their preferences. . . but in practice, not every party supporter is so diligent. This all gets pretty complicated; and in fact, with surpluses and transfers correct to two decimal places, PR-STV "is the most complicated system ever actually employed." (Dummett 1997: 127) Nevertheless, parties do tend to limit the number of candidates they nominate.

Of the other methodologies, the MBC and Condorcet, the former is indeed non-majoritarian while the latter, especially if there are 20 candidates on the ballot and therefore some 200 pairings to be counted, is considered to be rather complicated.

2.5.1 Quota Borda System (QBS)

QBS was invented by the late Professor Sir Michael Dummett under its original name, quota preference score (Dummett 1984: 284). As the term implies, it relates to both a quota and a Borda score. Briefly, it works as follows. Voters are asked to cast up to a fixed number of preferences; in a six-seater constituency, that number would probably be six. As in PR-STV, parties are encouraged by the mathematics of the count to nominate only as many candidates as they think they can get elected. Then, in the vote—and here it differs from PR-STV—QBS not only *allows*, it actually *encourages* the voter to submit a full ballot of, say, six preferences and, in this regard, it is similar to the MBC on which it is based. As noted above, however, the MBC is not proportional; so hence QBS—the introduction of the quota.

QBS   Quota Borda System

In a simple example of a QBS count, seats are awarded to those candidates who gain either a large number of 1st and/or 2nd preferences, that or a large MBC score. The count, then, is much easier than that of a PR-STV analysis: there are no eliminations and surpluses, and therefore no transfers, so no fractions and decimal places and so on. In a simple scenario, the count starts by adding up all the 1st preferences for each candidate—and a 1st preference is always a 1st preference, regardless of how many other preferences the voter has cast; next it totals all the 2nd preferences, and they too do not change; next, it collates all the points for each candidate and, as in an MBC, the points allocated for each preference do depend on how many preferences the voter has cast overall.

Seats are then awarded:

- in stage (i), to any candidate who has won a quota of 1st preferences;
- in stage (ii), to any pair of candidates who have two quotas of 1st/2nd preferences[8];

from henceforth, the votes received by candidates already elected are no longer included in the calculations;

- in stage (iii), to just one of any pair of candidates who have one quota of 1st/2nd preferences, the candidate with the higher MBC score;

and if seats are still to be filled,

- in stage (iv) to those with the highest MBC scores (Emerson 2007: 39–57).

To take a practical example, consider the Balkans. As noted above (Sect. 2.1.5.1), the 1990 TRS election in Bosnia was a sectarian headcount. The post-war 1996 election, now with the closed PR-list system chosen by the Organisation for Security and Co-operation in Europe, OSCE, and assumed to be an integral part of the Peace Process, had an equally sectarian outcome. So what could happen in a QBS election?

Consider a hypothetical six-seater Bosnian constituency in which the people are 30:30:30, Muslim:Orthodox:Catholic.[9] So each group might think it should be able to get two candidates elected. Now because many people think democracy depends upon majority vote decision-making, not only do many countries divide into two but,

---

[8]If x voters cast a 1st preference for candidate D and a 2nd for B, if y candidates cast a 1st preference for B and a 2nd for D; and if $x + y \geq$ one quota, the B/D pair is said to have a quota.

[9]Different groups in Bosnia and other parts of the former Yugoslavia are often referred to as ethnic or, at best, ethno-religious. But there are no ethnic differences in Bosnia, Croatia, the northern half of Serbia or Slovenia: except for the likes of a few Vlachs perhaps, the people are nearly all Slavs. Granted, in the south of the former Federation, the mainly Albanian speakers of Kosova are of a distinct and separate ethnicity. But the main difference in the northern part is one of religion: the Serb is often Orthodox, the Croat is usually Catholic, and many Bosniaks are Muslim. There is of course one other fairly big difference: 1000 years of history.

in a plural society which is itself divided into ethno-religious groups or whatever, each group may also tend to split into two, with one big party and one smaller one... along with a few other tiny ones perhaps. As in NI where there have usually been two mainly Catholic parties and two mainly Protestant, so too in Bosnia, there tends to be two main parties in each of the three religious groupings. So, in this hypothetical constituency, there could well be two or maybe even three candidates from the larger Bosniak party, one or maybe even two from the smaller Bosniak party, as well as the same from the Bosnian Serb and Bosnian Croat parties, plus perhaps a candidate or two from a cross-community party like the Socialists. In total, it could be that the ballot paper lists 5 Bosniaks, 5 Serbs and 5 Croats, along with 1 or 2 others.

Now in such a six-seater election, as noted, a full ballot might consist of six preferences. And because QBS is like the MBC, the electoral system itself encourages the voter to cross the gender gap and the party divide if not indeed, at least for the 6th preference, the sectarian chasm. In many peace initiatives, the democratic process is described as a vital ingredient thereof; therefore, any voting procedure should itself be inherently 'peace-ful'. The MBC and QBS fit the bill. The voter who wishes to use the election as an act of reconciliation can vote, not only for a candidate of her own religion, but also for one or more candidates of one or more of the other groups. What's more—and this is where QBS is so much better than PR-STV—the voter will know that her vote will be shared by the candidates she has chosen from those other groups: what she does in the polling booth is what will happen in the count, her vote will be shared by those for whom she has voted.

Granted, there may be more than five candidates from each religious group, in which case, of course, a voter could cast all of his preferences for just one set of candidates. In doing so, however, he would almost certainly cross the gender gap and, for some men, this can be a first step towards pluralism. At best, of course, just as many Northern Irish voters use PR-STV in a cross-party and even cross-community way, so too voters in a QBS election, if given this opportunity, would indeed cross the sectarian chasm. Generally speaking, it is the more moderate voters who do use their preferences; in contrast, many a DUP and SF voter support only their own party's candidates... as often as not, as instructed by party activists who hand-out what they call guidance at the entrance to the polling station—an act of "vote management" as it is called, which is almost by definition un- if not anti-democratic. What's more, such an active act of campaigning on polling day itself would be considered illegal in any OSCE-monitored election (see Sect. 4.2.4.7).

In other words, the moderate voter is more likely to give an accurate representation of his/her opinion. The thesis continues: the better the voting mechanism, the more moderate and more accurate will be the outcome. "The incentive structure [of] the electoral system is [so] important... what a dearth of imagination there has been in most countries in utilizing its potential for ethnic accommodation."[10] (Horowitz 2000: 651) A first step in any society which wishes to overcome the excesses of the extremist is to adopt preferential voting procedures in order to ensure

---

[10]Horowitz is not here talking about QBS, but his words still apply.

their influence is not greater than its proportional due: the MBC in decision-making and ideally, QBS in elections.

2.5.2 The Comparison's Assessment

On balance, then, from the list shown in Table 2.1, the most appropriate and most accurate electoral system is QBS. FPTP is Orwellian; PR-list is fairer but still too exclusive; PR-STV is good; but QBS is even more inclusive (Emerson 2010: 39–60). For obvious reasons of vested interest, politicians usually choose that which suits them and their party. Unfortunately, for some incomprehensible reason, human rights lawyers rarely if ever go into the detail of how some voting procedures can be terrible; while those who should understand, today's journalists and political scientists, seldom even mention QBS let alone discuss its advantages.

As noted, peacemakers often say that the democratic process is a vital part of the peace process; the electoral system itself should therefore be 'peace-ful'. Accordingly, when the OSCE and others observe elections, especially in conflict zones, they try to ensure that everything is indeed peaceful... well, almost everything. Every adult aged (16 or) 18 or more should be allowed to register to vote, including the sick and disabled and maybe too the imprisoned (but not necessarily the diaspora); everyone of perhaps a slightly older age should be eligible to stand, except for the likes of indicted (war) criminals of course; campaigning should be fair, with no government officials abusing their powers and/or state resources; expenditures should be limited not least to create a fair 'playing field'; press coverage should be balanced for all parties, and so on. On the day itself, polling stations should be neutral, with no activists campaigning outside the main gate, with not even a party flag within so many metres of the entrance. Party activists should be allowed to observe the elections, but only from an impartial perspective; they should have no access to the electoral register. And elections should be observed by domestic as well as by international observers. The OSCE looks at it all... almost.

For reasons probably related to the politics of power, however, it does not comment on the electoral system itself (see also Sect. 6.7.3). The OSCE tends to favour PR, so if it itself chooses the system, as in Bosnia in 1996 (Sect. 5.6.6), it normally opts for a single-preference form PR-list. If, however, a country chooses a different system, even a horrible one like FPTP or TRS, the OSCE says little or nothing. This is probably because the British and French respectively would get very upset if the OSCE criticised their hopelessly inaccurate and adversarial systems as being hopelessly inaccurate and adversarial.

2.6   Electronic Voting

As mentioned, a democratic election should be the coming together of all concerned to appoint those who, for the next few years, will govern society, hopefully to the best of their ability. Accordingly, the parliament should be elected by means of a preferential and proportional electoral system, at best, QBS; and that parliament should conduct its deliberations and make its decisions by means of a similarly inclusive voting procedure, the MBC. Given the advent of computers, there is no reason at all why electronic preferential decision-making should not be used in the elected chamber (Sect. 1.6), and little reason why e-voting should not also be used in elections.

Of the countries visited by the author during this journey, only two were using electronic voting for an election: Belgium (Sect. 5.2.2.1) and Mongolia (Sect. 6.7.3). Elsewhere, the record has not been so good. Ireland did a trial and gave up; in the Netherlands, electronic voting was banned in 2007; and not even Germany has tried, let alone other newer democracies like Bosnia.

There are those who argue that e-voting could be done from numerous venues, even from the home. This would not be good. It might mean that the husband could bully the wife, or the parents the adult child. In some countries, as in NI, it might even mean that a paramilitary group could then dominate a whole neighbourhood. As implied above, however, an election should be a social event. Accordingly, there should be a venue where the people meet, the polling station, so to cast either a paper or an electronic vote. One way is to ask the voter to fill in a paper ballot, as in Mongolia (Sect. 6.7.2), and she then feeds the completed ballot into the machine; another way, as was tried in Ireland but only once, lets the voter stand at a computer console, tap in his preferences and then zap the completed ballot into the count. Ideally, he should then get a little paper slip to confirm his vote, and he could then deposit this anonymous piece of paper into a ballot box so that, if need be later on, a paper count could also be conducted. It is most important to ensure, however, that no voter leaves the polling station with any paper evidence as to how he has voted.

2.7   Conclusion

It might well be the case that Xí Jìnpíng more closely represents the average Chinese citizen than does Theresa May the ordinary Briton, let alone Trump the common American. Whether the National People's Congress more accurately reflects Chinese society than the House of Commons mirrors Britain or Congress the US is debatable. If the relevant electoral system were more fair, however, then, to take the British example, parliament would be more pluralist; this would probably mean fewer Tories and fewer Labour, with rather more Lib-Dems and Greens and UKIP, the UK Independence Party. As Chap. 3 will argue, it is better to have everyone 'in the tent', in parliament, rather than left outside, disappointed if not disgruntled.

There are those, not only in the US, who fear that while the introduction of PR could lead to a more accurate reflection of the collective will, it could also prompt the emergence of nationalistic, sectarian and/or racial parties: the Irish party, a Polish party, a Christian or a Muslim party, and so on. With QBS, however, such fears would probably be unjustified; if an even more inclusive system, the Borda quota system were to be invented, such that the candidates' MBC scores were more important than their 1st/2nd preference count, these concerns could perhaps be further mitigated.

For the moment, however, use should be made of whatever is already available: an accurate electoral system by which to elect both an executive and a legislature; secondly, an accurate decision-making system for use in the legislature, in order to ensure the decisions taken represent the collective will of that parliament. If that chamber has been accurately elected, these decisions will also fairly accurately represent the will of the people. That's the theory.

In practice, or so this book argues, a PR-STV or, better still, a QBS election will produce a parliament which accurately reflects the true nature of society. In 1933, Hitler did not represent the average German. His party managed to get a high degree of representation, in part because the electoral system was Orwellian, i.e., single preference. Many extremist voters will not want to cast more than a single prefer-ence; more moderate voters will be content to do so. It is vital, therefore, that the democratic process should involve an electoral system in which the voter is encour-aged to participate and to the full. Each may support his favourite candidate; but each is also asked to cast her 2nd and subsequent preferences, to say who are her compromise candidates. If politics is the *art* of compromise, voting itself should be an *act* of compromise.

The effect of a QBS election and of MBC decision-making would be that:

- he who abstains takes no part in the democratic process;
- she who submits a partial ballot plays a partial part;
- but those who submit full ballots play a full part.

The democratic process is, yes, a social event. People or their representatives come together to make collective decisions. Compromise must be an essential ingredient of the entire process. Both in elections and in decision-making, Orwellian or single-preference voting procedures are inadequate. With a preferential and proportional electoral system, many of the chosen representatives will not be so extreme; and with preferential decision-making, their decisions could well be more fair and sound. Such a polity might be able to ensure, not the end of populism, but the curtailment of voting procedures which give the populist greater and unfair chances of success. So now comes the question of how to appoint the executive: it is time for the next chapter.

References

Dummett, M. (1984). *Voting procedures*. Oxford: Clarendon Press.
Dummett, M. (1997). *Principles of electoral reform*. Oxford: OUP.
Duverger, M. (1955). *Political parties*. London: Methuen and Co.
Emerson, P. (2007). *Designing an all-inclusive democracy*. Heidelberg: Springer.
Emerson, P. (2010). Proportionality without transference: The merits of the Quota Borda System, QBS. In *Representation* (Vol. 46, No. 2). London: McDougall Trust.
Horowitz, D. (2000). *Ethnic groups in conflict*. Berkeley, CA: University of California Press.
IDEA. (1997). *The international IDEA handbook of electoral system design*. Stockholm: IDEA.
Lijphart, A. (1995). *Electoral systems and party systems*. Oxford: OUP.
Luce, E. (2018). *The retreat of western liberalism*. London: Abacus.
McLean, I., & Urken, A. (1995). *Classics of social choice*. Ann Arbor, MI: University of Michigan Press.
Woodward, S. (1995). *Balkan tragedy*. Washington: The Brookings Institution.

Chapter 3
Governance: From Power-dividing to Power-sharing

*It is now arguable that the party system. . . may be less well
adapted to the needs of the twenty-first [century].*
(Garret FitzGerald 2003: 65)

Abstract As noted, many people believe in a form of majority rule which is based
on majority voting. But if the (simple or weighted) majority vote is inadequate, and if
the modified Borda count, MBC, is known to be more precise, democracy would
presumably be enhanced if the latter were adopted as the international norm for
democratic decision-making. As shown in Chap. 1, this MBC is indeed robust,
inclusive and accurate; but it is also non-majoritarian. If therefore it were to be
introduced, that which follows from majority voting—the crudest form of majority
rule—should also be reformed. Thus the basis of democratic governance, everywhere, could be that which is often advocated for post-conflict societies: all-party
power-sharing. Easier said than done, some might say; after all, many a so-called
stable democracy sometimes has great difficulty in forming a new, post-election
administration, even only a majority coalition let alone an all-party executive. With a
matrix vote, however, it can be both said and done quite easily. This
Chapter critiques current practice and (therefore) proposes an alternative.

3.1 Party Politics

Now there are those who believe "political parties remain an indispensible institu-
tional framework for representation and governance in a democracy" (Diamond
1999: 96). "Furthermore," he goes on, a party structure with "a limited number of
significant parties. . .appears to foster policy effectiveness and consistency" (*Ibid*:
98). As shall be seen shortly, (Sect. 4.4.1), it was not always like this; in England for
example, political parties emerged almost by accident. Going back even further, they
were not to be found in ancient Greece at all, "only groups of a more or less fluid

nature, the members of which might well be divided differently on different issues..." (de Ste Croix 2004: 198).

While some people were not madly in favour of partisan politics, others felt that "organised 'factions' were not only unnecessary but downright harmful," (Dahl 2000: 92). What's more, George Washington went so far as to say that the two-party system and "the alternate domination of one faction over another... [has] perpetrated the most horrid enormities [and] is itself a frightful despotism".[1]

It should also be noted that some electoral systems allow for the participation of independent, non-party candidates, and presumably the resulting parliament is no less democratic for that. Indeed, the idea that the two-party system can apply to any and every country is just nonsense, especially when, as in Afghanistan for example, in a parliament of 249 members, 100 of them are independents, and of the partisan members, any sense of allegiance to a particular party is often pretty weak. So maybe "the mass party... far from being inherent to any democratic system of government, may represent merely a phase of democratic development that is passing away" (Bogdanor 1994: 97). Hopefully, in the UK and maybe too in the US, Brexit and Trump will have hastened its demise, and the future will see the end not only of "the mass party" but also of that which is sometimes not much better, the mass or majority coalition.

To assume, therefore, that governance must be based on a binary format, with a government on one side confronted by an opposition on the other, is not necessarily wise, and may be neither necessary nor wise. From so much that is said in relation to conflict zones, it would seem that there must be, and that there are, other ways of doing things, of which more in a moment or two.

3.2   Concocting a Coalition

In many countries, the democratic process of forming a new government consists of two phases. Firstly, there is a free and fair election in which the people choose a parliament, albeit under an electoral system which, as was seen in Chap. 2, might not be fair at all; nevertheless, in other respects, the democratic process in this phase is often open and transparent. However, for the same extraordinary reasons which have now been mentioned quite often, nearly all concerned believe in simple majority rule, so laws and policies in parliament are adopted in binary ratifications, as often as not, majority votes of the very worst **A?**—"option A, yes or no?"—variety. Accordingly, the parties in parliament once elected, rather than share power, divide it into two: the larger 'half' of the MPs forms a government, while the rest become that which some might regard as an oxymoron, the "loyal opposition". In Mongolia, for example, (Sect. 6.7.2), "there is no notion of a loyal opposition" (Man 2011: 431). In the West, in contrast, many have become used to the idea that such a division is not

---

[1]His farewell address of 1796.

only desirable but integral, and it is all premised on the fact that laws are ratified by a (simple or weighted) majority vote.

If in the election, as can happen with first-past-the-post, FPTP, as in the UK, one party has won a majority (not of the votes perhaps but) of the seats,[2] that party then forms the government; all of it; the party leader becomes the new prime minister, PM, and she chooses her cabinet, deciding who is to be which minister, and so on. She is, to use Lord Hailsham's phrase, 'the elected dictator' (Hailsham 1978). If at some future date during the course of her parliament, she has a disagreement with a particular minister, she can sack him and have a re-shuffle. In the old Soviet Union, politicians out of favour could be sent to Siberia; the UK is not quite such a large country, so maybe the equivalent is to appoint the said minister as Secretary of State for NI.[3]

If in stark contrast to the UK, the country has a PR electoral system and enjoys a measure of pluralism, and if therefore it has a multi-party structure—as is the case in Belgium for example—then in all probability no one party gains a majority (of the votes or) of the seats. Some people think this is a problem, but mainly because they are so wedded to simple majority rule; thus they complain of "the disadvantages of all parliaments elected by PR methods, such as under certain circumstances increasing the power of small minority parties" (IDEA 1997: 84). It can be even worse when just one or two independent MPs hold the balance of power, the 'king-makers' as they are called (Sect. 4.3.4). It is not PR which is the problem, however, and nor was PR the problem in Germany in the Weimar Republic (Sect. 5.3.1); it was (and is still) the belief in and practice of binary majority rule. Accordingly, if and when the parliament is hung—that is, when there is no obvious majority party or coalition in waiting—there follows the second phase of the democratic process and, quite unlike the first which is definitely open and transparent, the second is often closed and opaque. The newly elected politicians close the doors, draw the curtains, and off they go upstairs to try and sort something out.

The subsequent negotiations can be pretty complicated. The party with the largest minority will want to be in charge, and will want certain key positions like the top job of PM and maybe too, that of certain important portfolios like the ministry of finance. But other parties may try to gang up against the largest and form an alternative cabinet. Either way, any parties joining a coalition will want to pick some nice 'cherries', the more important ministries. Underlying everything, of course, is the question of compatibility... sometimes. Will a party of the left want to join its opposite? Will one particular party wish to co-operate with another, no matter how large the latter, especially if its leader is accused of financial misdemeanours, to quote the case of Andrej Babiš in the Czech Republic?

---

[2]In 2015, for example, the party with just 36.9% of the vote won 50.8% of the seats, a majority, just! But not a just majority.

[3]In 1979, Jim Prior was appointed to be the UK's Secretary of State for Employment, but later on within the Cabinet, Prime Minister Thatcher described him as a 'wet'—yet again, politics was binary, with the other wing of her cabinet supposedly 'dry'; so two years later, she sent him off to the UK's wettest and most distant outpost, Belfast.

(Sect. 5.4.2). An even more emotional question concerns extremist parties, like those of the right such as *Alternative für Deutschland*, AfD, in Germany, or those (sometimes) of the left, like *Sinn Féin*,[4] SF, in Ireland: should the two largest parties form a grand coalition if this then means that the extremist party, as the third largest in parliament, thus becomes the official opposition? (Sects. 5.3.3 and 4.3.4).

A party with a very large number of seats and only just short of a majority might want to team up with a little fringe party. In 2017 in the UK, where a majority in the House of Commons was maybe as many as 326—the figure is a little uncertain because SF's seven members abstain (not from claiming office expenses and the like but) from voting—the Tories with 317 seats teamed up with NI's Democratic Unionist Party, DUP, which has only 10 MPs. The arrangement is called 'confidence and supply': the DUP promised to support the government in any confidence votes, while the Tories 'supplied' NI with a grant—or a bribe—of £1 billion. Some people find this sort of arrangement, by which an extremist party can thus gain far more influence than is its proportional due, by which the tail may thus sometimes wag the dog, rather distasteful. In 1999, for example, when the Freedom Party of Austria, *Freiheitliche Partei Österreichs*, FPÖ, with 52 seats, joined the Austrian People's Party, *Österreichische Volkspartei*, ÖVP, also on 52, in a majority coalition (Sect. 5.5.2)—a majority in the *Nationalrat* was anything greater than 92—the EU expressed serious concerns and actually imposed sanctions. In 2017, the same two parties joined forces in another similar administration, but few complained. There again, in the wake of the even shadier deal in the UK about which the EU was also silent, maybe it felt it could no longer be critical. It is all a worrying sign of the times.

3.2.1 The Mathematics of a Majority

But back to the theory. In a scenario where the biggest party has, say, 40% of the seats, it may well aim to form a majority coalition with one or more parties. 50% plus one would be a bit tight, of course; in such a situation, one sickness or death let alone a solitary rebel, could well spell the end; so maybe 54% would be considered optimal, to take the Armenian figure (Sect. 5.8.3.2). At that level, the big party can keep most of the ministries for itself and retain effective control. If however the partner is itself a large party of, say, 30%, then the resulting cabinet—a grand coalition—will in theory at least be very stable, but the larger party's perks of office will be fewer.

Forming a new government, then, can be difficult, and the greater the number of parties, the greater the number of possible combinations. Little wonder, in relation to some of the countries covered by this volume, many of the politicians involved have often taken quite a long time to do the necessary. In 2016 Ireland broke the Irish record for the number of days it took the newly elected *Dáil* (Irish parliament) to

---

[4]Gaelic for 'ourselves alone'.

form a government—70 (Sect. 4.3.4); one year later, the Netherlands parliament broke the Dutch record—225 days (Sect. 5.2.4.1); and in the same year, the *Bundestag* did the equivalent in Germany—161 days (Sect. 5.3.3). The world record, of course, goes to Belgium which, in 2010/11, took 541 days to set up a new administration (Sect. 5.2.2.1). Despite such problems, many western politicians nevertheless suggest that conflict zones like NI and the Balkans (let alone Syria and Afghanistan), where presumably the inter-party and inter-personal rivalries are much greater, should have not just majority but all-party coalitions! Indeed they should, but not—or so this book argues—in the pretence, once a peace settlement has been reached and everything has settled down again, that all concerned can revert to 'normality' and simple majority rule.

Sometimes, of course, the negotiations break down and forming a majority coalition proves to be too difficult; so, as was mentioned, while still believing in simple majority rule, those concerned set up a minority administration, as in the Czech Republic (Sect. 5.4.2). In such a structure, any bills passing through parliament will still require the support of a majority; so each topic is taken, one at a time, and on each piece of proposed new legislation, the government tries to woo support from at least one of the other parties.

3.2.2   Variations of 'Majority' Rule

All of these various forms of administration may be summarised for the countries concerned in Table 3.1—the acronyms are all spelt out in Chaps. 4, 5 and 6. Suffice here to say that, just as in most countries on most issues, only one decision-making voting procedure is held to be democratic—the simple or weighted majority vote; and just as, in contrast, nearly all the electoral systems in Chap. 2 are regarded as democratic, all that is except the North Korean variety; so too, all but the last form of government listed in Table 3.1 are considered to be only totally democratic… although sometimes, as in the theocratic rather than democratic Iran, only or mainly by those directly involved. {Some jurisdictions have changed from one form of governance to another, and they are listed in the rows identified chronologically as follows: NI (y) and (w); Ireland (j) and (a); the UK (k), (d) and (c); Germany, (ac), (n) and (t); the Czech Republic (o) and (b); Austria (u) and (p); Taiwan (af) and (h); Mongolia (z), (aa) and (i); and Russia (ad) and (ab).}

The resulting coalitions are often full of anomalies. Sometimes, as in Austria, the party which was the most successful in the election—like the Social Democratic Party of Austria, *Sozialdemokratische Partei Österreichs*, SPÖ, in 1999, with 65 seats (Sect. 5.5.1)—was then excluded from the government of two smaller parties, each of 52 seats. Sometimes, returning to the UK, the tiny DUP with 0.9% of the vote is included in the government while several much bigger parties—the Labour Party, the Lib-Dems and the Scottish Nationalist Party, SNP, with 40.0, 7.9 and 3.0% respectively—are all excluded (Sect. 4.4.3.3). But maybe one of the worst consequences applies to Turkey, for just as the Catholics in NI knew that they would

Table 3.1 Forms of governance encountered on the journey

	Government	Example	Party, or parties in coalition.	Numbers involved	Year
(a)	1-party minority administration	Ireland	FG + independents (with FF agreement)	66 + 7 of 157 (with 44 + 1 abstentions)	2016
(b)		Czech Republic	ANO	78 of 200	2017
(c)	confidence and supply		Tory + DUP	317 + 10 of 650	2017
(d)		UK	Tories	330 of 650	2015
(e)		Turkey	AKP	317 of 550	11.2015
(f)	One-party majority rule	Georgia	Georgian Dream	115 of 150	2016
(g)		Hong Kong	Pro-establishment	40 of 70	2016
(h)		Taiwan	DPP	68 of 113	2016
(i)		Mongolia	MPP	65 of 76	2016
(j)		Ireland	FG + Labour	76 + 37 of 165	2011
(k)		UK	Tory + Lib-Dem	306 + 57 of 326	2010
(l)		Belgium	4 parties	85 of 150	2014
(m)	2 or more parties	Netherlands	5 parties	85 of 150	2017
(n)	in a majority coalition	Germany	CDU/CSU + FDP	239 + 93 of 312	2009
(o)		Czech Republic	ČSSD + ANO + KDU-ČSL	50 + 47 + 14	2013
(p)		Austria	ÖVP + FPÖ	62+ 51 of 183	2017
(r)		Serbia	SNS + SPS	153 of 250	2016
(s)		{Iran	List of Hope +	121 of 290	2016}
(t)		Germany	CDU/CSU + SPD	246 + 153 of 355	2017
(u)	2 parties in a grand coalition	Austria	SPÖ + ÖVP	52 + 47 of 183	2013
(v)		Macedonia	VMRO-DPMNE + SDSM	51 + 49 of 120	2016
(w)		NI	DUP + SF	28 + 27 of 90	< 2016
(x)	An all-party coalition	Bosnia	SDA + SNSD + HDZ BiH	9 + 6 + 5 of 42	2018
(y)		NI	OUP, SDLP, DUP + SF	28 + 24 + 20 + 18	1998
(z)	One dominant party state	Mongolia	MPRP	176 of 295	1951
(aa)		Mongolia	MPRP	350 of 430	1990
(ab)		Russia	United Russia	343 of 450	2016
(ac)		Germany	NSDAP	661 of 661	1933
(ad)		USSR	CPSU	1958 of 2250	1989
(ae)	A one-party state	China	CCP	2980	2018
(af)		Taiwan	KMT		< 1992
(ag)		North Korea	Workers' Party of Korea	607 of 680	2014

never be in government—not until the 1998 Belfast Agreement that is—so too the Kurds in today's Turkey understand that, for the foreseeable future, they will never ever be asked to join a majority coalition (Sect. 5.7.1). Yet again, simple majority rule is a huge part of the problem.

In summary, then, nearly all western governments believe in binary majority rule and power-dividing, the very opposite of that which they advocate for peace settlements: all-party coalitions and power-sharing. Furthermore, many democracies operate in such a way that allows party leaders—at worst, in single-party adminis-trations, only one; or in coalitions, a tiny minority of just a few politicians—an almost complete monopoly as to who is to undertake which ministerial role in government.

Many elected representatives find it quite difficult to co-operate with those against whom, up until the election, they did compete. So no wonder forming a coalition can take a long time. Politics, however, is the art of compromise, they say; and the attractions of power normally mean that a solution will eventually be found, even if the resulting coalition defies mathematical, ideological and democratic logic.

3.3 Power-sharing

"Under [certain] conditions, [binary] majority rule is not only undemocratic but also dangerous, [not least] because minorities that are continually denied access to power will feel excluded and discriminated against and may lose their allegiance to the regime." (Lijphart 2011: 31–32). Accordingly, and especially in conflict zones like NI and Bosnia but the same also applies to Belgium and did apply to Czechoslova-kia, the relevant authorities have adopted a form of power-sharing, despite the fact that the latter is actually, as implied above, an opposite of binary majority rule.

A power-sharing structure, Lijphart suggests, consists of certain criteria, (*ibid*: 35–45), which include some if not all of the following: power should be decentralised in a federal or similar arrangement; parliament should be bi-cameral; elections should be by a system of PR, allowing for a multi-party structure; gover-nance should be subject to all-party coalitions; and ministerial posts should be shared. On decision-making, he suggests a system of supermajorities, something similar to the consociational system {which was advocated for Czechoslovakia in 1968 (Sect. 5.4.1)}, which was part of Belgium's post-WWII constitutional reforms (Sect. 5.2.2), which was abused or rather (not) used in Bosnia after the elections of 1990 (Sect. 5.6.5), and which was adopted for NI in 1998 (Sect. 4.2.4.2). Basically, if the (Czechs) (Flemings) (Bosniaks) (Unionists) say 'yes' and if the (Slovakians) (Walloons) (Bosnian Serbs) (Nationalists) say 'yes', and if the (Bosnian Croats also say 'yes'), then 'yes' it shall be. As shall be seen, this methodology of twin/triple majorities actually has many disadvantages, which is why this book would like to amend Lijphart's criteria by adding two more: decision-making should be preferen-tial, while elections too should be not only proportional but also preferential.

Sadly, as noted above, while many countries advocate national unity govern-ments and power-sharing for those plural societies which are involved in conflicts, they themselves continue to practice simple majority rule and power-dividing. Throughout the Troubles in NI, for example, London continually wagged the finger at Belfast with advice on PR elections and power-sharing in Stormont, without ever lifting a finger to reform its own system of governance. In regard to binary majority rule, Dublin was no better.

The one exception to all this is Switzerland. In 1959, without having an armed conflict to resolve, the Swiss nevertheless decided to institute a system of power-sharing by which all major parties would serve together in a seven-person Federal Council. They used a 'magic formula' as it was called of 2:2:2:1, so the three biggest parties chose two members each, and the fourth slightly smaller party chose one. With changes in the parties' electoral fortunes, the formula has now been changed to 2:2:1:1:1,[5] but the magic is still working well. "An additional informal. . . rule is that the linguistic groups be represented in rough proportion to their sizes: four or five German-speakers, one or two French-speakers, and frequently an Italian-speaker" (*Ibid*: 34).

A common feature of these three forms of power-sharing—in NI, Bosnia and Switzerland—is the fact that, in forming an all-party power-sharing cabinet, none of them rely on an election; instead, they have all concocted a formula of some sort. After all, if it takes hundreds of days for Belgium and Germany etc. to sort out just a majority coalition, forming a government of national unity, GNU, an all-party coalition, in a conflict zone, could take months if not years! So the three power-sharing countries have each devised a set of rules, if only as a pragmatic step to ensure that something actually happens. The NI form of power-sharing works on a formula by which each of the biggest parties allocate the ten ministries to them-selves, (Sect. 4.2.4.1), one after the other according to their electoral strength; the constitutional arrangements agreed for Bosnia, (Sect. 5.6.6), stipulate that the Pres-idency, for example, shall consist of one person from each of the three groups; and the Swiss have their magic.

It is often true to say that politicians like to be able to, as it were, control things; as often as not, they are not very keen on voting systems, especially if the results cannot be predicted; (see also fn. 31 in Sect. 5.9.2). Maybe this explains why, thus far, they have been reluctant to consider an electoral methodology; it is hoped that the following paragraphs will facilitate a change of mind.

3.3.1 Decision-Making in Parliament

As noted earlier, decision-making in most parliaments is usually based on simple or weighted majority votes. Thus, in the UK for example, a motion is moved; amend-ments are tabled; the Speaker decides in which order they shall be taken—and this ruling can sometimes be crucial; each amendment in turn is then debated and voted upon; and finally, the substantive is itself subjected to a vote. In 'normal' times—that is, when the government has a large majority—the process functions: the cabinet chooses a policy, the parliament debates it prior to a vote, and because the govern-ment has a majority in parliament, the government usually wins that vote. In effect,

---

[5]In the 2015 election, while five parties gained more than 10 MPs, a further seven parties were only in single figures.

therefore, the Executive thereby controls the Legislature, and parliament is little more than a rubber stamp. . . in 'normal' times. No wonder they like majority voting.

There is no reason at all, however, why decisions in parliament should not be taken by one of the other methodologies discussed in Chap. 1. Norway has provision for TRS decision-making, although the last time it was used was in 1972,[6] and the same TRS methodology has been used elsewhere in some referendums, (Sect. 1.5). The Danish parliament often takes plurality votes, though usually on the basis of only three options. While when debating amendments, the Finnish, Norwegian and Swedish parliaments resort to serial voting, a series of majority votes on a range of amendments arranged in sequence—the cheapest to most expensive, for example, as would be done for any single-peaked analyses (Sect. 1.6.3)—with votes taken on the two extreme options until only one remains; the latter, therefore, is the Condorcet winner. In other respects, these Scandinavian parliaments are similar to those of their southern neighbours in that they too often use majority voting, and they too split into government versus opposition, usually on the basis of majority coalitions.

That said, any parliament could decide to have a different *modus operandi*, and decision-making could indeed be based on a different voting mechanism such as AV, the MBC and/or the Condorcet rule, (or again, at least in theory, on approval voting or range voting). As the reader now knows, this book advocates the MBC. The Condorcet rule is indeed very accurate; it is still, however, majoritarian, and if its use were the norm, a majority in parliament could still dominate proceedings if it so wished. The MBC, in contrast, is non-majoritarian; nevertheless, along with Condorcet, these are the two best "interpretations of majority rule," (McLean and McMillan 2003: 139).

As noted, (Sect. 1.1.5), in many voters' profiles, the MBC social choice and the Condorcet social choice may often be one and the same; but they can differ—the Condorcet winner (*league champion*) may not have the best Borda score (*goal difference*). No voting procedure, of course, is perfect, to quote Arrow's impossibility theorem, (Arrow 1963). A Condorcet count can suffer from 'the paradox' as it is called (Sect. 1.1), when $A > B > C > D > A$, but not an MBC. While the outcome of an MBC, but not that of a Condorcet count, could be subject to an 'irrelevant alternative'; this suggests that for any given set of preferences on four options, the outcome of a three-option vote might be different from the outcome of a four-option poll, even though the fourth option is very unpopular.[7] It should be noted however that if the rules for the debate have been observed, (Annex C), the list of options chosen by the consensors will not include anything which is irrelevant in the minds of those concerned. On balance, therefore, because the MBC is the more inclusive, it has the support of this author.

---

[6]When choosing a site for the state oil company, the three cities could not be placed in any order, so parliament used TRS. Stavanger got 75 of the 150 votes, exactly 50%, to Trondheim's 49 and Bergen's 20, so Stavanger was declared the winner.

[7]In, say, a three-option debate on options *A, B* and *C*, the outcome might be *B*. If an irrelevant alternative, option *D* is introduced—irrelevant in so far as no-one likes it very much—the outcome in an MBC might then be different, but not in a Condorcet count.

Doubtless, if all concerned voted sincerely, any MBC/Condorcet combined social choice would be approved in any majority vote ratification. There will be occasions, however—as was seen in Tables 1.2 and 1.4—when an MBC social choice does not enjoy majority support (if that term implies 50% plus one or more of the 1st preferences). As Michael Dummett suggests, however, this need not be a primary concern. A democratic decision should be the outcome which, "is most generally popular with the electorate, or at least the most acceptable," (Dummett 1997: 71), and "the soundest method of identifying" such an outcome is the MBC. If in a five-option debate, the winning option is the 1st preference of only a few, but the 2nd preference of nearly everybody else, then that should do.

First things first, however: a non-majoritarian all-party power-sharing government may indeed be able to function on the basis of preferential decision-making by MBC; the first step for the newly elected parliament is to select or better still elect those who are to serve in such a GNU.

3.3.2   Electing an All-party Coalition: The Matrix Vote

Instead of negotiations both problematic and protracted, a more democratic approach could surely be an election. The difficulties are considerable of course, for the purpose of such an election procedure would be twofold: to produce an all-party coalition in which, firstly, each party would be fairly represented, and secondly, every minister appointed would be the one considered most suitable for the respective ministry.

In this computer age, however, such difficulties can be easily overcome. Suffice to say that the appropriate ballot paper would need to be not linear but tabular: one dimension, let's say the vertical, could be used to choose the most popular candidates—and the recommended methodology is the quota Borda system QBS, (Sect. 2.5.1), but see below; and a second dimension, the horizontal, would facilitate the appointment of each of the chosen candidates to a specific ministry, and this is best based on an MBC analysis, (Sect. 1.6.1). The complete voting procedure is called a matrix vote, (Emerson 2016).

3.3.2.1   The Ballot

Consider a simple example in which a parliament of just 20 MPs, again representing parties **W**, **X**, **Y** and **Z**, now with 8, 6, 4 and 2 seats each, seeks to elect a GNU. Initially, the MPs should use an MBC to decide how many and which ministries will be involved; to introduce the reader to the concept of the matrix vote, let it be assumed that they opt for a very simple government of only six departments, the ones identified in Table 3.2.

The QBS matrix vote is proportional. Therefore, party **W** may expect to win 40% of the six cabinet seats, which would be two or maybe three of them. On 30%, party **X** can expect two; **Y** can hope for one; and **Z** probably none. (This is indeed a very

Table 3.2 A 6 × 6 matrix vote ballot paper

Preferences		Ministers of:					
		Prime Minister	Global Warming	Finance	Foreign Affairs	Home Affairs	Environment
	Names of candidates						
1st							
2nd							
3rd							
4th							
5th							
6th							

simple example; a more complex setting is shown in Annex E.) Let it be assumed that the **W** party nominees for ministerial office are **W**i, **W**j and **W**k; that party **X** promotes **X**i and **X**j; and party **Y** proposes **Y**i.

Party **Y**, then, need not nominate **Y**i for the post of PM. Probably its best bet is to decide if **Y**i is well-recognised and a well-liked specialist, to nominate her for the ministry of her specialisation, which is, say, Environment. In contrast, the biggest party, **W**, might well decide to nominate candidates for the post of PM and one or two other ministries, those it considers to be the most important and/or for which it has appropriately talented candidates.

3.3.2.2 The Vote

When it comes to the vote, the party **W** members will probably vote for the **W** nominees in a way that ensures its two main nominees get a quota. There again, the party might decide to adopt another tactic, namely, to give all of its 1st preferences to its prime ministerial nominee, so to guarantee that biggest prize, while ensuring its other candidates also get a quota but on the basis of its MPs' different 2nd preferences, a quota for **W**j definitely, and another for **W**k perhaps.

Because the vote is PR, **W** is probably not going to get 4 members elected, let alone 6, so it would be pretty pointless for a **W** party MP to cast his lower preferences for other **W** members; the wiser course would be to vote for those of the other parties with whom he thinks co-operation might be more likely. Let it again be assumed that party **W** tends to co-operate with party **Y**, and **X** with **Z**. A second assumption is that:

- party **W** wants **W**i for the post of PM and **W**j for Finance;
- party **X** proposes **X**i for Foreign Affairs;

Table 3.3 A W party MP's 6 × 6 matrix vote ballot paper

Preferences		Ministers of:					
		Prime Minister	Global Warming	Finance	Foreign Affairs	Home Affairs	Environment
	Names of candidates						
1st	**Wi**	✓					
2nd	**Wj**			✓			
3rd	**Yi**						✓
4th	**Wk**		✓			✓	
5th	**Xj**				✓		
6th	**Yj**						

- party **Y** nominates **Yi** for the Environment; and finally,
- party **Z** supports the party **X** nominee, and hopes for party **X**'s help with **Zj** for Home Affairs.

In effect, then, as always, the parties are in competition with each other. A party **W** MP, therefore, will probably not cast a preference for **Xi** to be PM—he wants that post for his own **Wi**—but he might cast a lower preference for **Xi** to be posted to Foreign Affairs, for example. Accordingly, this party **W** MP might vote, in order of preference, initially for his own party nominees, then for his colleagues of party **Y**, and finally, for those of party **X** and/or **Z** whom he regards positively; all as shown in the sample ballot paper of Table 3.3. His choice of candidates is listed, in order of preference, in the left-hand shaded column; and his choice of ministerial appointments for his chosen half-dozen is shown in the un-shaded matrix.

Doubtless a party **X** MP would have a different set of preferences, as shown in Table 3.4.

In this 6 × 6 matrix vote, a full valid ballot will contain the names of six different eligible candidates in the shaded part of the ballot paper; and six ticks in the matrix, one tick in each column, and one tick in each row. In such a full ballot, in a 6-candidate QBS and MBC, a 1st preference is worth 6 points, a 2nd preference 5, a 3rd 4, and so on. So, in the above Table 3.3, the said party **W** member has given a 1st preference for **Wi** in the QBS election to be elected to cabinet, and 6 points for **Wi** to be appointed PM in the MBC election. In Table 3.4, the party **X** MP has given **Wj** a 6th preference in the QBS election, and so 1 point for **Wj** to be appointed Minister of the Environment. And so on.

There is just one small complication. To make sure that all the MPs can vote as they might wish, every voter may cast not just one tick per candidate as shown, but

Table 3.4 An X party MP's 6 × 6 matrix vote ballot paper

Preferences	Names of candidates	Prime Minister	Global Warming	Finance	Foreign Affairs	Home Affairs	Environment
				Ministers of:			
1st	**Xi**				✓		
2nd	**Zj**					✓	
3rd	**Xj**		✓				
4th	**Yi**			✓			
5th	**Wl**	✓					
6th	**Wj**						✓

three: a gold, a silver and a bronze tick (as described in Annex E). A party **X** MP, therefore, may vote for **Xi** to be PM, even though the bigger party **W** nominee will almost certainly win this posting. Then, in the count, if **Xi** is not chosen for the premiership, **Xi**'s gold sum will be transferred to its silver ministries, as instructed by all the appropriate silver ticks, (and if need be, subsequently, to the bronze ticks as well, but in practice this is unlikely—**Wi** will probably get her golden nomination of PM, and **Xi** will doubtless get his silver).

For the moment anyway, let it be assumed that a third voter, a party **Y** MP, votes as shown in Table 3.5; again, only her golden ticks are shown.

Table 3.5 A **Y** party MP's 6 × 6 matrix vote ballot paper

Preferences	Names of candidates	Prime Minister	Global Warming	Finance	Foreign Affairs	Home Affairs	Environment
				Ministers of:			
1st	**Yi**						✓
2nd	**Wi**	✓					
3rd	**Wj**			✓			
4th	**Wk**					✓	
5th	**Xi**				✓		
6th	**Zj**		✓				

3.3.2.3 The Count

To keep this example simple, its purpose is to identify the consensus of just these three voters. The count proceeds as follows. All the candidates' 1st preferences are totalled, as are their 2nd preferences; and so too their MBC scores. The matrix vote count is then conducted in two phases: first comes the election based on data recorded in the shaded left-hand column, to see which are the six most popular candidates; {as noted above, this is best done on the basis of a QBS election as shown in Annex E, (but see Sect. 3.3.3); in this current simple example, however, it is conducted as per an MBC election}. Then comes the second phase, an MBC analysis of all the sums in the matrix, and in this second phase, successful candidates are appointed to the relevant ministry in descending order, according to the sums received in the matrix.

The ticks having been converted into points, the three votes cast in Tables 3.3, 3.4 and 3.5 gives the preliminary result, as shown in Table 3.6. The right-hand column of MBC scores awarded to each candidate are an indication of the candidates' relative popularities. The bottom row of MBC scores is a measure of the relative importance of each ministerial post (but see below).

The points in the matrix are now added into sums, and the results so far are consolidated as shown in Table 3.7:

- by arranging the ministries in order of relative importance, with descending MBC scores, left to right, as shown in the bottom two rows: the upper row of scores are for the seven candidates listed, while the lower row shows the scores for all the points received by all candidates;

Table 3.6 The preliminary 6 × 6 matrix vote results

Preferences / The candidates	Ministers of:						MBC scores
	Prime Minister	Global Warming	Finance	Foreign Affairs	Home Affairs	Environment	
Wi	6, 5						11
Wj			5, 4			1	10
Yi			3			4, 6	13
Wk					3, 3		6
Xj		2, 4					6
Yj				1			1
Xi				6, 2			8
Zj		1			5		6
Wl	2						2
MBC scores	13	7	12	9	11	11	63

Table 3.7 The consolidated 6×6 matrix vote results

Preferences		Ministers of:						MBC scores
		Prime Minister	Finance	Environment	Home Affairs	Foreign Affairs	Global Warming	
	Successful candidates							
1st	**Yi**		3	10				13
2nd	**Wi**	11						11
3rd	**Wj**		9	1				10
4th	**Xi**					8		8
5th=	**Wk**				6			6
	Xj						6	6
	Zj					5	1	6
MBC scores	totals for 7	11	12	11	11	8	7	60
	totals for all	13	12	11	11	9	7	63

- by eliminating (nearly) all the unsuccessful candidates, but three of them have tied on 6 points for the last two ministries, so for the moment at least, the consolidated results will include seven candidates; and
- by arranging these seven candidates in order of their popularity, (as measured in this simple example by their MBC scores, as shown in the right-hand column), from top to bottom.

In effect, the matrix vote allows and actually encourages the MPs, not only to submit a full ballot—for such is in the nature of an MBC—but also to vote across the party divide—as happens in any QBS election. This, it is argued, is a pre-requisite of any good power-sharing governmental structure.

The MBC analysis takes place in descending order, as per the sums in the matrix of Table 3.7. The highest sum of 11 appoints **Wi** to the post of PM. The next highest sum of 10 gives the Environment to **Yi**. The sum of 9 puts **Wj** into Finance, and **Xi** goes to Foreign Affairs on a sum of 8. There are then two 6s in the matrix; one appoints **Wk** to Home Affairs, and one gives Global Warming to **Xj**. So even though **Zj** also has an MBC score of 6, she has a highest sum of only 5, and so loses not only her ambition of Home Affairs, but also her chance of being appointed to the cabinet.

3.3.2.4 The Result

The final result—admittedly, the consensus of only three voters—is as shown in Table 3.8. No-one wins everything, but everyone wins something.

The three MPs all submitted full ballots, each casting all six preferences, so each exercised $(6 + 5 + 4 + 3 + 2 + 1 =) 21$ points. Therefore, the total number of points cast is $3 \times 21 = 63$ points, but some of the points cast were given to candidates who

Table 3.8 The final 6 × 6 matrix vote results

Preferences / Successful candidates		Prime Minister	Finance	Environment	Home Affairs	Foreign Affairs	Global Warming	MBC scores
		Ministers of:						
1st	**Yi**			10				13
2nd	**Wi**	11						11
3rd	**Wj**		9					10
4th	**Xi**					8		8
5th=	**Wk**				6			6
	Xj						6	6
MBC	totals for 6	11	12	11	6	8	6	54
scores	totals for all	13	12	11	11	9	7	63

did not qualify as one of the (seven and then) six successful cabinet members, so the total of MBC scores, (60) and (54) shown in the bottom right boxes of Tables 3.7 and 3.8, will invariably be less than the total full score (63). The proximity of these two final scores is an indication of the overall level of consensus for this election, (Sect. 7.4).

3.3.3 A History of the Matrix Vote

The methodology was invented by the author, (Emerson 2007: 61–85). In theory, the first phase of a matrix vote count, the election of the members of cabinet, could be conducted by any proportional system, and initially, the chosen methodology was PR-STV, (Sect. 2.1.5.1). But the British cabinet has 21 ministers in addition to the PM; in Ireland there are 15 plus the *Taoiseach* (PM); and with PR-STV, election counts for such a large number of elected representatives can sometimes involve a huge number of stages and can therefore be very complicated. Not for this reason alone, it was therefore decided to use the simpler and more inclusive QBS.[8] The second phase, the analysis of the matrix itself, has also been tested and developed: initially it was done on the basis of a BC—with the $(n, n-1 \ldots 1)$ rule—but is now done with an MBC and the $(m, m-1 \ldots 1)$ rule, (Sect. 1.6).

---

[8]In settings where proportionality is not considered to be important, this first part of a matrix vote count can be conducted in accordance with an MBC count. In political scenarios, however, when parliament is electing a cabinet or a local council is choosing its committee chairpersons, it is wiser to use QBS.

Along with a forerunner of the MBC, a PR-STV prototype of the matrix vote was put to the test at a New Ireland Group, NIG, cross-community conference in Belfast in 1986 (Sect. 4.2.3), and since then it has been used by the NIG and, for a time, by the NI Green Party, NI GP. It has also been tested and demonstrated both at home and abroad, in Austria, Bulgaria, China and Germany, and has now been computerised. The most recent experiment was a 2016 Dublin-based public meeting in April of that year, when the *Dáil* (parliament) itself was in a post-election limbo, (Sect. 4.3.4).

The Chinese experiment was a little apolitical. Instead of running a mock-up election for the Chinese Communist Party's Politbureau Standing Committee, the students in Nánkāi University, Tiānjīn, were asked to choose four actors from a short list of ten, to play the leading parts in a hypothetical film which required a pretty girl, of course; a handsome feller, of course; a villain and a corrupt official, both also *de rigeur*. It worked: again, no one won everything but everyone won something, and to the surprise of this author, the overall winner was not China's most famous film-star, Fàn Bīngbīng, 李冰冰.

In essence, then, a matrix vote can be used whenever a certain electorate wishes to choose a fixed number of individuals to work together in a collective unit. All of a football club's fans, for example, and not just the manager, could choose their first division team. All the shareholders could appoint a management board. A matrix vote could also be part of the annual general meeting, AGM, of organisations in civil society, when electing their executive committees; after all, the talents required for those who aspire to be a secretary seldom coincide with those who would prefer to be the treasurer. Better that, surely, than a series of majority votes, which at worst might allow a faction to dominate everything.

Its most important main function, of course, is in peace-making: all the parties in a country's newly-elected post-conflict proportional parliament could thus elect an inclusive, all-party, power-sharing, coalition cabinet or GNU, and all within a matter of days.

3.3.4 The Procedure

In the wake of a general election, a parliament first elects a Speaker. He/she then draws up a list of all MPs who are eligible to stand for cabinet membership—all those who (unlike the current author) are under 70 years old, say; all who have not already served more than, oh, two terms in government; and all who have indicated that they do not wish to stand for ministerial office. In theory, the principle on which a true democracy could and maybe should operate is one that allows individuals to opt out of the possibility of being chosen, but not to opt in. It should certainly not allow for any Boris Godunov (Sect. 5.9.1) or Yuán Shìkǎi (Sect. 6.3.4) style of self-nomination or coronation.

Accordingly, the Speaker asks for the names of those who may wish to opt out of all or maybe just some particular ministerial appointments. Not everyone would want to be the Minister of Finance, for example, or in the Defence portfolio. On this basis, it should be possible for her to prepare a list of all those who are eligible and willing to stand for some or all postings.

Later, having stated who they wish to propose and for which post(s), the parties may engage in inter-party negotiations; a day or two should suffice, after all, many MPs will be in parliament for a second or third term, and many of them will already be well aware of their party and parliamentary colleagues' talents. Accordingly, the election may be held on day four or five, in a free un-whipped vote, and assuming everything shall be done electronically, the result could be declared at the most one week after the general election results were announced. Such a timetable would be applicable, not only to the election of an all-party coalition in any 'stable' democracy, but also to the appointment of just such an inclusive government in any conflict zone.

The premier shall not have the power to sack any cabinet member; that possibility shall rest only with the superior authority, the parliament. If at some stage of its term in office a member of the cabinet resigns, is imprisoned or dies, or no longer enjoys the confidence of the House,[9] the ballots shall be re-counted with all preferences cast for the said individual being re-allocated in accordance with the MPs' subsequent preferences. This will probably have the same effect as a minor re-shuffle, with the appointment of one new minister, and maybe a change of portfolio for one or two others.

3.3.5 Application

In a post-majoritarian polity, operating under a pluralist form of majority rule, a newly elected parliament could indeed use a matrix vote to elect a power-sharing GNU. Assuming no-one has been coerced by means fair or foul to vote tactically rather than sincerely—and that includes any ploys of the party whips[10]—the matrix vote result is bound to be a cabinet in which not only all relatively large parties shall be represented in fair proportion, but also all or nearly all the ministers shall be well-suited to their new portfolios.

It might also be pointed out that the matrix vote could also be used by the two or more parties concerned to elect a majority coalition, or even by the parliamentary

---

[9]And here too, the corresponding vote need not be binary.

[10]As was seen in Sect. 1.7.5, increasing the MP's freedom of choice tends to decrease the degree of control by which a party whip may try to order her to act as he demands. In like manner, a matrix vote offers the MP an even greater degree of choice: in the above example, choosing six cabinet members from a parliament of just a score of MPs to serve in six portfolios, there are over 2 billion ways in which an MP may vote—2,009,318,400 to be exact. When choosing a cabinet of a dozen from a parliament of an hundred to serve in 12 ministries, the degree of freedom is measured in trillions. The social choice scientist may calculate the number; the political scientist may simply use the word 'pluralism'.

party of just one party to elect a one-party administration. Any of the above methodologies would be better, surely, than an 'elected dictatorship' or that which is not much better, a process of protracted and secret negotiations.

There may be some who argue that the matrix vote is all a bit complicated. As with the more sophisticated electoral systems like PR-STV and QBS, however, it is simple enough: as the slogan has it, these electoral systems are actually as easy as 1–2–3 to use, and a little more difficult to count. The matrix vote is of course rather more complicated, but the users are all elected MPs, so they are meant to be quite clever. Even then, when filling in the ballot paper, it is easy enough: one golden tick in each column, and one in each row. The complications come in the count, but the electorate is never in the millions, it is usually just a few hundred. Secondly, the count can be done electronically; the Speaker needs to understand only how it works, and then press a button.

3.3.6 The Consequences

A party which is large enough in a general election to gain representation in the legislature should be allowed to take its seats. In like manner, a party which is large enough in parliament should be entitled to participate in government.

In the wake of the 2017 elections, in the British House of Commons, the DUP has 1.5% of the seats (on 0.9% of the vote); it should not, therefore, be in government at all![11] In Germany, in contrast, the AfD has 13%, so it should probably have two members in the 16-member cabinet.

Herein lies the essence of a more consensual polity. If there are extremists in society, as may indeed be the case in any country, then they should be entitled to stand for and be elected to parliament. Secondly, if their strength in parliament is sufficiently high, they should also be in cabinet. In either situation, however, they should be represented only to the extent which is their proportional due.

As Chap. 2 made clear, (Sect. 2.5.1), a preferential electoral system like QBS is more likely to facilitate a more accurate and therefore a more moderate outcome. Nevertheless, extremists do exist, but as long as they do not break the law, they should be allowed to participate alongside the rest of society. So, if sufficiently numerous, they should be represented in parliament. And to repeat, in those countries in whose parliaments they are strong enough, they should also be allowed to participate in government.

In a consensual polity, cabinets and the parliaments which elect them should operate in consensus, with decisions determined verbally and/or with the additional use of an MBC. In no way, therefore, could a tail, no matter how large, be able to wag the collective dog. Rather, the extremists would be in cabinet, in their proportional

---

[11]In a matrix vote, it is always possible for a talented member of a small party, or even a talented independent, to be elected to cabinet… if they get sufficient cross-party support.

due, hopefully to co-operate with their fellow members of government, most of whom would be always aiming to seek a consensus. If these extremists succeed in working with their fellow ministers in one parliament, they could well be re-elected to serve in a subsequent cabinet at the next general election. If not, hopefully, the public would vote for someone(s) else. In a nutshell, to quote the metaphor, society should allow any extremists to be, like the proverbial camels, *inside* the tent; either they learn to become more responsible, in which case they may well get re-elected; or, if they continue to 'piss around', they will be told, democratically of course, to 'piss off'.

3.4   Conclusion

As will be seen in Chaps. 4 and 5, simple majority rule and power-dividing have been, not only a cause of dysfunction in umpteen 'stable democracies', but also a major cause of violence in many plural societies. The list of the latter is long: Northern Ireland, the Balkans and the Caucasus; if caution is not exercised, it could also be the catalyst of violence in China; it has also been problematic elsewhere: in Rwanda, Kenya and South Sudan in Africa, and all over the Middle East where all too often the tale of violence and suffering is one of a Sunni/Shi'a majority dominating a Shi'a/Sunni minority; furthermore, a 'one-state' solution to the Israeli/Palestinian problem will probably never be found if all concerned pursue a political system of binary majority rule. As is recognised by some in NI and other conflict zones, however, the political choice of an economic policy or of a transport plan need not depend so immediately on an MP's confessional faith. Rather, decisions should depend upon the participants' agreeing to express and discuss their preferences.

What is required, therefore, is a willingness amongst politicians and political scientists, firstly, to question the adversarial structure which is simple majority rule, and secondly, to consider a win-win polity founded on more inclusive voting procedures. What is also required as a matter of urgency is for human rights lawyers to question the right of a majority to rule; after all, it may be wrong. There is a little more on this in Chap. 7.

References

Arrow, K. (1963). *Social choice and individual values*. New Haven: Yale University Press.
Bogdanor, V. (1994). Western Europe. In D. Butler & A. Ranney (Eds.), *Referendums around the world*. Washington, DC: AEI Press.
Dahl, R. A. (2000). *On democracy*. New Haven and London: Yale University Press.
de Ste Croix, G. E. M. (2004). *Athenian democratic origins*. Oxford: OUP.
Diamond, L. (1999). *Developing democracy*. Baltimore and London: The Johns Hopkins University Press.
Dummett, M. (1997). *Principles of electoral reform*. Oxford: OUP.
Emerson, P. (2007). *Designing an all-inclusive democracy*. Heidelberg: Springer.

Emerson, P. (2016). *From majority rule to inclusive politics*. Heidelberg: Springer.
FitzGerald, G. (2003). *Reflections on the Irish state*. Dublin: Irish Academic Press.
Hailsham, L. (1978). *The dilemma of democracy*. London: Collins.
IDEA. (1997). *The international IDEA handbook of electoral system design*. Stockholm: IDEA.
Lijphart, A. (2011). *Patterns of democracy*. New Haven: Yale University Press.
Man, J. (2011). *Genghis Khan*. London: Bantam Books.
McLean, I., & McMillan, A. (2003). *Oxford concise dictionary of politics*. Oxford: OUP.

Part II
The Practice

Chapter 4
Majority Voting in Belfast, Dublin and London

> *Stressing the rightness of the principle of majority rule* (He, of course, was not the only politician to believe in (binary) majority rule), *[Abraham Lincoln] warned that government must cease if the minority refuses to acquiesce...*
>
> (Emerson R 1966: 304).

Abstract Throughout Britain and Ireland, people use majority voting, and in politics, they believe in a binary form of majority rule. The consequences have been huge, and this Chapter looks at those which have afflicted the author's home town of Belfast, the land of his father, Ireland, and then his mother's England.

4.1 Introduction

Some parts of the world have neutral words to describe a group of nations which are, of course, different but nevertheless share some similarities: the Low Countries, the Balkans and the Caucasus. "The British Isles," in contrast, is a geographical term which is, as it were, biased: it includes Britain[1] which is British, and another island which is not, Ireland. Within these islands there are two nation-states: the first is the United Kingdom, , which joins Britain and Northern Ireland, NI, so the latter is not in Britain and some would argue that, therefore, it is not British... but others disagree; the second is the Republic of Ireland, RoI. In the bigger island, there is England, Scotland and Wales; the smaller island is home to NI and the RoI. And over all these

---

[1]The fact that there is no mention of the word 'Great' as in Great Britain is not only because the use of this word implies that other countries are perhaps not so great, but mainly because the word in its Serbo-Croat translation—'velika', as in *Velika Srpska*, Greater Serbia, or *Velika Xarvatska*, Greater Croatia—was and still is part of the problem in the Balkans.

© Springer Nature Switzerland AG 2020

P. Emerson, *Majority Voting as a Catalyst of Populism*,
https://doi.org/10.1007/978-3-030-20219-4_4

(and other) differences, people have often fought and died. Today, thankfully, they just argue.

4.2   Northern Ireland

Ulster says *'NO!'*

The Rev. Ian Paisley, MP.

4.2.1   A Protestant State for a Protestant People

For a blatantly sectarian reason, many people in NI believe in majority rule. When the border was 'invented'—or maybe 'concocted'—as part of the 1920 Settlement, the island of Ireland was divided into two, and the northern bit was designed to have a majority of Protestants. In fact, Ulster is a nine-county unit, but there were too many Catholics in three of the counties—Cavan, Monaghan and Donegal—so those three were hived off into the Republic... except for a bit of Derry (or Londonderry), which the Protestants were rather fond of. Therefore NI is not Ulster, but only part of it; and the most northerly part of Ireland is actually in the South, Malin Head in Co. Donegal.

So, like the peninsula of Korea (Sect. 6.6.2), Ireland was divided into two, while Yugoslavia (Sect. 5.6.1) and the Caucasus (Sect. 5.8.1) were/are even more complicated. Britain claimed sovereignty over NI, but so too did the RoI. The two nations were in conflict, but the war between the two, the Troubles of 1969–1994, was as it were a proxy war: for most it was a sectarian conflict fought largely in the six counties of the North.

As part of the 1920 Settlement, both NI and the RoI were 'given' the PR-single transferable vote electoral system, PR-STV (Sect. 2.1.1). Those involved obviously thought quite hard about this; for some strange reason, however, they did not think about decision-making... so democratic decisions in both parts of the island were still to be made by majority vote, and both enjoyed, or endured, simple majority rule. The Protestants up North then used this majority facility to abolish PR-STV and replace it with the majoritarian (and much more British) first-past-the-post, FPTP. Politicians in the South also tried to get rid of PR-STV (and go 'British'), but the people said 'no', twice (Sect. 4.3.3).

In 1969, with majority rule a major cause of discrimination in housing, jobs and so on, the situation exploded. It was the start of the 'Troubles', the violence. So in 1972, Westminster imposed 'Direct Rule' to regain the reins of government, and re-introduced PR-STV; decision-making in local councils and so on, however, remained majoritarian.

4.2.2 The Border Poll

The violence quickly escalated and in that year of '72, the number of casualties was at its worst. In response, Ted Heath, the British Prime Minister of the day, opted to hold the so-called 'border poll', a plebiscite on the future of NI, in order to "take the border out of politics," (Bogdanor 1994: 37). In fact, of course, it did no such thing. The chosen question was a **AB?** type choice (Sect. 1.1.2) of two options: option *A*, "Do you want NI to remain part of the UK?" or option *B*, "Do you want NI to be joined with the RoI outside the UK?"

At that time, the Protestants were a majority, forming about 60% of the population, so they voted for *A*. The Catholics were a minority, turkeys do not vote for Christmas, and they abstained; in fact, the Social Democratic and Labour Party, SDLP, campaigned for a boycott. The turnout was 58.7%. So nearly all the Protestants voted, and nearly all the Catholics did not. The result was indeed Stalinist: 98.9% wanted *A*, a mere 1.1% voted for *B*.

The lesson was not learnt. As shall be seen in Chap. 5, minorities in the Balkans and the Caucasus also abstained. And so too, for that matter, did the hapless Crimean Tatars in 2014. For some extraordinary reason, however, while the border poll only made matters worse, elsewhere in the UK—not least in Scotland in 2014 (Sect. 4.4.3.2) and even more so in regard to Brexit (Sect. 4.4.3.3)—people continued to believe in binary referendums.

4.2.3 The Anglo-Irish Agreement

In 1985, in what was still the Soviet Union, Mikhail Gorbachev came to power and initiated his policy of *perestroika* (re-construction) (Sect. 5.9.2). As a direct result (and for a few other reasons), NI was no longer of any significant strategic importance to the UK, so later that year, like night follows day, the Anglo-Irish Agreement was signed. It was only on 9.11.1990, however, that the then NI Secretary, Peter Brooke, declared that Britain has "no selfish strategic or economic interest" in NI, so opening up the possibility of constitutional change if not, indeed, that of a united Ireland.

Interestingly enough, there was no comma between the word 'selfish' and the word 'strategic' (de Bréadún 2008: 6)... because, of course, there were huge *selfish* interests of the political variety, as shall now be explained. Both of the ruling parties in Westminster—Tory and Labour—believe in simple majority rule, as do all the others, unfortunately. With whom a particular party forms a majority sometimes matters, it seems, not one iota; and while both major parties have sometimes found it quite difficult to come to any arrangement with the Liberals or their successors, the Lib-Dems (though on some occasions, both have succeeded), the two big parties have always thought it would be quite 'handy' to be able to have a few MPs in the House of Commons who were not particularly concerned with the politics of

Britain—the Unionists—and with whom, therefore, co-operation might be easier. The latter maintained the Labour Party in power in 1978, for a time (Sect. 4.4.2); and in 2017, the Tories came to a disgraceful agreement with the extremist and sectarian Democratic Unionist Party, DUP (Sect. 4.4.3.3), whose very name is an oxymoron (Sect. 7.1).

But back to 1985 and the Anglo-Irish Agreement. No sooner had it been signed than there were howls of protest on the streets of Belfast, and to a crowd of 100,000 people outside the City Hall, Paisley, the leader of the DUP, screamed, "Ulster says 'NO!'" so implying that democracy can be based on an **A?** type 'yes-or-no' question (Sect. 1.1.2). One week later, on this author's initiative, six of us stood at the same venue, in silence, with a poster which read, "We have got to 'say yes' to something." (See also Sect. 5.3.1). At the very least, the relevant question should have been of the **AB?** variety, at most multi-optional.

In order to demonstrate the use of this type of question, a prototype of the MBC was put to the test in a series of cross-community public meetings organised by the New Ireland Group, NIG. The first, in May 1986, was a gathering of over 200 (see also Sect. 3.3.3—it was also a first experiment for the matrix vote), and over the years the two voting procedures have been developed and refined; in 1991, for example, albeit with paper ballots, electronic voting was used for the first time (the first time for the organisers, that is), an event which also saw the participation of two guests from Yugoslavia (Sect. 5.6.2). Participants in these meetings included the press, the public, professors of political science and lots of politicians: several local councillors, one NI party leader, members of all the political parties in NI, even those related to paramilitary groups, several future Members of the Legislative Assembly, MLAs (NI's elected chamber, which was to come into existence with the 1998 Belfast Agreement), two members of the European Parliament, MEPs, and two *Teachta Dála*, TDS (MPs from the *Dáil*, the Irish parliament), one of whom was the then future and, in 2018, the current President of Ireland, Michael D Higgins.

The 1986 meeting was a huge success: the participants met, debated, proposed various constitutional arrangements, cast their preferences, and thus found their collective consensus.[2] Despite all of this, while due consideration was given to multi-candidate electoral systems, for some quite inexplicable reasons, multi-option voting for decision-making was not even mentioned during all the official talks leading up to the Belfast (Good Friday) Agreement.

The story runs like this. As a result of talks between the SDLP and Sinn Féin, SF, the latter came to the realisation that violence was actually counter-productive; that given the demographics in NI, the Catholics would soon be in a majority, and that which could not be achieved by force of arms—a united Ireland—could nevertheless be achieved by force of numbers. Hence, in 1994, the Irish Republican Army, IRA, announced a cease-fire. The Peace Process was born.

---

[2]NI to have "devolution and power-sharing with a Belfast-Dublin-London tripartite agreement."

4.2.4   The Belfast Peace Agreement

A major part of the NI problem had always been the almost universal belief in a form of majority rule based on majority voting. After all, it was this belief which had allowed the Unionists to have all the power, because they were the majority. *Ergo*, the mainly Catholic Nationalists, a permanent minority, had no power. And hence the violence of 1969, etc.

As the basis of the Peace Process, it was decided that this problem of binary majority rule could be ameliorated by a different sort of binary majority rule: instead of the Unionists dominating the Nationalists, which was just naughty, from now on, the 'nice guys'—the Ulster Unionist Party, UUP and the SDLP—would dominate the 'not so nice guys'—the DUP and SF; and this would be lovely.[3] Discussions then ensued as to the details necessary for a power-sharing peace settlement: the electoral system, power-sharing in the Executive, and decision-making; but a non-majoritarian polity was not even mentioned let alone discussed.

4.2.4.1   Elections and Power-Sharing

Proportionality, of course, was very important. So the Talks agreed to retain the PR-STV electoral system in 18 six-seater constituencies, which was then reduced to 18 five-seaters for the 2017 elections. So that was OK.

The top executive position of First Minister would be shared with a Deputy, one of each of the two most popular and 'nice' parties; so that was proportional, or at least balanced. In addition, the 10 ministers (were not to be elected by a seemingly unmentionable matrix vote but) were to be appointed in a process of 'cherry-picking' by which each party could choose one of its own members to be one of the 10 ministers, taking it in turns, as determined by the election. In 1998, the order was UUP, SDLP, DUP, SF, UUP, SDLP, DUP, SF, UUP, SDLP; so that was proportional as well: 3-3-2-2. The fact that the combination of all the executive posts gave an overall ratio of 4-4-2-2, which was *not* proportional, was just sort of ignored, not least by the 'nice guys'... because of course, they were the beneficiaries.

For those first elections in 1998, then, everything worked according to plan. The results were UUP, SDLP, DUP, SF at 28-24-20-18 and, when divided by the d'Hondt divisors of 1-2-3-4..., the ratio was indeed UUP:SDLP:DUP:SF = 3:3:2:2.

Unfortunately, of course, 'what can go wrong will go wrong' (Murphy's Law—which the Russians call *zakon butebroda*, the law of the sandwich[4]), and in the next

---

[3] As elsewhere, as for example in the Balkans (Sect. 2.5.1), every group in a divided society tends to divide itself into two. In NI, therefore, which is already divided into two, each 'half' is also split down the 'middle', so there are the four 'main' parties: the DUP and UUP, facing the SDLP and SF.

[4] Закон бутерброда. If dropped accidentally, a slice of bread and butter will always land 'butter side down'.

Assembly elections of 2003, the 'nice guys' lost, and the cherry-picking was now to be done to a different order. Seats won were DUP, UUP, SF, SDLP = 30, 27, 24, 18 which is still 3-3-2-2. But by the next election in 2007, it had gone completely wrong. It was now DUP, SF, UUP, SDLP = 36-28-18-18 [which also made for a rather messy ratio, mathematically speaking, as the DUP's 36 (when divided by d'Hondt divisor of 4) and the two 18s of the UUP and SDLP (when divided by 2) all tie on 9, so there were three individuals of varying 'nicety' competing for the last two 'cherries'].

4.2.4.2   Decision-Making and Power-Sharing

Decision-making was also due to go wrong, and in a much more serious manner. The basic idea was again that the 'nice guys' would win. Accordingly, decisions on certain 'key' issues, the term used in the Agreement—elections of the First and Deputy First Ministers, standing orders, the budget, etc., [Belfast Agreement 1998: Strand 1.5 (d)]—were to be subject to a 'consociational' vote. This term, which dates from 1603 (Lijphart 1977: 1), refers to a form of decision-making which is based on questions of the **A?** or **AB?** Variety (Sect. 1.1.2). The theory, then, as noted earlier (Sect. 3.3), is that if a majority of Unionists say 'yes' and if a majority of Nationalist say 'yes', then 'yes' it shall be.

The methodology has quite a few disadvantages. The first is that the question posed is still dichotomous, which as Chap. 1 explained, is not the best way of doing things... especially in a society which is itself divided. Secondly, in order to carry out such a vote in the Assembly, everyone has to know who is 'Unionist' and who is 'Nationalist', so the very agreement perpetuates that which in theory it was supposed to overcome: sectarianism. Thirdly, any MLAs who do not want to be designated in such a sectarian manner may opt out and call themselves 'Other', but that means they have little or no influence in the relevant decision-making. Fourthly, the very methodology means that both the Unionists and the Nationalists have a veto; if either bloc says 'no', then that's it, *impasse*, and nothing happens. Which is one of the reasons why the NI Executive collapsed in January 2016. In all, the Belfast Agreement "remains grounded in the very structures it aspires to transcend... [it] reinforces and perpetuates sectarian division," (Taylor 2009: 320).

Decisions may also be taken in referendums, of course. So while the Dayton Agreement for Bosnia rules out any referendums at all (Sect. 5.6.6), the NI Agreement is the absolute opposite.[5] Indeed, without provision for a referendum on the future constitutional status of NI, there would probably not have been an

---

[5]Another feature of the two post-conflict settlements is also very different. In Bosnia, any persons accused of war crimes can be indicted and sent to The Hague for trial and, if proven guilty, sentenced and punished. In NI, however, there were no war crimes at all, apparently; admittedly, some individuals were found guilty of murder and sentenced accordingly; but no one in higher authority took any blame at all and instead of any being indicted, two of them were appointed as First and Deputy First Ministers.

agreement... or not one which SF would have signed. As it stands, however, there is to be a referendum, if the Secretary of State "shall" so decide—and the Agreement says he/she "shall"—not 'may' but "shall"—"if it appears likely... that a majority of those voting would express a wish that NI should cease to be part of the UK and form part of a united Ireland." (Agreement, Annex A 1998: Schedule 1.2). So, as in Scotland (see below), it could be 50% plus one. The question, it says, shall be of the "*A* or *B*?" variety. If the answer is *A*, stay in the UK, then the referendum may be re-scheduled, every seven years or so... and the process becomes a "never-end-'em" to quote one wit on BBC Radio 4. If, however, at any future re-play, the outcome is *B*, then that will be that, apparently, for ever... even though *B* is only *a* united Ireland, not *the*, just *a*—a constitutional arrangement which has yet to be defined. And it's called a Peace Process.

To take a sporting analogy again, it's a bit like a football game between Manchester United and Manchester City, which United wins, 3-nil; so there's a re-match, and again they win, 4-2; and again, 2-nil; but then, in the fourth tie, City wins 1-nil... and that's it. They are the Champions, for ever amen, until the end of time!

There are two further aspects of this referendum idea which are very worrying. Firstly, the consociational basis of decision-making, as used in the NI Assembly, could not work in society at large without there being two electoral registers, which would all be horribly sectarian. It could and did (not) work in Cyprus,[6] where the two communities are so separate; but in NI, where many communities are mixed, where countless couples are in mixed relationships, it would be dangerous if not also almost impossible.

The even more serious point is that, with majority voting as noted, everything might depend on just one vote. Granted, the referendum will probably not be held, unless the NI Secretary thinks option *B* has a *comfortable* majority... whatever that means... but if defined as a precise percentage, that too could be determined by a singleton. In effect, the constitutional status of NI could change by a margin of one vote, 'x' percent plus one ... unless, the day before polling day, someone kills two Catholics, in which case the result would be 'x' percent minus one, so NI would stay in the UK. And it's called a Peace Process.

4.2.4.3 The Principle of Consent

By law, when two persons consent to have sex, both must agree. In the Belfast Agreement, in contrast, 'the principle of consent' applies only to a majority: it is a marriage without a bride.

Sometimes the Agreement talks of "*a* majority" (Constitutional Issues, 1 (i) and (iii) etc.), and sometimes of "*the* majority" (1 (ii) and (v) and so on)—the difference

---

[6]In 2004, Kofi Annan's peace proposal—an **A**? type 'yes-or-no?' proposal—was accepted by 64.9% of the Turkish Cypriots but rejected by 75.8% of the Greek Cypriots. In effect, the plan was thus vetoed.

is of course huge. At the moment, x percent want to stay in the UK, and they are mainly Protestant—*the* majority; while y percent, mainly Catholic, would like a united Ireland—*the* minority. (Anybody else, z, apparently does not count—or rather, is not counted.) At the moment $x > y$. If w percent of Protestants change their minds, and if $x - w < y + w$, then it could mean a united Ireland. Or, which is more likely, if y increases from its natural birth-rate to y', while x does not keep pace, then at some stage, maybe, $x' < y'$. So today, x is "the majority," while in tomorrow's terminology, $y + w$ and/or y' are both described as "a majority". In the Belfast Agreement, the articles both definite and indefinite are used with abandon but remain, definitely, undefined.

There is provision in the Agreement for any individual in NI to as it were make a compromise: everyone is entitled to hold a British passport, or an Irish one, or both. Very good. Collectively, however, the principle of consent means that there can be no collective compromise; for society as a whole, it is either/or; we are either all British or we are all Irish. Very bad. And it's called a Peace Process.[7]

4.2.4.4   The Patten Commission

In 1998, the Conservative politician Chris Patten—from 1992 to 1997 he was the last British Governor in Hong Kong (Sect. 6.4.2)—wrote his report on the future of NI policing. He knew full well that NI was divided into two; he nevertheless suggested only one new name for what had been the Royal Ulster Constabulary, RUC, and that was the Police Service of NI, PSNI.[8] So, given the nature of NI society, it was utterly predictable that the Protestants would want the former and the Nationalists the latter.

He also suggested that recruitment to the new police force should include a definite number of Catholics, in order to reduce the Protestant bias; but that was as if everybody in NI is either/or; as if there are no minorities; as if there is no Chinese community, for example, let alone any other ethnic and/or religious minorities. Extraordinary!

4.2.4.5   The Referendum

The Belfast Agreement was duly signed on 10.4.1998, Good Friday, and the referendum—yet another **AB?** question, "Do you support. . .?"—followed on 22nd May. On a turnout of 81.1%, 71.1% voted in favour. It was a great day, so much so

---

[7]In similar fashion, many pollsters and others act as if everyone in NI is either 'this' or 'that', as if there were only two denominations and two aspirations. In so doing, they exacerbate the most bitter of society's divisions.

[8]At a seminar on this topic hosted by the de Borda Institute, participants were offered seven possible names, and the one which received the highest level of support from the audience of community workers, the best possible compromise, was the name of 'The Police'. http://www.deborda.org/1999-ulster-peoples-college/

that, as a journalist with the *Belfast Telegraph* the late Barry White commented, there was an unwritten agreement among his colleagues in the media that none of them would criticise the Agreement. As is obvious from this book, however, the current author had many reservations about the convoluted decision-making procedures, with some matters to be put to a straight majority vote and other key questions to be subject to weighted consociational majorities, mainly because everything was to remain dichotomous. So, he asked, if and when a policy enjoys a simple but not enough for a weighted majority, "is the question of whether or not [the question] is a key question itself a key question?" The conundrum was published but, on the insistence of the editor of NI's political journal, *Fortnight*, anonymously; they used the name Waldo Ralph—not perhaps the perfect disguise[9] (Emerson [Ralph] 1998: 16).

4.2.4.6 International Conflict Resolution

As part of the Peace Process, the government of South Africa invited all the parties which had been elected to NI's forum in 1996, to go and look at the post-apartheid Peace Process. It might perhaps have been more appropriate for them to go to Yugoslavia, but there, of course, the locals speak a different language. The visit nevertheless had positive benefits; the IRA cease-fire, which had just broken down, was restored, and the NI Peace Process was soon back on track.

Going back earlier, to 1969 when the Troubles first started in NI, the British had sent the British Army to restore order. Instead of such a partial presence, however, if the peacekeepers had been from continental Europe, maybe the violence of later years would have been less severe. Furthermore, if some of them had been Yugoslavs, who knows, the benefits might also have had a beneficial influence on events in the 1990s Balkans.

4.2.4.7 International Election Observation

In 1990, the UK signed the Copenhagen Agreement on observing elections, so to promote good practice (Sect. 2.5.2). Democracy was defined as if it involved the election of "at least one chamber"[10] and in this way, Britain's unelected House of Lords could still be regarded as sort of OK. The idea, then, was that Britain and other very democratic countries should observe elections abroad, especially those in any of the new democracies. It was not supposed to mean that observers from abroad

---

[9]The author nevertheless campaigned in favour of a 'yes' vote, sticking up posters and so on. His attempts to warn of the dangers in the Agreement on the steering committee, however, were not entertained.

[10]Article (7.2) of the 1990 Copenhagen Document asks participating states to "permit all seats in at least one chamber of the national legislature to be freely contested in a popular vote."

would come to the UK to observe British contests! Indeed, in those days, impartial observers were not even allowed to enter any UK polling station. Eventually, however, the inevitable happened: the first OSCE observers to come to the UK came to NI in 2002; they were only three of them, and they too were not allowed to enter a polling station. Now, however, they can go inside.

If they had been, they would have seen that NI polling stations are not administered according to international standards: even today, polling stations are not neutral; ballot papers are not anonymous; voters are not left unmolested as they enter the polling precinct; and voters' identities are not kept secret from the party activists, some of whom are actually inside the polling stations, being told by the officials that, yes, this voter is called Paddy Murphy, and that his number on the register is 1234 or whatever. Thus the party activist knows exactly who has voted and who not. This is horrible. But it is all legal. What happens next—and this *is* illegal but it still happens—is as follows: towards the end of the day, data on who has not yet voted is passed to the activists waiting at the entrance, and they then go off to round up any stragglers.[11] Needless to say, the author has published on this topic; (Emerson 2005: 6–7); the response of the authorities has been minimal. If, however, elections were conducted more fairly, it is probably true to suppose that the extremist parties on both sides would not be so successful.[12]

4.2.5 Conclusion

A veto has been compared to a gun in an Anton Chekov play: if a pistol is sitting on the mantelpiece in Act I, it will be fired in Act II. So sure enough, the veto is there in the Belfast Agreement, and it has indeed been used. Bang, and everything has now broken down. After the 2016 Assembly elections, the 'nice guys'—the UUP, SDLP, GP and Alliance Parties—formed an opposition, while, between themselves, the DUP and SF shared all the Executive posts, except for that of Justice. But then, on 16.1.2017, this semi-power-sharing government collapsed and, at the time of writing nearly two years on, despite numerous attempts and coercions from elsewhere, it still has not been re-convened. It can only be hoped that one day, those concerned will (read this book and) consider a less majoritarian polity.

---

[11]The worst instance witnessed by the author was in a North Belfast polling station when a very sick old man was brought in. He was already crying if not dying. And he stood there, at the entrance of the room, holding his voting card, shaking and sobbing, "What do I do now?"

[12]The author stood as a candidate in 15 NI elections, and was thus able to observe the activities of many polling stations in many elections under FPTP, PR-list and PR-STV. His first contest was in 1977, at a time when SF did not participate in the democratic process at all. He lost. "Well done," some said in passing afterwards, "Better luck next time." And another whispered, "Never mind love, I voted for you . . ." she paused, cast her eyes over her shoulders to check no-one was listening, and then added, "seven times."

The requirement for photographic ID was introduced shortly afterwards.

One simple change would be to stipulate that the newly elected Assembly should indeed elect the Executive. If some MLAs prefer to abstain in this election, then so be it; in like manner, when NI goes to the polls, the outcome depends only upon those who have voted; so, if the DUP and SF want to abstain, no problem, let the other MLAs vote, and let the world carry on, without being held to ransom by the spoil-sports. Unfortunately, of course, the Belfast Agreement was in large part written by those who would then be its operators, with all too little restraint from any human rights provisions.

4.3 Ireland

> We shall have small groups of seven or eight.
> We will not have parties on definite lines of political cleavage.
> > Kevin O'Higgins on *Dáil Éireann*, the Irish Parliament (Lyons 1986: 475).

4.3.1 Ireland, The Constitution, Bunreacht na hÉireann

Like the British (and many others), the Irish also believe in majority voting. Accordingly, this section looks at the role Ireland has played viz-a-viz the North; then at its own power-sharing arrangements; and finally, on a more positive note, on Ireland's contribution to participatory democracy.

Majority rule in NI was widely recognised as problematic, not least in the Forum for Peace and Reconciliation, a Dublin Government initiative to facilitate the work of the NI Peace Process. It started its discussions on 28.10.1994 and most participants agreed that any final resolution of the problem should involve two majority vote referendums, one in the North as mentioned above and the other down South. SF disagreed; they wanted an all-Ireland referendum. And the Green Party, GP, disagreed[13]; it wanted a preferential vote. Alas, the media and everyone else were mainly interested in SF's position.

But back to the beginning, and Ireland, the Irish Free State as it was originally called, got its independence in 1922 in the Anglo-Irish Treaty. Unlike its British neighbour, Ireland has a written constitution, and the original 1922 version was replaced in a referendum in 1937 (Irish Government 1937). Article 6.1 declares that, "All powers of government...[have the right] to decide all questions of national policy, according to the common good." Later, when talking of the two Houses of the *Oireachtas* (the *Dáil*, the parliament, and the upper chamber, the *Seanad*), it states that, "All questions... shall... be determined by a majority of the members present and voting..." Similarly, on referendums in Article 47.2, it goes on to say

---

[13]The author was part of the GP delegation to the Forum.

that any proposal submitted to a referendum shall be accepted if "a majority of the votes cast. . . shall have been cast in favour. . .".

So the Constitution contradicts itself if, except in a few instances when a majority is overwhelming, the common good—Rousseau's "general will"—does not necessarily coincide with a majority will. Such divergence is likely if, in a multi-optional debate, the supposed majority will is identified in a binary ballot (Sect. 1.8).

4.3.2   Politics as Normal

Despite these contradictions, and despite the aspiration of Kevin O'Higgins quoted at the beginning of this section, the *Dáil* soon settled into a two-party adversarial polity. In 1927, W.T. Cosgrove of *Fine Gael*, FG, won 47 of the 152 seats to the 45 of *Fianna Fáil*, FF (and SF lost nearly all of their seats). Initially, FF was on an abstentionist ticket, but in August they joined in and called for a vote of confidence, which they thought they could win albeit with a majority of only one. But a certain TD, the member for Sligo, was invited to a pub and given a Guinness or few; he was soon in a paralytic drunken stupor, at which point, he was bunged onto a train for the West. Meanwhile, because of his absence, the vote in the *Dáil* was a tie. So the chair used his casting vote, and Cosgrove survived by a margin of this one vote. "Resign, resign!" cried the opposition. But he replied, "One vote! That is democracy." (Letters, *Irish Times*, 7.3.1996 and Jordan 2006: 154).

4.3.3   PR-STV

A few years later, like the Unionists in 1929, and for the same obvious reasons of vested interest, the FF Government wanted to change the 'Irish' electoral system of PR-STV (Sect. 2.1.5), to the British FPTP version (Sect. 2.1.2). There was, however, the small problem of the Irish constitution, so a referendum was held at the same time as a presidential election on whether or not the people wanted this change. The FF candidate was Éamon de Valera or Dev as he was popularly called, and the FF slogan used was "Vote Dev and yes." Come the election in June 1959, however, lots of people said Dev and 'no': 'yes' to Dev by 56.3%, but 'no' to FPTP by 51.8%. Not wishing to abide by this "will of the people," the Government held another referendum in 1968, but the people now said an Ulster-like 'NO!' by the much bigger margin of 60.8%. (Lakeman 1974: 267). And that was that. Not because of but despite certain politicians, Ireland still has PR-STV.

4.3.4 Coalition Governments

Even though the RoI was more aware than most that binary majority rule was a major cause of the problems in the North, the Irish Parliament itself has continued to practice this form of democracy… as has the British Parliament, of course (Sect. 3.3). As a result, and for the last 30 years, the *Dáil* has usually relied on a majority- or maybe only a minority-coalition. Needless to say, whenever the results of a general election have been finely balanced, forming an administration has caused one or two problems.

Such was the case in 1982. The election in February that year gave FF 81 seats, just three short of a majority. FG had 63, which was well short, but maybe, if they joined up with Labour on 15 and a few independents, they could cobble up something. So Garret FitzGerald—nicknamed Garret the Good—offered one of the independents, a new TD called Tony Gregory, £1m for his working class Dublin constituency, in exchange for support. £1m, umm, that's a lot of money![14] Essentially, it was a bribe. Charlie Haughey of FF, offered £100m. That was a bigger umm. So that was another that: Haughey became the *Taoiseach* (PM), again—he had held the post in 1979. Not for long though. Later that year, when his finance bill proposed budget cuts, Gregory and some other left-wing TDs withdrew their support, so another election was held, and FitzGerald became *Taoiseach*, again—his first stint had been in 1981—and he remained in post until 1987, when Haughey became *Taoiseach* again again.

In this, his third tour of duty, he was in charge of a minority administration but in 1989 and '92, FF joined up with the Progressive Democrats, PDs, which was logical enough—after all, the PDs were an offshoot of FF. Next, FF joined up with Labour, which was not so logical but, there again, nor is politics; FF was soon back to the PDs, twice, before teaming up with the GP as well in 2007. In the next 2011 elections, as a result of this administration's rising unpopularity, the junior coalition party suffered terribly (as happened in the UK with the Lib-Dems in 2015), and the GP lost all of its TDs.

Five years later, another election was due. So on 23.2.2016, the de Borda Institute held its Dublin launch of *From Majority Rule to Inclusive Politics* (Emerson 2016a), to explain how a newly elected parliament could elect its new administration. Three days later, the 'free and fair' general election was indecisive, or so said those who believe in binary majority rule: yet again, no one party had a majority of the seats, and this time as well, there was no obvious two-party coalition in waiting. So, as sometimes happens in continental Europe, the very democratic election was followed by a very dubious series of inter-party talks, as the newly elected TDs tried to sort something out behind closed doors.

In the mean time, while the politicians were on the top-floor of Leinster House, members of the public met in an open meeting, hosted by the de Borda Institute with

---

[14]At that time, the Irish £, the punt, was almost on a par with sterling, the English £.

The Irish Times, Dublin City University and an NGO called CIVIQ.[15] It was an experimental role-play *Dáil* in which, on arrival, every participant drew a name out of a hat and adopted the persona of a TD; they first discussed amongst themselves, 'party' by 'party' as it were, who they should nominate for which ministry and in which order of preference; next, in 'inter-party' talks, each group negotiated with one or more of the other 'parties', to try and get some measure of co-operation; and finally, electronically of course, they voted. After a short delay which should have been a couple of nano-seconds (but was actually a few minutes), the result was duly displayed.   https://static1.squarespace.com/static/56a9f0a9e0327c33e479d003/t/ 58ce437217bffcb09bc71644/1489912696683/IJSEES_VOLUME1_1.pdf—page 56.

At last, the matrix vote (Sect. 3.3.2)—by now some 30 years old—had been recognised by the (Irish) media and academia. Not that the politicians took any notice. Instead, doubtless out of a sense of fear from the growing strength of SF (Sect. 3.2), the main opposition party, FF, actually decided to support a minority administration of FG and a few independents in a rather unusual or even grand 'confidence and supply' arrangement, with a big party supporting the even bigger one.

4.3.5 Participatory Democracy

In many countries, lots of people are experimenting with various forms of participatory democracy: focus groups, deliberative polling, citizens' assemblies, constitutional conventions and so on. Like the citizens' assembly held in British Columbia in 2004, some of them are initiated by the Government; others, in Iceland for example, have been bottom-up.

The Canadian exercise was concerned with the electoral system; it looked at all the options and then held a vote on just two of them. Obviously, the people behind that initiative had wanted everyone to want PR-STV, so that in any future election, everyone would be offered 'a range of candidates'; so they dictated that everyone would *not* be offered 'a range of options' but that the final decision would be a two-option ballot—"change, yes or no?"

The final outcome was a majority of 57.7% in favour, but the rule required a weighted majority of 60%, so the majority lost. Ah well, that's democracy. A second vote in 2009 also failed. . . or, depending on the reader's point of view, succeeded. Yet again, it seems, academics and others who are madly in favour of preferential voting in elections, are equally madly in favour of binary voting in decision-making. It is truly quite extraordinary.

---

[15]https://www.civiq.eu

Ireland had its own Citizens' Assembly in 2016. It was tasked by the Government to look at a number of topics, the most contentious being the question of abortion. But first, a quick word on decision-making in Ireland; it goes back a few years.

In 1996, at the time of the Forum for Peace and Reconciliation (Sect. 4.3.1), the Government asked a Constitution Review Group to examine the entire document. As implied earlier (Sect. 1.1.1), this team of 15 lawyers, professors and doctors concluded, not only that, "Democracy works on the basis of a decision by the majority," (Whitaker 1996: 398) but also, that "the referendum system has worked well in practice," (ibid: 469). This is *after* the NI border poll of 1973 (Sect. 4.2.2), and *after* the dreadful referendums in the early 1990s in the Balkans (Sect. 5.6.2). Even south of the border, it came *after* the 1995 referendum on divorce reform, which scraped home by less than 1%. As elsewhere, so too in Ireland, many academics believe in and do not question majority voting. It is indeed at least odd.

4.3.5.1 Abortion

In 1992, a referendum attempt to reform what was an old-fashioned law on abortion—to describe it in the mildest of terms—failed by quite a large margin. The problem, of course, did not go away, and the Government produced a Green Paper, (Irish Government Undated), which agreed there were considerable problems with any binary ballot. Prior to that 1992 referendum, it argued, "the debate became bitter and polarised..." (*op. cit.*: 126), as binary referendums often do. Furthermore, the proposal was rejected, "apparently, by those who disliked its restrictiveness as well as by those being opposed to abortion being legalised... on any ground." (Ibid.: 166.) (Sect. 1.1.2). Accordingly, the Green Paper suggested there were seven possible options. Now some of them applied to 'what' should be done, the abortion law itself, and others spoke of 'how' it should be done, in the constitution, in the *Dáil* or wherever. So, concentrating on the former 'what' question, the de Borda Institute proposed a multi-option referendum of five options; (correspondence, 10.12.1999).

As a result, on 17.5.2000, a delegation from the Institute met the Joint Committee on the Constitution to ask for just such a five-option ballot. The options would be chosen independently, it was suggested, and people would then have the opportunity to cast their preferences on (one, some or at best) all of these options, as in an MBC. But, intervened Liz McManus TD, a politician with a different idea of politics, the elected TD should allow a referendum to include only those options with which she is in agreement: "I could not agree to put forward an option... which I would have a moral objection to." (Joint Committee on the Constitution 2000: 24). So, assuming there is no consensus in the *Dáil* on some topic or other, there will always be those who oppose pluralism.

On 7.3.2002, the referendum was duly held, and it was binary. It lost by a margin of less than 1%. "The people have spoken," said the *Taoiseach*, Bertie Ahern, when the result was declared. "So, what did they say?" the author asked in a letter to *The Irish Times*, 8.3.2002. And still the problem did not go away.

In the wake of the Whitaker Report, the Irish Government reconstituted an All-party *Oireachtas* Committee on the Constitution in 2002. Next, in 2012, came a Constitutional Convention, a meeting of 66 members of the public and 33 politicians, and it considered a number of options, not least that of same-sex marriage. This was then taken to a referendum and the result was a surprise to many: approved by 62.1% in 2015; Ireland had joined the twenty-first century.

The subject of abortion, however, they did not consider. Hence the Citizens' Assembly of 2016, and in this one, all 99 participants were randomly-selected civilians. It was another top-down initiative, tasked to consider abortion and a few other controversies.

4.3.5.2 The Citizens' Assembly

For some old-fashioned reason, the Assembly was instructed by the *Dáil* in its terms of reference to ensure that, "all matters before the Assembly will be determined by a majority of members present and voting, other than the Chairperson, who will have a casting vote in the case of an equality of votes."

To be fair, the Assembly Secretariat did try to use some non-binary techniques, including (though without naming it as such) a Borda methodology. And why not; after all, as was suggested to them by this author, a consensus could be identified in this way, and then any consensual outcome could be confirmed in a binary ballot, so to comply with the terms of reference. Sometimes, however, and this despite the fact that the Assembly was advised by a number of experts, the organisers found the mathematics a bit difficult. When voting on Question 9 in Ballot 4, for example, on what to do in instances of rape, there were five possible options: and each 'citizen' was allowed to vote on whether an abortion should be allowed A, never; $B1$, up to 12 weeks; $B2$, up to 22 weeks; $B3$ with no restriction; or C, if they preferred not to state an opinion. The results of 86 valid votes were A 9, $B1$ 23, $B2$ 25, $B3$ 25 and C 4.[16] The chair then used her casting vote and the outcome was declared to be $B2$.[17] But 26 is not, of course, a majority of all the Bs, all 73 of them, let alone of all 82 of the A/B voters, let alone of every member of the Assembly present and voting, 86. If instead of this plurality vote, an MBC had been used, with the four options placed in order of sequence on the x-axis, and if the MBC set of results had also shown a single peak curve (Sect. 1.6.3), it would have been possible to calculate the collective will of the Assembly very accurately indeed.

These arguments were put to the Citizens' Assembly Secretariat, and the latter agreed enthusiastically to hold a meeting to discuss decision-making. But this was then cancelled. The Steering Group decided they should be consistent: in other

---

[16]https://www.citizensassembly.ie/en/Meetings/Ballot-4-Results-Tables.pdf

[17]https://www.citizensassembly.ie/en/The-Eighth-Amendment-of-the-Constitution/Final-Report-on-the-Eighth-Amendment-of-the-Constitution/Final-Report-incl-Appendix-A-D.pdf

words, having been consistently inaccurate, they would continue to be inaccurate. Extraordinary. Advisers, however, do not like to be advised.

4.3.5.3 Pluralism

The tale nevertheless has a happy ending, well almost. At a subsequent session of the Assembly, when debating the conduct of referendums, it made "a number of recommendations in respect of multi-option voting, namely:

- 76% voted in favour of allowing more than two options on a ballot paper in a constitutional referendum;
- 52% voted in favour that when there are more than two options on the ballot paper in a constitutional referendum the outcome should be decided by PR-STV."[18]

So after over 20 years of campaigning on this issue, multi-option voting, at least in referendums, has at last been recognized as possible and, what's more, recommended as desirable. At some stage in the future, preferential voting in decision-making might even be introduced into the *Dáil*. For some ridiculous reason, however, the Citizens' Assembly decided to make this recommendation by a binary vote. In effect, therefore, the 'citizens' decided to advocate a more consensual decision-making procedure by means of a less consensual procedure... which is a bit like agreeing to the Belfast Peace Agreement by first going outside to have a punch-up. Secondly, on the advice of seven political science experts, who it seemed wanted to confirm that binary voting is still absolutely fine, the Assembly took another binary vote on how a multi-option referendum should be counted, and it opted for PR-STV. Which of course is impossible: PR applies to elections in which more than one candidate is being elected; it cannot apply to decision-making in which only one outcome is sought. What an extraordinary set of ill-advised advisers! What they meant, of course, was AV.

4.3.6 Conclusion

Ireland's contribution to democracy world-wide has not been great. It got off to a very bad start in 1818, when an Irishman became the first person to win 100% support in a referendum: Bernardo O'Higgins it was, and thus he became *El Supremo,* the Chilean dictator.

Since Ireland gained independence, however, while its record in decision-making has not been the best, its use of a good electoral system has been fine—even if the constituencies do vary in size from 3-member to 5-member, which tends to make an

---

[18]https://www.citizensassembly.ie/en/Manner-in-which-referenda-are-held/Manner-in-which-referenda-are-held.html

election a bit of a post-code lottery, especially for any candidates in and supporters of a small party.

Another fine feather in the Irish cap relates to the above Citizens' Assembly. Apart from some of the decision-making which was indeed a bit dodgy, the exercise in general was excellent and widely recognized. It may yet lead to a polity in which a representative democracy can function alongside certain elements of a more direct structure.

4.4   Britain

The UK's constitution is "a set of understandings which no one understands."
                                                          Quoted in A.C. Grayling (2017: 72).

4.4.1   Britain, Two-party Politics

For some strange reason, people in Britain still believe in majority voting, and the home of the industrial revolution is still using two instruments which are over 2000 years old. One is the spade, which is still quite useful for the home gardener; out on the farm, however, it has long since been replaced by all sorts of machines. The second one is the simple or weighted majority vote; in theory, it has been bettered by various multi-option methodologies... but in practice, it is still ubiquitous.

If binary questions are used in the home—will you do the washing up or won't you?—the relationship has probably already started to break down. When the two are still one, they rarely use dichotomies—shall we go to Bangor for our holidays dear, yes-or-no? Life, after all, is multi-optional. The question is open: where shall we go, dear?

For reasons which are explicable, and mostly associated with vested interest, people in business and politics still use the primitive and blunt instrument of majority voting; and for reasons which are quite inexplicable, its use in politics is seldom questioned by the media or academia. Accordingly, in this section, the text first looks at the history of English democracy, and then at its more contemporary majoritarian mistakes—the biggest of which is Brexit.

Legend has it that everyone present was equal when, back in the fifth century, King Arthur met with his Knights of the Round Table—everyone except, of course, the King himself. Unfortunately, however, when the first palace of Westminster was built in the eleventh century, the architects designed a debating chamber of two halves, with one set of seats facing the other. It became the home of the English Parliament in the thirteenth century and it is often called the mother of parliaments; for some reason, this description continues despite umpteen signs of democratic dementia.

Initially, of course, the monarch was in charge. Then, in 1215, King John was not so strong, so the barons of England, like the boyars of Russia a bit later on (Sect. 5.9.1), managed to get some power for themselves, and the deal was Magna Carta: this was the first step towards a democracy, the crown was not above the law. Accordingly, on occasions of major importance, the king was required to go to the parliament, as for example in 1532 when Henry VIII wanted to annul his first marriage. He thought he would be more likely to get a majority in favour if the MPs stood in full view of everybody—while, of course, his executioner was in The Tower, whetting his axe—and thus parliament had its first open division. Henry got what he wanted, his second wife. Whether or not she wanted him, history does not say.

Initially, there were no political parties as such, and every MP was simply the member for 'this' or 'that' constituency—or 'rotten borough'. One side of the parliament consisted of the well-heeled of well-established families; those opposite were more the *nouveau riche*. They debated. They argued. They took majority votes. So they divided. Of course. Indeed, it was not long before terms of abuse were being hurled from one side of the House to the other. You "whig" shouted one half, a word which meant "a money-grabbing Scots Presbyterian." That was pretty rude. You "tory" responded the other even more venomously, an "Irish Papist bandit;" in those days, a term of total abuse.

Thus was born the British two-party system (Churchill 1956: Book II, 294), the Whigs or the Liberals as they were later called on one side, and the Tories, the Conservative Party, on the other. These two parties shared the spoils of office, as it were taking it in turns after each election to form the government, arguing about everything, with just the exceptions of the National Government in 1929 during the slump, and the two coalition governments during the two World Wars. Yes, they argued about everything; well almost everything; the exception came when their vested interests coincided, and Britain's choice of FPTP "was shaped throughout by the needs and interests of the party leaders, and settled, symbolically, in a private inter-party conclave." (Bogdanor 1981: 113).

This two-party system continued throughout the eighteenth and nineteenth centuries... until eventually a third party came along, the Labour Party. Something had to give... FPTP caters for only two main parties (Sect. 2.1.3) ... so there was a hiccough, the last Liberal PM was David Lloyd George in WWI, and the two-party system returned to full strength in the 1920s. Since then, the Labour and Conservative Parties have argued about everything... except FPTP of course and, oh yes, the atomic bomb.

4.4.2 The Binary Bind

It had been feared by many—John Stewart Mill, for example—that democracy would bring about a legitimized form of mob rule. Slowly, however, the franchise was extended, firstly to all adult males, later, with the suffragettes, to all adults. MPs were elected, supposedly to represent the entire country; but parliament then divided into two, government versus opposition. Sometimes, it seemed, the latter opposed the former for the sheer sake of it; indeed, "The whole constitution was arranged so that men might quarrel," to quote Lord Balfour's depiction. There was one other subject, however, on which they were all agreed, and this involved all of them—Labour and Tory and Liberal et al.: all decided, or it was just assumed, that all decisions had to be resolved by a majority vote. How else could they argue?

In the eyes of many, the full franchise meant that Britain qualified as a mature democracy (Runciman 2018: 216). This is really extraordinary! Britain uses a most immature decision-making voting procedure, majority voting, and one of the most immature electoral systems, FPTP. Yet umpteen political scientists describe this British democracy as 'stable' and 'mature', and so too the political structure in the States. Even when it produces a Trump?

A clear sign of senility occurred in 1978. James Callaghan was the PM, having inherited a three-seat majority from the previous, 1974 election. This Labour Party administration, however, was old and frail. There was a resignation or two, and then one terribly democratic Labour MP did something without any consultation at all with either her constituents or even with her party leadership; she died. So on 2.3.78, there was a by-election. Labour lost. A vote of confidence was called. So hence the Lib-Lab Pact, with the Liberal Party supporting Labour, and Callaghan survived for a little longer.

It lasted only to 7.9.78. The Liberals thought that there would then be a general election. But no, the supposedly left-wing Labour Party jumped over the moon and joined the definitely right-wing UUP[19] by giving them a bribe of a few more Westminster seats, all FPTP of course, and Callaghan survived to fight another day. But having got what they wanted, the fickle UUP followed the Liberals and pulled out as well.

Another vote of confidence was called for 28.3.79. Everyone got terribly excited, and the journalists did their sums. The Tories were going to vote 'no', of course; Labour 'yes', of course; Liberals 'no', of course; the Scottish National Party, SNP, the Welsh, of course of course... and it all came to 325 to 325, a draw, with one MP still to be counted: Frank Maguire, the member for Fermanagh and Tyrone, by trait a republican, by trade a publican. So lots of journalists came over to his pub to ask, 'which way will you vote?' 'What are you having?' he replied, and sales were brisk. But he said nothing. He realized, however, that the entire future of British politics was in his Irish hands, so off he went on one of his rare visits to London where he was entertained in the Labour Party whip's office to a whiskey, Irish of course. 'Which way are you going to vote Frank?' 'It's a grand day,' says he. 'Yes, I'll take another whiskey.' But he said nothing.

It was time for the debate. The MPs gathered. They met. They spoke. They all said what everyone else knew they were going to say. But Frank said nothing; he just sat there. Eventually, the division bell was called, and almost as in Henry VIII's day,

---

[19] A similar feat of political acrobatics was performed in the Czech Republic in 2017 (Sect. 5.6.3).

the MPs stood to vote. But Frank did nothing, he still just sat. Callaghan lost, by one vote. A general election was called. Margaret Thatcher was elected and remained in power until 1987. Gee thanks Frank. His debrief was very brief: "I wanted to abstain in person."

4.4.3 Multi-option Debates But Binary Voting

Why is it "that, despite the plurality of groups in an environment (rarely are there only two), polarity frequently emerges?" (Horowitz 2000: 182). The biggest cause is probably because, as the reader now knows, most people—but not, it is hoped, the reader—believe in majority voting. Sometimes, the debate is indeed multi-optional, and such was the case in 2003 when the House of Lords debated the question, already 100 years old, of Lords reform.

There were seven but then a short list of just five options 'on the table'—all elected, 80:20, 50:50, 20:80 or all appointed. Believing in simple majority rule and practicing simple majority voting, as by and large most of the Lords and Ladies do, it was decided to take five majority votes. But that is "daft," said Lord Meghnad Desai, "if people answer yes or no to [five] options," there won't be an answer. "How would we decide what the House had chosen, if a majority was reached on four of the [five] options?" (Hansard 2003). Daft indeed.

And daft it became. They took five majority votes and lost the lot! So no decision was taken, and the problem, already as noted 100 years old, was to remain unresolved for longer. "The right way," he argued, "is to ask us all to rank the [five] options from one to [five] and then add up those rankings." (*Ibid.*) A BC, in all but name.

Voting in parliament was always binary, of course, and often daft. By the same logic—if that's the right word—voting in referendums was binary as well. But not quite always. In 1948, the British Government legislated for a multi-option referendum to be held in Newfoundland, one of the world's first multi-option plebiscites![20] It started as a proposal for a two-option referendum because, as often happens in top-down politics, those in charge chose the choice. The folks in Halifax, however, had a different opinion: they wanted a third option on the ballot paper. They protested. Oh all right; it was added; and in an 88% turnout in both rounds, it won the second round of the TRS ballot with 52%. (Emerson 2012: 164). The precedent, therefore, was set... but never repeated.

---

[20]The first, on the question of prohibition, was in New Zealand in 1894.

4.4.3.1 Electoral Reform

It took only five days of negotiations after the 2010 general election for the Tory and Lib-Dems to form a coalition government. As part of the deal, David Cameron promised the Lib-Dems, who with their predecessors the Liberals have long since wanted PR-STV, a referendum on electoral reform. Indeed, the history goes back to the nineteenth century (Sect. 2.1.5.1), but unfortunately, when the Liberal Party was itself in power in the early part of the twentieth century, it sort of forgot.

In 1998, Lord Roy Jenkins chaired an *Independent Commission on the Voting System* which, as part of its work, sent three commissioners to New Zealand to look at the fascinating experience from 'down under'. In 1992, the Christchurch Parliament tasked a Royal Commission on the NZ electoral system to be really independent and, as a result, the commissioners drew up a short list of five options. Accordingly, the people were given a five-option referendum, to be conducted like a sort of TRS. It was compared to a hand: there was the thumb, FPTP, and four fingers, AV, AMS, MMP and PR-STV.[21] If, in the first round, a majority supported any of the four fingers, there would then be a second round between the thumb and the biggest finger. In the first round, MMP was a huge finger on 58%; and in the second round, with an 83% turnout, it beat FPTP by 54%.

For some very naughty reason, although Lord Jenkins' final report includes a two-page section on NZ, it makes no mention at all of the latter's pluralist approach to decision-making. (Jenkins 1998: 20–21). Admittedly, the Commission's terms of reference wanted a recommendation for "an alternative"—supposedly just one of them—with a view to holding an **AB?** type two-option referendum (Sect. 1.1.2) at some future date. But while the good Lord chose to talk "well outside [his] terms of reference" in relation to the size of the parliament (ibid: 21), he chose *not* to talk at all about a real choice, about multi-option voting. It was, therefore, not truly independent, or so this author argued at a public session of the Commission held in Belfast. The reason may lie in the fact that, just as both of the main parties had a vested interest in FPTP, so too, they both have an interest in binary voting. Multi-option voting cannot be so easily controlled. Meanwhile, the outcome of the NZ poll was MMP, "contrary to the interests of both major [NZ] parties." (Hughes 1994: 171).

As it transpired, the Jenkins Report was soon lost in the archives, because Labour won a massive majority in the 1997 election, and Tony Blair, who had thought he might need some help from the Lib-Dems, changed his mind. They all do.

In 2010, however, the Lib-Dems were in coalition, so electoral reform was back on the agenda, and Cameron asked his first of three 'which' questions for the 2011 referendum: 'which do you want, everybody? my 1st preference, FPTP, or would you like my 2nd, AV?' The Liberal Party's 1st preference, PR-STV, was not

---

[21]AMS, the Additional Member System, is like MMP but while there are indeed two counts, one by FPTP and one by PR, there is only the one ballot in AMS, but two in MMP. The resulting party structure with AMS is smaller than the German two + two, and with AMS, the two bigger parties tend to be larger, and almost as large as in FPTP.

allowed, and nor was anybody else's for that matter. So the question of the **AB?** variety was "AV or FPTP?" neither of which is PR. For the many thousands of those who would have wanted to vote for PR, this was like asking a vegetarian, "beef or lamb?" The Electoral Commission, however, decided the question was fair, the referendum went ahead, and the people voted for FPTP by 67.9%. But no one can say for sure whether the will of the people was in favour of FPTP; OK, when given the choice of only these two, they opted for FPTP; but nobody knows whether or not the British people would actually have preferred a form of PR. In New Zealand, they do know "the will of their people" much more accurately, and they now have MMP, the German system of PR.

4.4.3.2   Scotland

In 1979, Callaghan had given the Scottish a referendum on devolution, but he wanted none of it. So he adjusted the rules to insist that such an outcome would be approved, not necessarily if it won support from a majority of the voters, but only if it won the support of 40% of the total population. In the vote itself, the majority won but no it didn't, and Callaghan won: a majority of 51.6% voted in favour, but this was only 32.9% of the total electorate. So that was yet another that.

No it wasn't. In 1997, there was a second referendum. Unlike Callaghan, Blair actually wanted the Scots to want devolution; the SNP wanted independence to be included on the ballot and argued for an AV multi-option ballot (SNP 1992: 1–6); but Blair did not want the Scots to want independence so the referendum question was binary, 'Do you want what I want you to want, 'yes-or-no?' Devolution won by a landslide, 74.3%. So that was a different that...

... until 2014, when there was yet another referendum, this time on independence. The SNP still wanted three options[22]—the status quo, maximum devolution ('devo-max' as it was called) or independence—but Cameron wanted his second 'which' to be another binary question: 'Which do you want, status quo or independence?' He thought he would win; the SNP's Alex Salmon just wanted the right to hold a referendum, which could always be repeated later on in another 'never-end-'em', so he settled for the two-option question; and when signing the 2012 Edinburgh Agreement, both leaders "made clear they will abide by the result, even if it is 50% either way plus a single vote." The *Guardian*, 16.10.2014. That, after all, is democracy, they say. Status quo or independence? was the question of the **AB?** variety, even though it was asked as, "Independence, yes-or-no?" as in an **A?** type of poll. Again, for reasons which they have never explained, the Electoral Commission thought the question was fair. This too is quite extraordinary.

So everything was set for 2014, the ballot papers were printed, and the campaign started. But, umm, the SNP was doing rather well. Cameron panicked, and even

---

[22]In the wake of the 2014 referendum, it seems the SNP's enthusiasm for multi-option referendums has waned a little.

though postal voting had already started, the three party leaders in Westminster, Tory, Labour and Lib-Dem, signed "the vow" and changed the question: the status quo now meant 'devo-max'. "A No vote," they pledged, "will deliver faster, safer and better change..." (Daily Record, 15.9.2014: 1), which is an unusual interpretation of the word 'no' but never mind. Two days later, the vote was held, and sure enough, the winner was 'devo-max'. But nobody voted for it. They couldn't. It wasn't on the ballot paper. Nevertheless, 55.3% did say 'no' to independence, so that was the final that. For a generation. Perhaps.[23] With the debate about the UK's relationship with the EU in such a mess, the prospects for Scottish independence are waxing again.

4.4.3.3   Brexit

Cameron's third 'which?' was 'a wicked which' (Emerson 2016b).[24] His 2013 "pledge to hold an 'in or out' referendum... had been designed to fend off [the UK Independence Party] UKIP and critics in his own party" (Clarke et al. 2017: 140).[25] Yet again, as seemingly always, the question was to be binary, 'in or out?' 'yes or no?' but, as shown in Chap. 1, an **A**? ballot in which the voters answer 'positive or negative' is incapable of facilitating the identification of the will of the people.

In a two-party system, the two big parties might 'tolerate' a party or two in the middle—for with FPTP, any middle ground party will doubtless be pretty small—but neither would want serious competition on its side of the divide. Cameron's problem was either UKIP and/or the Tory Brexiteers; but the latter's campaign was "...a politically illegitimate effort by the right wing of a political movement to effect... changes which they could not achieve as a self-standing political party" (Grayling 2017: 11).

A multi-option question, even if only a plurality vote (Sect. 1.1.3), might have identified the collective will. As suggested in a press release issued by the de Borda Institute in February 2016,[26] four months *before* the fateful referendum in June of that year, there could have been three options on the agenda: the UK in the EU, in the EEA or in the WTO? (Sect. 1.1.1). At least, then, the voters would have been able to vote positively which, as noted, is a fundamental requirement of any democratic decision-making voting mechanism (Sect. 1.1.4). It is worth repeating that a 'yes-or-

---

[23]In all other respects, it was a beautiful referendum, at least in Edinburgh; the atmosphere between the two opposing sides was polite and charming. The Electoral Commission had invited guests from all over the world to witness this event—the author met Kenyan, Mexican and South Korean observers—but none alas from Ukraine. 2014 was also the year of the Crimean referendum, and the word "*Shotlandiya*" was used by Russian separatists in Eastern Ukraine (Sect. 5.9.4).

[24]https://www.greeneuropeanjournal.eu/david-cameron-and-the-three-whiches/

[25]For some extraordinary reason, the authors describe lots of factors which influenced the Brexit result, but they do not even mention the biggest one of them all: the crude binary vote on which it was based.

[26]http://www.deborda.org/press-releases/ number 7.

no?' cannot facilitate a proper decision-making process. Now on this occasion, the Electoral Commission did have something to say: they did not like the 'Should the UK remain a member of the EU' nature of the original question, which after all is too like a 'yes-or-no? **A?** type question, so they changed it to 'remain or leave?' But that is also like a 'yes-or-no? The change was, at best, semantic.

The vote, then, in theory a non-binding ballot, was divisive. Of course. Binary votes often are. If the referendum had been a multi-option poll, the campaign would have been more nuanced, the divisions in society less bitter, and maybe, who knows, Jo Cox MP, the Labour Party 'remain' campaigner, would still be alive. She was murdered on 16.6.2016, just a week before the referendum. And, at the time of writing, November 2018, England is now more divided than ever.

The de Borda press release was ignored by both the media and most of academia. The referendum was duly held and, on a 72.2% turnout, 51.9% said 'leave'. And that, so many said, or shouted, or screamed, was the will of the people, even though nobody knew what this undecipherable and 'un-understood' word 'leave' actually meant.

Accordingly, and because Britain is so mesmerised by "the mystique of the majority," [(Dummett 1997: 71) (Sect. 1.1.3)], there then started another binary argument as to whether or not it meant a 'soft' or a 'hard' Brexit.

It is probably fair to say that, in 1990, before their Government decided to appoint a Royal Commission to look at their electoral system, many New Zealanders did not know the meanings of such acronyms as AMS and MMP (Sect. 4.4.3.1). By the time various lobby groups had campaigned for this or that system, and the Commission had debated the merits of each, and the press had commented on all of these proposals, and so on and so forth, people did understand these terms. Hence, by the time the referendum was held, many voters were reasonably aware of everything that was involved, and (nearly) all of them were able to vote positively. Accordingly, the outcome had a good chance of being accurate.

With Brexit, the opposite is the case. Prior to the referendum, very few people were aware of what phrases like 'customs union' and 'Canada plus' actually meant. It was a classic case in which majority voting can indeed be the catalyst of populism (Sect. 1.1.6). The people voted 'no', or 'leave'. But few knew what the word implied. And, with members of the Tory Party tearing themselves apart, they still don't know. Nobody knows.

In such a scenario, getting anything done is actually quite difficult... unless, of course, the PM has a large majority in parliament and, if necessary, is prepared to use the whip. Theresa May was therefore tempted to hold an election, so to increase her rather slim majority. The tactic back-fired, totally. She lost her majority and had to set up the horrible 'confidence and supply' arrangement with the DUP (Sect. 3.2.2). In theory, the British Government is meant to be impartial to the Belfast Peace Agreement (Sect. 4.2.4), but how can a party be neutral to a problem of which it is a part? And how (the hell) can such a sectarian party as the DUP possibly be fair to (itself and) SF? The arrangement is on very shaky ground, especially when trying to stand on water on a border in the Irish Sea. As of now, the DUP, "which cannot form a government at home [in NI] is dictating the future of the entire UK." (The

Guardian editorial, 15.10.2018.) It can only happen because people still believe in majority voting as the basis of a binary form of majority rule. It is extraordinary, bizarre even.

Given all of this, it is hardly surprising that some people are calling for a second referendum, not necessarily of the 'never-end-'em' variety. After all, if Cameron goes to Brussels, sorts something out, asks the people 'yes-or-no?' and gets 'no' for an answer, and if then his successor, Theresa May, goes to Brussels and tries to sort something else out, logically, there should then be a referendum on 'her' proposal. But if it's to be another 'yes-or-no?' query, and if the answer is again 'no', the process could proceed *ad nauseam*, 'no' 'no' and 'no' to everything. Which, as mentioned earlier, is the nature of populism.

At the time of writing, November 2018, there are again at least three options 'on the table': (a) a May/EU 'withdrawal agreement'; (b) no deal (or WTO); and (c) back to 'remain'. If everything is to be decided in parliament, the outcome may well be influenced by all the Tory/Labour whips seeking first and foremost their party advantage, or the long-term hopes of the SNP, or the sectarian whims of the DUP, or maybe the abstentionist SF. Maybe a second referendum could give a more unpolluted outcome. If, however, it is to be (a) versus (b), the 'remain' crowd will feel duly aggrieved; if it is to be (a) versus (c), there could well be social unrest. Whether the decision is to be taken in parliament or in the country at large, therefore, if it is to have any chance of being fair, the final vote should be multi-optional and, ideally, preferential.

Perhaps the only definite factor in all this is that parliament is to have what is called a 'meaningful' vote. {This presumably suggests that some (binary) votes are 'meaningless'—which is indeed true.} It should mean that the MPs will be able to consider all options, including that of (c) a second referendum. But no. In British parliamentary terms, it means that the House will have the opportunity to debate Brexit, possibly in the form of option (a), yes or no, which could mean (a) or (b). So what do the (c) supporters do? Majority voting is not only inaccurate and inadequate: it is also totally inappropriate. And one horrible possibility is that Theresa May will get a majority, because some MPs will support her option 'x' only because they dislike the alternative option 'y'. So that which supposedly gets majority support will not have majority support; binary voting can be nonsensical.

4.4.4   Conclusion

Many aspects of British democracy—the rights of assembly, to peacefully protest, to stand for office, habeas corpus, the freedom of the press and so on—are excellent. Its electoral system, however, is appalling and FPTP is (not *the* but) *a* cause of so many problems elsewhere in the world, as for example in Zimbabwe where Robert Mugabe also enjoyed being the 'elected dictator'. . . while his people suffered the consequences. Another part of the problem is Britain's decision-making voting mechanism—majority voting, and its consequence, binary majority rule and the two-party system. The mind-set is stuck: democracy, they say, is binary majority rule. So democratic decisions, they go on, are taken by a majority vote. And they do go on.

Maybe the biggest consequence of the whole Brexit debate, however, will be the demise of the two-party system and the realisation that, "if the problem ain't binary, you don't use binary voting." As Chap. 3 acknowledged, all-party power-sharing might be difficult, but it has to be better than the current binary politics.

Cameron's decision to hold a referendum was based largely on the needs of his party; and May's determination to pursue a 'hard' Brexit, not least by including the likes of Boris Johnson in her cabinet, was also designed, first and foremost, to keep her party together. Binary politics was, and still is, the problem.

4.5 Overall Conclusion

Majority rule was and still is problematic in NI. Irish democracy would be so much healthier if it were to use preferential decision-making not only in referendums but also in the *Dáil*, and most definitely in its advanced work on deliberative democracy. While in Britain, Brexit is likely to lead to the break-up of the UK, as Scotland opts to opt out and seek independence. In this case, of course, the 'Union', a noun, will no longer exist, so the justification for its adjective, Unionist, will be at best question-able. The Unionists of NI have long since managed to claim the adjective 'British' even though they are separated from its noun 'Britain' (although, as was mentioned, they are still part of the other geographical noun, the 'British Isles'). But if the UK is to be no more, the chances for a united Ireland become stronger. In a nutshell, the DUP may have duped themselves into oblivion.

Even without any changes in Scotland, the very fact that NI is not the same as Finchley—Thatcher's old constituency—might mean that NI holds its referendum as per the Belfast Agreement earlier than the DUP would have wanted, because of Brexit.

Other long-term consequences of Brexit may also be very meaningful. Hopefully, people will at last begin to question the very structure of politics: our collective obsession with majority vote decision-making along with our blind acceptance of that which follows, binary majority rule; secondly, Britain might at long last decide to change its often hopelessly inaccurate FPTP to something a little more suited to the twenty-first century; this could lead to more frequent coalition governments; and then, with the introduction of electronic preferential decision-making leading to the demise of the whip system, there might at last be all-party power-sharing. Let us pray.

For what would have been the consequences if, for example, the 2011 referendum had actually, like its NZ equivalent, been multi-optional? It is quite possible to imagine that the UK would then have opted for some form of PR. In which case, firstly, Cameron would probably not have won a majority in 2015, and some of the Tories, possibly the more extreme ones, would have lost their seats; as a *quid pro quo*, a few of the pro-'remain' Lib-Dems might have retained theirs, and a few pro-'remain' Greens might also have gained representation. Thirdly, the DUP would then have had less than 10 MPs, and SF less than 7. In which case, NI could also have sent some non-abstaining 'remain' MPs to Westminster.

Admittedly, with a change in the electoral system to PR, UKIP would doubtless have gained representation in Westminster, so without a change in Westminster's decision-making procedures, maybe the Tory Party would have ditched the Lib-Dems and joined UKIP in a majority coalition. So there could have been a Brexit referendum after all.

There again, if the reforms outlined in Chaps. 1–3 had been implemented, and if the UK had therefore had an all-party coalition, with UKIP MPs in cabinet alongside those of the Lib-Dems and the GP, not to mention others of the SNP, but only at most one member of the DUP, such a cabinet would probably not have come to a consensus to hold a binary referendum on Brexit. And this horrible political story could actually have been a pleasant tale, with the UK still in the EU, and with far less racism on the streets of what is now a far from 'merrie' but still a very 'olde' England.

References

Bogdanor, V. (1981). *The people and the party system*. Cambridge: Cambridge University Press.
Bogdanor, V. (1994). Western Europe. In D. Butler & A. Ranney (Eds.), *Referendums around the world*. Washington, DC: The AEI Press.
British/Irish Governments. (1998). *The Belfast agreement.*
Churchill, W. S. (1956). *A history of the English-speaking peoples*. London: Pluto.
Clarke, H., Goodwin, M., & Whiteley, P. (2017). *Brexit: Why Britain voted to leave the European Union*. Cambridge, MA: Cambridge University Press.
de Bréadún, D. (2008). *The far side of revenge*. Cork: The Collins Press.
Dummett, M. (1997). *Principles of electoral reform*. Oxford: Oxford University Press.
Emerson, P. (1998). The election: Possible outcomes. *Fortnight*, No 371.
Emerson, P. (2005). Yet again, NI elections fail to meet international standards. *Fortnight*, No 436.
Emerson, P. (2012). *Defining democracy* (2nd ed.). Heidelberg: Springer.
Emerson, P. (2016a). *From majority rule to inclusive politics*. Heidelberg: Springer.
Emerson, P. (2016b). David Cameron and the Three 'Whiches'. *Green European Journal*.
Emerson, R. (1966). *From empire to nation*. Boston: Beacon Press.
Grayling, A. C. (2017). *Democracy and its crisis*. London: One World.
Horowitz, D. (2000). *Ethnic groups in conflict*. Berkeley: University of California Press.
Hughes, C. (1994). Australia and New Zealand. In D. Butler & A. Ranney (Eds.), *Referendums around the world*. Washington, DC: The AEI Press.
Irish Government. (1937). *Bunreacht na hÉireann. Constitution of Ireland*. Dublin: Government Publications.
Irish Government. (Undated). *Green paper on abortion*. Dublin: Stationary Office.
Jenkins, R. (1998). *The report of the independent commission on the voting system*. London: The Stationery Office.
Joint Committee. (2000). *Public hearings on abortion*. Dublin: Leinster House.
Jordan, A. J. (2006). *W. T. Cosgrave, Founder of modern Ireland*. Dublin: Westport Books.
Lakeman, E. (1974). *How democracies vote*. London: Faber and Faber.

Lijphart, A. (1977). *Democracy in plural societies*. New Haven: Yale University Press.
Lyons, F. S. L. (1986). *Ireland since the famine*. London: Fontana Press.
Runciman, D. (2018). *How democracy ends*. London: Profile Books.
SNP. (1992). *A multi-option referendum – let the people decide*. Edinburgh: SNP.
Taylor, R. (Ed.). (2009). *Consociational theory*. London: Routledge.
Whitaker, T. K. (1996). *Report of the constitution review group*. Dublin: The Stationery Office.

Chapter 5
Continental Europe: Are We All Little Bolsheviks?

> ...beginning about the ninth century, movements for self-government developed in the Italian cities and then spread northward, 'forcing bishops and barons... to share power with the burghers, and in the end often yield to them altogether'.
>
> (Samuel P. Huntington 1996: 71).

Abstract Although majority voting was first found to be inadequate by Pliny the Younger in Rome in the year CE 105 (Sect. 1.1.1), most people today, from Brest to Brest-Litovsk, still believe in majoritarianism. This chapter looks at some of the effects in this belief, briefly in western Europe, in some detail in the Balkans and the Caucasus, albeit with a little interlude in Turkey, and finally in the country which suffered more than any other from these ideas: Russia.

5.1 Introduction

In 1648, the nations of Europe signed the Treaty of Westphalia, so to bring an end to the calamitous wars of religion that had plagued the continent for centuries and, except for Ireland where the fighting continued off and on for a further three and a half centuries, and the Balkans where similar battles re-emerged in the 1990s, the Treaty was partly successful. From henceforth, Europe was to be ruled by independent sovereign states, each respecting the other, which was fine... and each competing with others, which ended in another disaster, the two World Wars. At the end of the second conflict, the continent was divided by the Iron Curtain,[1] and then that too collapsed in the 1980s.

---

[1]The author crossed this border, with his bicycle, in 1986, firstly, when travelling from West to East Germany, and later, from East to West and back again, through Checkpoint Charlie in Berlin.

© Springer Nature Switzerland AG 2020

P. Emerson, *Majority Voting as a Catalyst of Populism*,

https://doi.org/10.1007/978-3-030-20219-4_5

Continental Europe now consists of supposedly stable and mature democracies to the west, a few post-dictatorial newcomers like Greece, Portugal and Spain, and some even more recent ex-communist democracies to the east, most of them former members of the Warsaw Pact. Nearly all of their inhabitants now use majority voting as the basis of a binary majority rule. The consequences have sometimes been chaotic; at worst, in the Balkans and the Caucasus, wars.

This tale tells the story of each country visited, as the author travelled from the Low Countries, via '*Middel* Europe' and the former Yugoslavia, to Turkey and the Caucasus and, after a sojourn into Asia in Chap. 6, to Russia.

5.2   The Low Countries

In 1991, the good folks of Vlaaringen had a referendum...on whether or not to have a referendum.

(Holsteyn 1996: 130).

5.2.1   Introduction

Like so many other Europeans, both the Belgians and the Dutch use majority voting and believe in simple majority rule. The Belgian capital, Brussels, is of course home to the European Parliament which, while still using its own version of majority voting, does not and could not base its governance on majority rule. The next three sections will look at all three institutions, the two national and, in the middle, the one continental.

5.2.2   Belgium

Belgium, a plural society, was declared to be a constitutional monarchy at a National Congress in 1830. So, first things first, they looked for a king and in the following year—OK, he'll do—King Leopold I was crowned on 21st July. The country was and remains divided, although often united on the football pitch. There are the mainly Dutch-speaking Flemings of a more Protestant heritage on one side, 58% according to one estimate,[2] and the primarily French-speaking and rather more Catholic Walloons on the other, 41%, with Brussels in the middle, the capital, a mixture of both if not everything; and there is also a tiny minority of 1% of German-speakers. But these statistics imply that there are no mixed marriages, and no ethnic

---

[2]*Belgium as a Crucial Test of Consociationalism: the 2007–2011 Political Crisis* by Zsofia Pales, writing in 2011.

minorities, and no nothing if it's neither 'this' nor 'that'—the pollsters are part of the problem, as they were and still are in NI (Sect. 4.2.4.3, fn 7).

Belgium has its problems, of course, and one of the biggest conundrums occurs after pretty well every election: how to form a new majority government. Gradually, with one crisis after another, a consociational structure of governance has emerged, very much on the lines advocated by Arend Lijphart (Sect. 3.3). Powers were devolved to the regions, the electoral system was PR, both languages were on a par, and government was shared with equal numbers of Dutch- and French-speakers... but for some reason, decision-making was still to be based on dichotomous choices. Granted, the approval of any key decision was to depend on "super-majorities" (Lijphart 2011: 39), so they agreed that laws "pertaining to the... communities and regions... require two-thirds majorities in both houses [of parliament, and] majorities within the Dutch-speaking group as well as within the French-speaking group in each of the houses." (*Ibid*). Furthermore, if three-quarters of either were worried, they could 'ring the alarm bell' and, in effect, veto whatever caused them concern. Overall, therefore, while many aspects of their modern democracy were indeed to be modern, decision-making was still to be based on the ancient binary theme.

On the positive side, in 1958, the three countries of 'BE'lgium, the 'NE'therlands and 'LUX'embourg, set up the 'Benelux' Economic Union—(now why could not the people in the British Isles be equally 'wise' and organise a 'W'ales, 'I'reland, 'S'cotland and 'E'ngland federation?)[3] But the consociational structure has had some negative consequences, perhaps best summed up in the term 'ethnification'. It means that, as powers were devolved to the regions, many of the political parties became as divided as the nation. For example, there was the Social Christian Party—a name which in a multi-religious society is somewhat oxymoronic because democracy is meant to be for everybody whereas such a party was maybe only for the Christians (Sect. 7.1); in 1968, this then split into the Flemish and Walloon versions—so both of the new names were then double oxymorons. That said, within each 'family' (as they are termed), the two 'sister parties' usually got on fairly well together: the two socialist parties, for example, or the two sets of Greens. Nevertheless, just as the Belfast Agreement has institutionalised sectarianism in NI (Sect. 4.2.4.2), and just as the Dayton Agreement has had the same effect in Bosnia (Sect. 5.6.6), "ethnification of other policies [in Belgium] became prevalent, for example, imbalances in the funding of schools or scientific research, or the routing of the high speed train, etc. In all these instances policies which would not necessarily put the North against the South became interpreted in such a way due to the consociational ethnic divide of the country" (Quoted in Pales 2011: 31).

---

[3]One of many good ideas from the late Senator John Robb.

5.2.2.1   Elections and Governance

Belgian elections are rather better than its decision-making. Voting, which can be on paper or electronic, is compulsory, but voters can always vote for 'none of the above' if they want to. The system is PR-list, open (Sect. 2.1.5), and it allows for multi-candidate voting. Admittedly, it is not as 'free' as PR-single transferable vote PR-STV, or the quota Borda system QBS, in that the voters cannot use preferences, and nor can they cross the party divides; but they can vote for more than one candidate. The ballot paper offers a list of names under each party, and the voter may choose a number of candidates, as long as they are all from the one list, i.e., the one party.

This PR system means that the Belgian parliament has lots of parties, 13 of them at the last count. In 2010, the Fleming parties won 27, 17, 13, 13, 12, 5 and 1 seats; and the Walloons got 26, 18, 9, 8 and 1. The 'socialist family'—26 + 13—was the biggest, it (or they) said, not least because the Fleming party with 27 seats did not have a Walloon sister party. So that "we're the biggest," was not a good start to the inter-party negotiations. Eventually, after 541 days, the rabbit was pulled out of the hat: the parties of 26, 18, 17, 13 and 13 = 87 joined together, a handsome majority out of a total of 150, but the cynic might complain that it was then almost time for the next election.

Unfortunately, not an awful lot has changed in Brussels since that fiasco and, after the 2014 election, with the socialist family down by three seats and now out of government, a coalition of just four parties still needed 135 days to sort themselves out (or in).

5.2.3   The European Union

Since the start of the Renaissance in the fourteenth century, European philosophers and scientists have done wonders. That said, when Giscard d'Estaing's Commission proposed a new set of voting rules as a basis for the Treaty of Nice, everything centred on majority voting, albeit by different mathematical formulas... and all the thoughts and ideas of so many European social choice scientists, some of whom were mentioned earlier (Sect. 1.6.2), were not even considered.

The European Parliament could not work well if it operated according to the usual procedures of simple majority rule. So it has devised a different set of regulations like that of a rotating presidency, which apparently is fine. (But if it is fine for the EU, why can't the UK, for example, have a rotating PM?) In the parliament itself, all the various parties in Brussels or Strasbourg tend to fall into officially recognised groups, if that is they exceed the minimum requirement of at least 25 MEPs from at least seven countries, and that too is fine; after all, as the proverb relates, birds of a feather flock together. Unlike most other parliaments, however, the house itself does not divide into two; there are none of the 'usual' government-versus-opposition divisions; and in this author's book, that is fine as well.

Decisions are based on weightings. Germany for example, which is the biggest country, has 96 MEPs, while Malta, the smallest, has three. In terms of population, of course, the former is about 200 times bigger than the latter, but never mind. Then, come the vote, Germany, the UK, France and Italy, have 29 votes; Spain and Poland, 27; Romania 14; Netherlands 13; and so on down to Malta with 3 votes. And a decision shall be taken if it has the support of three majorities: a majority of countries, a majority of voting weights and a 62% majority of the total population. It is all very complicated... and *very* majoritarian.

5.2.3.1 The Vision

For many, the EU is a dream, the biggest of all lessons from WWII, the coming together of the nations of Europe in what, at last, may be a continent at peace. It is now under threat, not only from the prospect of Brexit but also from the rise in so many countries of various euro-sceptic parties; and the danger is that, in the next EU elections scheduled for May 2019, the use of single-preference electoral systems will artificially augment the success of these extremists (Sect. 2.7).

5.2.4 The Netherlands: A Question of the Question

Like so many other Europeans, the Dutch also use majority voting and practice simple majority rule. On 6.4.2016, a referendum was held on an 'Association Agreement' with Ukraine. The question was another **A?** style of yes-or-no: do you approve of this agreement? In a 32.3% turnout—which therefore surpassed the threshold of 30%—a majority of 61.0% said 'no'. But were they voting on Ukraine? Or were they thinking about the EU? On balance, it seems to be another instance of how it can be inappropriate to ask a simple **A?**-type 'for-or-against?' question. At the very least, it should have been in an **AB?** format: "Do you wish the EU to accept the Association Agreement...?" or "Do you wish the EU to reject the Agreement...?" But maybe, even then, the anti-EU vote would have supported the latter option.

5.2.4.1 A More Consensual Polity

Even within a majoritarian milieu, some countries like the Netherlands try to make their politics a little more consensual than that which is the norm in the UK. Accordingly, instead of the various political parties in each municipal authority competing against each other in a mayoral election, "the mayor is appointed by the province's [King's] Commissioner" (Netherlands Ministry of Foreign Affairs 2000: 44). So rather than pretending to be non-partisan—which many Mr./Ms. Speakers in

Britain's House of Commons and mayors in local councils nevertheless do very well—the mayor is indeed neutral with the responsibility to facilitate agreements.

In a similar fashion, if and when the newly elected parties find it difficult to form a new government—which, as in Belgium, is nearly always—an *informateur* is appointed to try and get some of the parties to reach an agreement. After the last 2017 election, the top eight parties had 33, 20, 19, 19, 14, 14, 5 and 5 seats. One of the 14-seat parties said that if the 33 is to be in, then it, the 14, will be out. One 19 said that if the 33 is not to be in, then it, on 19, will be out. And all 7 of them said if the 20 is to be in, then all of them will be out. The 20, of course, is the extremist Party of Freedom, *Partij voor de Vrijheid*, PVV. So the task was quite difficult, but eventually, after 225 days—not a world but a Dutch record—an agreement was made: 33, 19, 19 and 5, which adds up to 76, a majority of one.

5.2.5 A Little Conclusion

As noted in Chap. 1, from one side of the Euro-Asian landmass to the other, there is this ubiquitous obsession with majority voting. It is so strong that, even in those places where it is obvious that ordinary majority rule is inadequate—as is definitely the case in both of the above Low Countries—those involved try and concoct a pragmatic variation on the majoritarian theme. Disputes are still binary. It seems that, despite the capabilities of computers, which could make multi-option and even preferential voting so easy, consideration is never given to changing to a multi-optional basis of decision-making. It really is extraordinary. Given the roughly equal demographic balance in Belgium, it would be relatively easy to establish a threshold—a consensus coefficient, CC, as it is called (Sect. C.2)—such that, if surpassed, all concerned could rest assured that the said policy option had adequate support from across the divide, without institutionalising that divide. It would also be sensible for every newly elected parliament, instead of spending days, weeks and months negotiating a majority coalition, to instead decide to use a matrix vote and *elect* an all-party power-sharing administration, and do it all within a week.

To change the democratic basis, therefore, could be relatively easy. Unfortunately, for the moment anyway, every political party believes in binary majority rule. Preferential voting could facilitate the de-ethnification of Belgian politics; it could certainly make for a less convoluted form of decision-making in the European parliament; but maybe its biggest impact could be in the Netherlands, where the PVV is waiting for the day when it gets 50% plus one of the parliamentary seats. At which point, if it were to happen, the PVV could take over, at worst to mimic a majoritarian descent into totalitarianism which is what happened in neighbouring Germany in 1933. Dutch democracy could die. If there is to be reform, it has to happen now; tomorrow it may be impossible.

5.3   Germany

> When the generation that survived the war is no longer with us, we'll find out whether we
> have learned from history.
>
> Angela Merkel, quoted in The *Guardian*, 30.8.2018.

5.3.1   A Horrid History

For some reason, people in Germany a century ago believed in simple majority rule.
Accordingly, after the abdication of the Kaiser, although elections in the Weimar
Republic were held under a form of PR-list, decisions were taken by simple or
weighted majority vote.

The politicians of the day had to tackle huge problems, not least those imposed by
the Treaty of Versailles or the other serious difficulties arising from the 1929 slump.
Little wonder, then, that populism was on the rise. Forming a government was
difficult, to put it mildly. "Under an electoral system of proportional representation,
in which the relatively numerous parties held radically different opinions on a range
of domestic and foreign, it was extremely difficult to form any sort of stable coalition
government with majority support in parliament" (Fulbrook 1991: 46). In this quote,
the author is blaming the messenger, as if the electoral system is the problem when
actually it is the decision-making procedure; but she is not alone (Sect. 3.2).

While electing a government was nothing if not problematic, dismissing one was
dead easy: a vote of confidence was all that was required. For this reason, the post-
WWII constitution has provisions for what is called a constructive vote of
no-confidence. So those who do not like an existing government, option A, must
propose an alternative government, option B. They have to say 'yes' to something
(Sect. 4.2.3). In other words, instead of an A? type of question, it has to be in an **AB?**
format (Sect. 1.1.2). The difference is enormous! Unfortunately, however, this very
sensible reform applies only to votes of confidence.

But we return to Weimar. In the 1930 elections, the National Socialist German
Workers' Party, *Nationalsozialistische Deutsche Arbeiterpartei*, NSDAP or
Nazi Party, came second to the Social Democratic Party of Germany,
Sozialdemokratische Partei Deutschlands, SPD, but "there was [still] no basis for
a parliamentary majority in support of any viable coalition cabinet" (Fulbrook 2002:
174). On 30.1.1933, Adolf Hitler was inaugurated as Chancellor. In a nutshell, Hitler
came to power democratically.

The elections which followed shortly afterwards, on 5.3.1933, came just
six days after the Reichstag fire, which was blamed, violently, on the Communist
Party, *Kommunistische Partei Deutschlands,* KPD, with part of the anger directed at
the SPD as well. Needless to say, with this sort of publicity, the Nazis came out on
top, with 288 of the 647 seats, though not yet a majority (of 324 or more).

Hitler's first decision was the Enabling Act, by which the multi-party state was
turned into a one-party state. Because of everything that followed in its wake, it is

hardly surprising that so many politicians today, not only in Germany but in other countries too, believe in a multi-party democracy, [even if, as in the UK and US, it is only a two party structure—(Sect. 4.4.1)]. He needed a two-thirds majority, 432. He therefore banned the KPD, 81 seats, to require only 378 votes, and his SS (*Schutzstaffel*—Protection Squadron) kept some of the SPD away as well. Next, he wooed the Centre Party, 74, with the prospect of sectarian, NI-style, separate education: "The Catholics in particular were rather reassured by Hitler's insistence that the position of Christianity would be untouched in the future" (*ibid*: 68). So Hitler got what he wanted. In a nutshell, he not only came to power democratically but he also became the dictator democratically. In the next election, in November, the one and only party, the Nazis, won all 661 seats, and only 7.9% did not support the Nazi nominees by submitting votes which were invalid.

There was one other sort of democratic decision: Hitler, like Napoléon and Benito Mussolini before him and quite a few other dictators since, held a number of referendums. On the same election day of November 1933, 93.4% agreed to the Nazi government; one year later, 88.2% approved of Hitler as the Chancellor; on 29.2.36, 98.1% made him the Führer, and on 10.4.1938, 99.7% of Austrians voted for *Anschluss*, the union of Austria with Germany. In all four referendums, the turnout figures were above 90%. The rest, as they say, is history. The lessons are plenty.

5.3.2   West and East Germany

After the war, in 1949, The Federal Republic of Germany, FRG, had another attempt at creating a fair but functioning polity, part of which was a new written constitution, the Basic Law. *Inter alia* it states: "Article 38 (Elections). (1) Members of the German Bundestag shall be elected in general, direct, free, equal, and secret elections. They shall be representatives of the whole people, not bound by orders or instructions, and responsible only to their conscience" (Federal Government, Germany 1949: 57). That sounds like the end of the party whip system, which would be good. Interestingly enough, like many other constitutions and legal documents, it refers to a general election without specifying the electoral system, but it was also decided in 1949 to adopt the mixed-member proportional electoral system, MMP (Sect. 2.1.1). In other instances of elections, it is more specific: the Federal President shall be elected by a plurality vote, [Article 54(6)], and the Federal Chancellor by a majority vote [Article 63(2)] or, if that fails, by another plurality vote.

On decision-making, however, it contradicts itself: "The fact that Members of the Bundestag take decisions on behalf of the whole German people... is a requirement... for majority decision-making" (Introduction 2: 18). That sentence, this author suggests, is pure gobbledegook. With regard to a vote of no confidence, however, the law is not ambiguous: it needs a majority (Articles 67–8), while amendments to the constitution require a two-thirds majority (Article 79).

As far as referendums are concerned, it stipulates that "All state authority... shall be exercised by the people through elections and other votes" [Article 20(2)]. In effect, however, referendums at the state level have been banned. That was definitely a lesson from the pre-war years. But such ballots may and do still take place in the Länder, subject to a majority of those voting, as long as the turnout is at least 25% [Article 29(6)]. So that is a lesson unlearnt. And here's another: binary ballots still take place in the Bundestag; so much for the voting procedure advocated by their compatriot, Nicholas Cusanus (Sect. 1.6.2), although admittedly he was talking about an election.

As noted, a follow-on from Hitler reflected a very understandable abhorrence of any one-party structure, though maybe the new constitution goes a little too far in the opposite direction: "Political parties shall participate in the formation of the political will of the people..." [Article 21 (1)].

Meanwhile, on the eastern side of the Curtain, the German Democratic Republic, GDR, adopted its own constitution, all under the guidance of the Socialist Unity Party, a Marxist-Leninist party set up in 1949. To a certain extent, the structure was similar to that of West Germany, for it envisaged a bicameral structure of two elected chambers chosen by first-past-the-post, FPTP—perfect for a communist state!—and in the People's Chamber (*Volkskammer*), decisions were to be taken by majority vote—yet more totalitarianism. The one difference of note was that this constitution stipulated a system of power-sharing: any party with 40 members of the 400-seat chamber would then be in government, the theory being that members of the proletariat should work with those of the bourgeoisie... at least initially.

5.3.3 A Post-war History

The first elections in the FRG, in 1949, gave success to a new party, the Christian Democratic Union, CDU, *Christlich Demokratische Union Deutschlands,* and Konrad Adenauer was then elected Chancellor "by one vote—his own." He went on to lead five majority coalition governments until 1963, and the CDU continued as the strongest of three coalition partners, until Willy Brandt of the SPD took over in 1966, when *détente* was in the air. The democratic structure was working well, it seemed.

In 1982, however, the Free Democratic Party, FDP, *Freie Demokratische Partei,* which had been in coalition with the SPD, jumped horses as it were and joined a different majority coalition with the CDU and Christian Social Union, CSU, *Christlich-Soziale Union in Bayern*, the CDU under Helmut Kohl. In a party structure like the German one, where there are two big parties plus a few little parties, if and when the two large are of about the same size, then a small party can be the decisive factor (like the Irish king-maker, Sect. 4.3.4). Kohl remained in power until 1998, and the legacy he wanted he got: Germany was re-united in 1990.

As was suggested in Chap. 3 and as is the experience in the Low Countries, it is sometimes rather difficult to form a majority coalition. Consider for example the situation in the Bundestag in 2005, when the general election produced the following result: the CDU/CSU 226; the SPD, 222; FDP 61; The Left, 54; and the Green Party, GP, 51: 614 seats in all, so 308 was needed for a majority. Mathematically, such a sum could be achieved either by the two big parties in a grand coalition, or by either of the two big parties joining any two of the three smaller parties in any one of six possible majority coalitions. For those who believe in majoritarianism, any one of these seven possibilities would be only *totally* democratic. Extraordinary. In the end, they opted for Germany's first grand coalition.

Sorting out that 2005 grand coalition government took the parties 64 days. Four years later, there was another majority coalition, which needed only 30 days. Back to a grand in 2013, when 67 days were required, and in 2018, Germany did what the Dutch had just done (Sect. 5.5.2) and broke its own record—161 days. This, however, was new territory: the extremist *Alternative für Deutschland*, AfD was now in parliament.

The CDU/CSU were on 246; the SPD had 153; and the next biggest party was this AfD on 94. Then came the FDP on 80, The Left on 69 and the GP on 67. The nightmare scenario, then, if the grand coalition of 2013 were to continue, was that the AfD would become the official opposition. This, after all, is the logic of binary majority rule. So no wonder the negotiations took such a long time.

5.3.4   A Little Conclusion

It is an amazing fact but, in Germany of all places, so few of the lessons from Weimar have actually been learnt. They still believe in binary majority rule. Like the PVV in the Netherlands (Sect. 5.4.2), the AfD is waiting for the day when it gets 50% plus one. Afterwards, of course, it will again be too late.

Some of the lessons of Weimar have been learnt. The constructive vote of no confidence is a tiny or rather huge advance on the previous provisions. Why majority voting in the Bundestag is still of the **A?** type, however, is at least odd. The decision to ban (binary) referendums at the national level was also perhaps very sensible, but if they can be so terrible at that level, surely they could still be terrible in the Länder.

Why other forms of decision-making for use in both parliament and referendums were not even contemplated is also extraordinary, apart from the fact that multi-option decision-making is seldom considered in any jurisdiction. Every nation, it seems, uses majority voting; and most have binary majority rule; hence that which may be the biggest threat to European civilisation since its re-emergence in the renaissance... is called democracy.

5.4   The Czech Republic

> Unlike its neighbours, Czechoslovakia never succumbed to any form of dictatorship [in the inter-war years], even when bad times arrived.
>
> (Elizabeth Wiskemann 1966: 19).

5.4.1   A Little History

Czechoslovakia came into existence at the end of WWII. The western part, today's Czech Republic, had been under the Austrians, while Slovakia had been ruled by the Hungarians. Similarly in Yugoslavia, Croatia and Bosnia had been under the Austro-Hungarians while Serbia's imperial overlord had been the Ottomans. In the 1990s, both of these 'federations'—Czechoslovakia and Yugoslavia—fell apart, but only the Czechs and Slovaks did so peacefully. And today, the ultimate irony, all of the resulting new nation states are trying to come back together again by joining the EU.

As was said earlier (Sect. 1.4), the right of self-determination was established without consideration for the million Germans living in the Sudetenland. On 29.9.1938, the British and French governments signed the Munich Agreement, so to carve up what had been Czechoslovakia. The Poles then joined in and sliced off a bit for themselves; this was surely one of the most short-sighted acts of any government, because the Munich Agreement was *a* if not *the* cause of the Molotov-Ribbentrop Pact which led to the subsequent division of Poland—not for the first time in its history[4]—and then WWII.

When hostilities came to an end, Czecholsovakia (like Korea) was occupied by both Soviet and US forces, but both pulled out on 1.12.1945, the only loss being the most eastern part of the country which was ceded to the USSR.[5] In the following year, elections were held. Having won the largest share, 93 of the 300 seats, the Communist Party formed a coalition. Two years later, the coalition partners resigned, so the communists took over. Czechoslovakia was now firmly in the Soviet orbit, 'safely' behind the Iron Curtain.

There had been an uprising in the GDR in 1953, there was the Hungarian Revolution of '56, and then, in 1968, it was the Prague Spring.[6] Yet again, the tanks came in, but there did follow some constitutional change. Czechoslovakia

---

[4]Poland was partitioned three times: in 1772, 1790 and 1795, with the three surrounding empires of Austria, Russia and Prussia slicing off various bits until there was nothing left.

[5]The powers-that-be in the Kremlin always liked the Soviet Empire to be, like its predecessor the Russian Empire, contiguous. Accordingly, they wanted common borders with the satellites, and chopping off the eastern tip of Czechoslovakia gave the USSR a common border with Hungary as well. It was not a very long border, but wide enough for the tanks which then rolled in to Budapest in 1956 at the time of the Hungarian Revolution.

[6]Poland's biggest protest came a little later, with the rise of Solidarity, *Solidarność*, in 1980.

became a Federation, and the new rules for decision-making stated that, "A decision is adopted if a majority of all the deputies elected in the Czech Socialist Republic and a majority of all the deputies elected in the Slovak Socialist Republic have voted in favor..." (Constitutional Act of 27.10.1968 on Czechoslovak Federation, Article 42).[7] Amazing: this 'Sovietski' wording could have been taken straight out of the Belfast Agreement, except that the latter was only to be written 30 years later!

In Czechoslovakia, this formula worked without a hitch throughout the Soviet period, mainly because decisions of such import were not taken in Prague and/or Bratislava but in the Kremlin in Moscow. It meant, however, that both the Czechs and the Slovaks inherited, as it were, the power of veto (while the Moravians in the middle had nothing). By 1989, with Gorbachev's *perestroika* four years old, everything was changing. The Berlin Wall was down, Moscow was holding elections, Prague was now home for the Velvet Revolution... and then, in part because of the above constitutional arrangements for consociational voting, there came the velvet divorce. It all happened very quickly without a referendum let alone a war: in the wake of the June 1992 "elections... in which the principle party leaders in the two constituent republics committed themselves to separation," Czechoslovakia fell apart (White and Hill 1996: 165). But these two parties won only 48 and 24 of the 150 seats contested; a further nine parties had gained representation, and "public opinion, as expressed in polls, appeared not to favour that development."[8]

5.4.2   Today's Republic

Because they have PR elections, the Czech Republic has a multi-party structure; and because they believe in simple majority rule, they have perhaps more problems than would otherwise be the case. The 2013 elections led to a three-party coalition, the Czech Social Democratic Party, *Česká strana sociálně demokratická*, ČSSD, on 50, a new populist party Action of Dissatisfied Citizens, *Akce nespokojených občanů*, ANO, with 47, and the Christian Democrats, *Křesťanská a demokratická unie—Československá strana lidová*, KDU-ČSL, who had 14. Basically, the two biggest parties were just four short of a majority, 101, so they jumped over four other parties and joined up with the smallest party of all—and it's called democracy.

There was a bit of a crisis in May 2017, when the Socialist PM resigned because the populist ANO leader was accused of financial misdeeds. So the president intervened, the PM sacked the populist from the coalition, and all was well. Well nearly. In the next election on 22.10.2017, the ANO won with 78, and the ČSSD were down to 15. Meanwhile, criminal proceedings had been initiated against the above populist, one Andrej Babiš, so nobody wanted to join in a coalition with him!

---

[7]http://czecon.law.muni.cz/content/en/ustavy/1968/

[8]The author's frequent visits to Czechoslovakia and its successor states—his first was in 1988—have all indicated that many in both the Czech Republic and Slovakia regretted this separation.

But he had won, damn it. So on 13.12.2017, he set up a minority government. After Christmas, on 16.1.2018, there was a vote of no confidence and he lost, so it was back to the drawing board… until eventually, on 15.6.2018, a new coalition was formed: the populists, ANO, the Socialists, ČSSD, and the Communists.

5.4.3 A Little Conclusion

In the UK in 1978, as was mentioned (Sect. 4.4.2), the left-wing jumped over the Liberals and Conservatives to make a coalition with the most right-wing Ulster Unionists. The events in Prague in 2017 culminated in an even bigger contortion: the most right-wing populists with the most left-wing Communists. But that's what can happen with binary majority rule: anything.

The Czechs (and Slovaks) suffered for far too long under bolshevism, and now they bear the consequences of majoritarianism which, linguistically, is the same thing (Sect. 5.9.2). A non-majoritarian polity could be less troublesome.

5.5 Austria

"Oh, I'm feeling very old," said the old peasant farmer in a village not far from Prizren.
"Don't worry," the current author replied, "I'm pretty old myself."
"Ah, but I was here under the Austro-Hungarians."
        A conversation between a local and the author, then an international trainer in
                                                                                    Kosovo in 2001.

5.5.1 A Little History

Austria's First Republic started after WWI with the collapse of the Austro-Hungarian Empire and the end of the monarchy. It lasted until the supposedly democratic referendum of 1938, *Anschluss* (Sect. 5.3.1), a cause of WWII; and 1945 saw the birth of the Second Republic.

A PR-list electoral system, with the fairly low threshold of 4%, is conducted in nine constituencies, so with a parliament of just 183 members, Austria has a four–six party structure. For many of the post-war years, there was a grand coalition, with a right-wing Chancellor and a Vice Chancellor of the left. In 1966, however, the right-wing Austrian People's Party, *Österreichische Volkspartei*, ÖVP, won a majority, so there was one-party majority rule, and then it was the turn of the Socialist Party, *Sozialdemokratische Partei Österreichs*, SPÖ, which ruled either by itself or again in a grand coalition with the ÖVP. There was just the one exception: in 1983. Like the UK's Labour Party in 1978 (Sect. 4.4.2) and the Czech ANO just mentioned (Sect. 5.4.2), the SPÖ on 90 seats also jumped over the moon and joined up with the

12 MPs of the Freedom Party, *Freiheitliche Partei Österreichs*, FPÖ, which admittedly in those days was not as extreme as it was shortly to become.

Next, in 1999, the SPÖ won 65 of the 183-member parliament; the ÖVP and the FPÖ both had 52. So the two little dogs joined forces, to put the biggest dog into opposition (Sect. 3.2). The EU complained, not about the arbitrary way binary majority rule can be (ab)used, but about the inclusion of the FPÖ; so it imposed sanctions... only to revoke them after six months. The FPÖ then had a bit of a crisis and lost heavily in the next 2002 election: they now had just 18 seats compared to the SPÖ's 69 and the ÖVP's 79; the coalition nevertheless continued.

It was back to a grand SPÖ/ÖVP coalition in 2006, and this survived for a further two elections until 2017 when, yet again, the ÖVP on 62 joined the FPÖ on 51 to leave the SPÖ with 52 in opposition. What's more, it all happened relatively quickly: just 56 days after the election, on 18.12.2017, a new government was formed (Sect. 3.2). The EU said little.

5.5.2   A Very Little Conclusion

Extreme right-wing parties are on the move in many European countries. To give any of them more influence than is their proper electoral due is surely a mistake. A polity based on a government of national unity, GNU, would doubtless be the wiser course.

5.6   The Balkans

All the wars in the former Yugoslavia started with a referendum.[9]

Oslobodjenje,[10] 7.2.1999

5.6.1   The Historical Context

In one of the great migrations of history, the Slavs came to the Balkans in about the fourth century.[11] In later years, their settlements were divided into two when the two empires, the Austro-Hungarian and the Ottoman, confronted each other on the banks of the Sava. So today's Slovenia is 'in Europe' and the Balkans start on the Croatian

---

[9] *Su svi ratovi u bivšoj Yugoslaviji počeli nekim referendumom.* Author's translation.

[10] Sarajevo's legendary newspaper.

[11] At about the same time, the Gaels went from this part of Central Europe to Ireland. At home one evening during the 1997 election observation mission in Herzegovina, where many of the locals spoke of this land as if it were Serbian—*"Ovaj je Srbije,* this is Serbia"—the author joked that this region was actually part of the old Irish Empire. Whereupon all the women laughed... and all the men did not.

border, they say in Ljubljana. But Croatia is 'in Europe' as well, and the Balkans are over there, south of the Sava, they say in Zagreb; Europe meets Asia, they continue, in Zemun, the western suburb of Belgrade. Accordingly, whereas in fact there should be just the one history, there are actually lots of them in the Balkans—at least one in each of today's nation-states. What follows is a distillation.

In the nineteenth century, when Turkey became the sick man of Europe, the peoples of what was to become Yugoslavia—the word was first coined in 1848 (Thompson 1992: 253)—rose up in revolt. Other rulers took their opportunities, and the Austrians annexed Bosnia in 1908. Then came the two Balkan wars, when three 'little dogs'—Serbia, Montenegro and Bulgaria—rose up against the 'big dog', Turkey... and won; whereupon the little dogs started to fight amongst each other, and the big dog joined in again.

Serbia was on the rise. Austria was concerned. The Archduke was assassinated in Sarajevo by Gavrilo Princip, a young man who, having been rejected by the recruiting sergeant in the Balkan Wars, wanted to prove that he was indeed old enough to fight (Glenny 1999: 251)... and thus he started WWI. In its wake came Yugoslavia. Initially, it was called the Kingdom of Serbs, Croats and Slovenes, which did not say much for the Bosnians, let alone the Kosovars, but all the Yugo-(Southern-) Slavs were now in one country, as were a few others like the Roma, the Jews, and the Albanian-speakers in Kosovo.[12] As the saying went, it was one country with two alphabets, three religions, four languages, five nations, six republics and seven neighbours.

In 1941, it was invaded by the two Axis Powers of Italy and Germany, whereupon a fascist puppet state, the *Ustaše*, was set up in Croatia. As in Germany, here too there was a concentration camp, Jasenovac. Jews, gays and gypsies were all targeted, but its main function was against the Serbs: the aim was to expel a third, convert a third, and kill a third (*Ibid*: 499).

Resistance was mixed: there were the rather ineffective Četniks, who were mainly Serb, and the very motivated Partisans, who were multi-multi. The latter were led by one Josip Broz, the son of a Croat father and a Slovenian mother, affectionately (and sometimes not quite so affectionately) known as Tito—(in Serbo-Croat, it sort of means 'you, that', a good name for a dictator). Winston Churchill chose to support the Partisans (McLean 2009), and the rest is another history. Yugoslavia lost a million casualties, some killed by the enemy, others through internecine violence.

In 1945, the country was renamed the Socialist Federal Republic of Yugoslavia. "We are not yet ready for democracy," Tito explained in 1953 (Djilas 2000: 49) and, in words a little similar to those of Kevin O'Higgins (Sect. 4.4) added, "We will not have a multiparty. We will have a multigroup system!" (*ibid*: 156). What they did have, however, was "a new constitution, the longest such document in the world" (Glenny 1999: 593), an attempt to give all the various types of Slavs as well as the Albanian-speakers in Kosovo and the Hungarian-speakers in Vojvodina a

---

[12]Kosovo usually ends with an 'o' when spelt by the Serbs, but with an 'a' if written by an Albanian-speaker.

supposedly fair share of their politics, and all under an umbrella of socialism. "Each republican party controlled its own cadre, and republican-level elections and party congresses preceded the federal. To combat fears of majority tyranny, voting rights emphasised minority protections through consensus, parity, and proportional representation of republican-based organisations" (Woodward 1995: 40–1).

Unlike the British Empire which was far flung, the Soviet/Russian Empire was (and still is) a contiguous block (Sect. 5.4.1, fn 5). Josef Stalin, the Soviet dictator from 1922–1952, wanted that common border with Poland, Czechoslovakia, Hungary and Romania, to enable him (or his successors) to control everything, if need be by sending in the tanks. The three states of Bulgaria, the GDR and Yugoslavia were, so to speak, once removed: Bulgaria was no problem, and even asked to be the 16th republic in the USSR; the GDR proved to be a bit more difficult, and Soviet tanks were deployed to East Berlin during the 1953 uprising; but Tito was more distant and definitely 'his own man'. The break came in 1948, and shortly afterwards, Yugoslavia was a leading voice in the Non-Aligned Movement.

The West, if not everyone, sees many phenomena in a binary context: your enemy's enemy is your friend. If Nicolae Ceauşescu, the notorious dictator in Romania was anti-Soviet, then by all means invite him to Buckingham Palace in 1978 and ask the Queen to give him a cup of tea. Yugoslavia was also, post 1948, a friend; the US gave it considerable financial aid and, as a result, its post-war economy did rather well.

In 1985, however, with Gorbachev taking over in Moscow, the former enemy, the Soviet Union, was now a friend and the Cold War was over; so Yugoslavia was no longer needed. Like so many others, the bureaucrats in the International Monetary Fund, IMF, believe in majority voting, especially when pragmatics so dictate. It did not take them long; they wanted the Yugoslav loans to be repaid. Accordingly, "in October 1986. . . the IMF began to tie conditions for new credits to political reform. Its first demand for re-strengthening the governing capacity of the federal administration. . . was to change the voting rules in the National Bank from consensus to majority decision" (*Ibid*: 74). "Their assumption was that these changes would restore the government's capacity to. . . repay debt" (*Ibid*: 82). It was a fatal step towards war.

5.6.2   The Collapse of Yugoslavia

It is sometimes very difficult for politicians to talk about economics—a subject which even many economists do not understand—but it is easy for the former to talk about nationalism. The various republics of Yugoslavia held their first post-communist, multi-party elections in 1990; apart from Montenegro where a PR-list system was used, they all used the two-round system, TRS, [as did Russia in its first post-*perestroika* elections (Sect. 5.9.2.1)], and all of the republics had a whole host of political parties competing; it usually takes a little time for a country to settle down into a definite party-structure. In many of these Balkan contests, the main victor was nationalism. Thus, in Serbia, the winner was Slobodan Milošević.

Meanwhile, in Croatia... Well democracy, they say, is binary majority rule and power-dividing, which might involve a coalition government, and Franjo Tudjman "chose to form a grand coalition of all parties except the Serbian Democratic Party, which [then] left the parliament..." (*ibid*: 119). Pure sectarianism. Pure majority rule. A cause of war.

There again, democracy might mean power-sharing. In Bosnia (see below), the elections were indeed a sectarian headcount (Sect. 2.1.3), but then Alija Izetbegović "formed what was in effect a [GNU], constructed out of a formal recognition between all three major parties" (Malcolm 1996: 223).

Initially, "Although many [in the West] acknowledged Slovene, Croatian and Albanian aspirations, preoccupations with stability in the Soviet Union and the risks of its disintegration if a precedent was set in Yugoslavia dictated the hope that Yugoslavia would remain intact" (Woodward 1995: 164). It was a crazy situation in which international agreements allowed for both separatism and no separatism: there was "the stark contradiction... between two central articles of the Helsinki Final Act: the commitment to the self-determination of nations; and the principle of the violability of borders" (Silber and Little 1995: 161). The West chose the latter, so to support Gorbachev in the USSR, and therefore, implied by the same logic, Milošević in Yugoslavia.

In January 1991, however, after disturbances in Lithuania, the West changed its mind (Sect. 5.9.2.1). In the Soviet Union, it would no longer uphold the position of the sane and sober Gorbachev, and shifted its allegiance to Boris Yeltsin, who especially towards the end of his career qualified for neither adjective. At about the same time—after all, one communist federation can be much like another (and both were spelt with a capital 'yu')—the West dropped Milošević because he was an extremist... in exchange for Tudjman, who was an extremist. As Izetbegović noted, contrasting the two was like choosing between leukaemia and a brain tumour.

Referendums were to play havoc in both federations. In 1991, Gorbachev tried to keep the USSR together by holding a huge referendum, and the world's largest majority, 105 million, voted in favour... but the Soviet Union collapsed within a year. In Yugoslavia, a proposal for an all-Yugoslav referendum was vetoed by Slovenia, which then held its own referendum on 23.12.1990. Croatia followed on 19.5.1991 but, in an effort to pre-empt the latter poll, the *Krajina* held theirs one week earlier.[13]

For once, the British were against partition; or were they? They had divided Ireland of course, as well as Palestine and India. But on 2.12.1991, Lord Carrington warned against any recognition of Slovenian and Croatian independence, for it "might well be the spark that sets Bosnia-Herzegovina alight" (Woodward 1995:

---

[13]The *Krajina* are three regions in Croatia which had been and were still peopled by Serbs, initially as a bulwark against the Muslims of the Ottomans. And hence the word 'krajina' from 'kraj' or 'border region', (as also in the word 'Ukraine').

184). "It would mean a civil war," he continued, "I put this as strongly as I possibly could" (Silber and Little 1995: 220). Izetbegović also pleaded with Germany, the main protagonist of recognition in the European Community, EC—the forerunner of today's European Union, EU—"for it would mean war in [Bosnia]" (Woodward 1995: 184).

There now follows one of this book's greatest criticisms of majority voting: all too often, when the choice is binary, those voting on one topic about which they feel passionate are prepared to exchange their support with others who are more committed to a different topic—it is what the Americans call 'log-rolling'—and each supports the other by voting in favour of the other's as well as their own proposals.[14] So it was that, in exchange for a 'yes' in support of the UK PM John Major's grubby little policy on the EC's social charter, Britain agreed to join Germany in its support of the Slovenian and Croatian claims for independence. It was another fatal step towards war.

One month earlier, the EC had set up the Badinter Commission. And one month before that, the New Ireland Group, NIG, had held its fourth consensus conference in Belfast, to which they had invited a guest from Sarajevo, Mr. Petar Radji-Histić. The purpose was plain: for heaven's sake, no binary plebiscite in Bosnia! (Sect. 4.2.3). Alas the Commission, five Supreme Court judges under the chairmanship of Robert Badinter, found little wrong with the practice of binary voting, and they told the people(s) of Yugoslavia to just go ahead. The effect was tragic, not least in Bosnia, where the EC's "insistence on [binary] referendums... provided the impetus... to create ethnically pure areas through population transfers and expulsions as a prelude to the vote" (*Ibid*: 271).

It was a huge mistake.[15] Yugoslavia then held a plethora of referendums—in the various republics, and in various parts of these republics. The outcomes of some of the former category of votes were recognised by the international community; most of the latter were not; and sometimes, as in regard to Kosova, there was a change of mind. Overall, however, and as noted at the head of this section, referendums were often a cause of war.

5.6.3   Serbia at War

In 1389, at the Battle of Kosovo Polje, the Turks inflicted a defeat on the Slav forces under Prince Lazar. Serbian histories make little or no mention of Albanian forces. Albanian sources, however, say their predecessors were definitely there. While according to some Ottoman writings, the defeated army consisted of "mercenaries

---

[14]Such distortions could also occur in multi-option voting, but almost certainly not to the same divisive and corrosive extent.

[15]When asked in 2008 if he had any reflections on all this, Robert Badinter replied, "The answer is negative." (Private correspondence, 30.7.2008).

from Serbia, Albania, Bosnia and Hungary" (Malcolm 1998: 62). In conflict zones, as noted earlier, histories often vary.

As imperial rulers, the Ottomans were not the worst. If someone wanted to get on in life, then it would help if he were a he and a Muslim he. If another male just wanted to maintain his Orthodox faith, then that was also acceptable. So the Serbs were often peasant farmers, while a Moslem Bosnian, for example, could readily seek high rewards in the service of the Bey.

Everyone was aware of their differences, of course, and the late nineteenth century saw "the first attempts at modern statistical surveys of the population of the Kosovo region." "It also saw the first stirrings of nationalist ethnographic arguments: such disputes, about who was in the majority... have continued with unremitting acrimony to this day" (*Ibid*: 193–4).

In 1987, the 46-year-old Milošević, an elected member of the Serbian Communists, went to Kosovo Polje to play the nationalist card. "You will not be beaten!" he shouted, addressing another crowd of about a million in 1989 (Silber and Little 1995: 224), on the 600th anniversary of the great battle. Despite this blatant sabre-rattling, the West continued to support the maintenance of Yugoslavia and by implication its leader. In the 1990 elections, Milošević won the presidency with a massive 65.3%, and in the parliamentary contest, his Socialist Party of Serbia, SPS, *Социјалистичка партија србије, СПС*, came top at 46.1%. Then, in 1991, as stated above, the West switched its allegiance to Tudjman.

With the outbreak of war in Bosnia in 1992, Milošević was known to have very close contacts with the Bosnian Serb rebel leader, Radovan Karadžić, so when the Dayton negotiations were under way, the West changed its mind again, and the Serbian leader was as it were re-admitted into the fold of 'almost nice guys'.

Just a few years later, however, he was back in the doghouse again, this time over Kosova, and the West changed its mind for the third time. The situation was certainly tense. The Organisation for Security and Co-operation in Europe, OSCE, an organisation of 54 nations, had deployed a number of unarmed observers to try and make sure that violence did not erupt. On 24.3.1999, however, a much smaller organisation of then only 19 nations, the North Atlantic Treaty Organisation, NATO, displaced the OSCE and deployed a much larger number of personnel, so to commence a bombing campaign.

One week earlier, on 18.3.1999, while other signatories had duly penned their names to the Rambouillet Agreement on Kosova, Milošević had refused to add his own signature. So NATO bombed. He still refused. So NATO bombed some more. The bit he did not like was the clause about a referendum. Kosova had already had a plebiscite on independence in 1991, when 99.9% of an 87.0% turn out had voted in favour. (Just as in NI in 1973), the majority of Kosovars (Protestants) had all voted 'yes' and the minority of Serbs (Catholics) had abstained (Sect. 4.2.2). History, as always, repeats itself.

As with many other 'small' ballots, in the *Krajina* and *Republika Srpska, RS*, the West had not recognised this 1991 Kosovar poll. Now, however, in 1999, they had changed their minds, again, and they would accept a majority decision. But why have a vote when you know what the answer will be? Umm, good question.

Nevertheless NATO continued to bomb, and Milošević still refused to sign. Eventually, the former Russian PM Viktor Chernomyrdin went to Belgrade to renegotiate the agreement; so the referendum clause was removed; and Milošević then signed. So the bombing had been a complete waste of time, effort, resources and, most importantly, of lives!

5.6.4   Post-war Serbia

In the Serbian parliamentary elections of December 2000, it was all over. The slogan was "готов je, *gotov ye*, he is finished," and Zoran Dindić of the Democratic Opposition of Serbia, DOS, *Демократска опозиција Србије, ДОС*, won on 64.1%. So Serbia was now democratic, simple majority rule was the order of the day and, in the opinion of the international community, that was fine.

At the next contest in 2003, the Serbian Radical Party, SRS, *Српска радикална странка, СРС*, of Vojislav Šešelj—like Milošević, he was another indicted war criminal—came top on 27.6%. That was not good. But the three parties of DOS, only two seats short of a majority, managed to cobble up a coalition with the Socialist Party, so majority rule was still, apparently, just fine. Thus it continued after the 2007 election, except this time, it did not last very long. The coalition collapsed, new elections were held in 2008, and after 57 days of negotiations, a new majority coalition was established, but they were of pro-EU parties so that too, at least in the eyes of the West, was OK. The 'nice guys' were still in charge, just.

What can go wrong. . . and in the next election, it was the turn of the 'not-so-nice'. A pro-EU off-shoot of Šešelj's Radical Party, the Serbian Progressive party, SNS, *Српска напредна странка, СНС*, topped the poll with 24.1%, whereupon they joined forces with the Milošević's old party, the SPS. . . so maybe majority rule was not so good. In the 2014 contest, the SNS had an absolute majority but nevertheless continued to rule in coalition.

5.6.5   Bosnia-Herzegovina: Steps to War

Like all the other Yugoslav republics, Bosnia had its own elections in 1990. "One village drowning in a sea of green crescents, which proclaimed the (Muslim) Party of democratic action, SDA, *[Stranka demokratske akcije]*, would give way to another where the *šahovnica* (denoting the Croatian Democratic Union, HDZ—BiH, *[Hrvatska demokratska zajednica—Bosne i Hercegovine]*), was sovereign, or where every wall was covered with. . . the acronym SDS, the Serbian Democratic Party, *[Српска демократска странка]*." "Many doomed settlements were a jumble of all three" (Glenny 1996: 147). The election was indeed a sectarian headcount, another cause of war. If it had been preferential, at least then the voters might have been able to give a more exact expression of their opinion. In the circumstances,

PR-STV might not have been enough to secure the election of Ante Marković (Sect. 2.1.5.1). Maybe QBS could have saved the day (Sect. 2.5.1), just maybe.

"The three national parties had secretly agreed before the elections to form a coalition government" (Silber and Little 1995: 232,) a GNU (Sect. 5.6.2). Here too, as in theory in the Czech Republic in 1968 (Sect. 5.4.1), as in practice in Belgium (Sect. 5.2.2) emerging from the 1960s, and as in NI in 1998 (Sect. 4.2.4.2), the structure was one of consociationalism. In these three 'split-into-two' jurisdictions— NI, the Czech Republic and Belgium—it meant that each side could veto the other. Bosnia was even more divided, so any one of its *three* sides could apply the veto and, "In its eighteen-month-long existence, the Bosnian parliament failed to pass a single law" (Glenny 1996: 148). Instead, like thieves after the crime, they fell out. . . another prelude to war.

When divided by religion (as in the election, where voters were able to declare only a single 1st preference), Bosnia was 40:30:20—Muslim:Orthodox:Catholic. But at that time, 27% of the marriages in BiH were mixed (Thompson 1992: 91). Surely, therefore, lots of persons had 2nd preferences, if only for the partner or the child, for the husband, wife, son- and/or daughter-in-law.

Then came the referendum, the next step to war. Any two of the three religious/ nationalist groupings—40 + 30, or 40 + 20, or 30 + 20—could form a majority against the other one. That was one *huge* disadvantage of such a binary vote. Secondly, how were voters in mixed relationships meant to vote? Thirdly, what about those who wanted a compromise? Or peace? A binary referendum was obviously totally inappropriate. Admittedly, the Badinter Commission had stated "that a vote would be valid only if respectable numbers from all three communities of the republic approved" (Woodward 1995: 280), but that "respectable number" was never defined.

In the wake of the war in Croatia, a Serb/Croat alliance was probably impossible, {even though "Serb and Croat leaders were now meeting in secret to plan the partition, between them, of Bosnia-Herzegovina" (Silber and Little 1995: 204)}. So the Muslims and the Catholics—30 + 20—ganged up to vote 'yes'. "Karadžić had warned that a referendum would mean war" (Thompson 1992: 326), and sure enough, on "the day of the referendum, barricades were thrown up by Serb militants around various parts of Sarajevo" (Glenny 1996: 166).

That 30 + 20 tactic was a totally artificial 'marriage of convenience'. Before a year had passed, and even while both the Bosniaks and the Bosnian Croats were still fighting the Bosnian Serbs, these Muslim and Catholic forces had a war between themselves: it lasted from 18.10.1992 to 23.2.1994. As a methodology of decision-making for the newly emergent Bosnia, majority voting was plainly totally inappropriate.

The main war was also quick to rage. Peace efforts abounded, like the Vance-Owen Plan in 1993, but it only offered more divisions, this time into ten different semi-autonomous regions. "Milošević asked whether decisions would be taken by majority vote, or by 'consensus'.[16] A system of majority vote would always allow a coalition of Moslems and Croats to out vote the Serbs. 'Consensus', on the other hand, would give each nation, in effect, a veto" (Woodward 1995: 308). The plan got nowhere, and not only because, like Paisley in Belfast (Sect. 4.3), *RS* also said 'no'! On 15.5.1993, *RS* had a referendum[17]—everyone had a referendum—and 92.5% spoke in the negative; another meaningless **A?** question.

There were the three *Krajina* in Croatia—three Northern Irelands. The first, Okučani, was ethnically-cleansed by Croatia in Operation Flash on 1.5.1995. Partly as a consequence, in July, there was the massacre in Srebrenica, where the UN peacekeepers happened to be Dutch; this war crime was led by the Bosnian Serb rebel commander, Ratko[18] Mladić. {His father had been killed during WWII in the Jasenovac concentration camp (Sect. 5.6.1).} Never again, was the cry. One week later, it happened again, in Žepa, supposedly being looked after by the Ukrainians. The next one was to be Goražde, where the British were in charge. If but internationally, therefore, this was more serious. The Americans offered to help in the only way they know how—from the air—and the war turned. "Give us bombs for peace," pleaded President Bill Clinton's chief negotiator, Richard Holbrooke (Holbrooke 1998: 132), as Croatia pursued its own policy of ethnic cleansing, now in the larger Knin *Krajina*. "I urge you to go as far as you can," he advised Tudjman, "but not to take [the *RS* capital] Banja Luka" (*Ibid*: 160).

5.6.6   Bosnia's Peace Process

So then there was Dayton. It was called a peace-agreement but, like its Belfast equivalent, it was much more a cease-fire arrangement. The mainly Orthodox *RS* got a lot of what it had been fighting for, and it now became an 'entity'—if in doubt, concoct a new word. The slightly bigger 'half', 51% of the Bosnian landmass, was the other entity, the mainly Muslim/Catholic Federation of Bosnia-Herzegovina.

A further parallel with the Belfast Accords is the fact that the final document is full of majoritarian gobbledegook. "All decisions in both chambers shall be by a majority of those present and voting," it says. "The Delegates and Members shall make their best efforts to see that the majority includes at least one third of the votes of Delegates and Members from the territory of each Entity." But that is a minority of each. "[If not], the Chair and Deputy Chairs shall... attempt to obtain approval within three days of the vote. If those efforts fail, decisions shall be taken by a majority of those present and voting, provided that the dissenting votes do not include two-thirds or more of the delegates or Members elected from either Entity."

---

[16]The word 'consensus' is often assumed to mean unanimity, with all parties having the power of veto, the very use of which would imply that there was no consensus.

[17]Prior to and then during the war, *RS* had a total of five referendums.

[18]Ratko is a recognized first name in Serbia, but the Serbo-Croat word for 'war' is 'rat'.

{(OHR 1998). The General Framework Agreement for Peace in Bosnia and Herzegovina, Annex 4, Article IV, 3 (d).} There is more: "... provided the decision... is approved by a majority that includes a majority of Delegates from [a majority of] the Bosniac, Croat or Serb peoples." [*ibid*: Annex 4, Article IV, 3 (g)]. Balkan consociationalism.

In effect, like the Good Friday Agreement, Dayton also perpetuates the very sectarianism it is trying to overcome. Prior to the 1992–1995 war, the Joint Presidency was to consist of seven persons: two of each plus one Yugoslav. Post Dayton, it was to be a three-person team, only one of each (*ibid*, Article V), one elected from the *RS* Entity, the remaining two from the other Entity. So, anyone wishing to be a candidate had to designate themselves, like an MLA in the NI Assembly (Sect. 4.3.4.2). The language sounds fine: "To ensure the will of the people serves as the basis of the authority of government... [*ibid*: Annex 3, Article V (7)] there will be free elections" [*ibid*, Sect. 7.1]. But the voters will not be free to support a non-sectarian candidate, or to cast a second and any subsequent preferences. So the presidential candidates have to be sectarian, and so too do the voters. This then led to a challenge by the Social Democratic Party, *Socijaldemokratska partija Bosne i Hercegovine,* SDP, and quite right too.

Despite everything that had happened in the elections of 1990 and the referendum of 1992, the international community had the bizarre notion that, as soon as Bosnia held an election and thus became democratic (again), everything would be just fine. The first post-war elections were held in 1996, now under a system of closed PR-list chosen by the OSCE (Sect. 2.5.1), but, as noted, this too was a sectarian headcount.[19] Bosnia is now the most politicised of all states, with elected chambers in the one country, in the two entities, and in the ten cantons—with everything designated by sectarian geographical criteria. It was a cease-fire agreement, and at least it stopped the killing.

It is not, however, a peace agreement, and even now, in 2017, the problem persists. In a word, a major cause of the problem was and still is majoritarianism. *RS* still wants that which the Dayton Agreement does not allow: a referendum. So they are looking at Catalonia, just as Catalonia looked at Scotland. And if Catalonia can get away with an illegal referendum, then why not yet another referendum in *RS*? It is back to the Russian dolls of self-determination again: inside every majority, there's a minority trying to get out (Sects. 1.4 and 5.9.1).

The Bosnian Croat leadership is no better. Here too they believe in majority rule but, as a 20% minority, this can be problematic. The obvious solution, as exemplified

---

[19]By coincidence, a presidential election campaign was underway in the US at the same time. The Bosnian election was supervised by the OSCE, and the author was an observer in Derwenta, in *RS*. It was an amazingly complex logistical exercise, for every internally displaced person, IDP, was allowed to vote, either in their new residence or as if in their old. The vote took place on the Saturday. On the Sunday, lorries crisscrossed the country, taking ballots from Tuzla to Srebrenica, from Sarajevo to Zvornik, etc., etc. The ballots were then all mixed up, so that no-one could know any one ballot's provenance, and the count started at 9 o'clock on the Monday, to proceed non-stop until all was done: 6 pm on the Wednesday. Some of the locals joked that the acronym OSCE actually meant, 'the Organization to Secure Clinton's Election'. And they were right!

in the cantons, is to gerrymander the constituencies so as to guarantee majorities. But this has now been taken to a new art: the word gerrymander has to be replaced by a new term, gerrymeander, as constituencies are concocted which aren't even contiguous. Meanwhile—and this should have a bearing on all the shenanigans that the Bosnian Serbs and Bosnian Croats are up to—in Bosnia as a whole, the Muslims are now in a majority; alas, it seems to have no bearing at all.

The Bosnian story is so sad. Majoritarianism was a cause of its war and yet, as in Belfast, it is still regarded as the basis of its post-war settlement. Unfortunately, for some quite inexplicable reason, and this despite the war which cost 100,000 lives, the West still does not question this major cause of that conflict. The quotation with which this section started—"All the wars in the former Yugoslavia started with a referendum."—now applies to the 2014 referendums in Crimea, which Vladimir Vladimirovich Putin recognised, to the plebiscites which followed in Donetsk and Luhansk, which initially he did not recognise, and the continuing war in Eastern Ukraine (Sect. 5.9.4).

5.6.7 Macedonia, an Ancient History

Alexander the Great, 356–323 BCE, ruled an empire which stretched via Armenia and Iran, all the way to the Fergana Valley, which the Chinese also ruled for a time during the Hàn Dynasty, 206 BCE–220 CE. As noted above (Sect. 5.6.1), the Slav peoples arrived in the Balkans in the fourth century of this era.

There are those in today's Macedonia who are desperately trying to emphasise their sense of national identity, not least with ersatz statues to the said Alexander and so on, and this is partly because many of their four neighbours—Serbian, Bulgarian, Greek and Albanian—think that the northern, eastern, southern or western part of Macedonia actually belongs to them.

Shortly after Slovenia and then Croatia held their referendums on independence, Macedonia did the same, on 8.9.1991. Yet again, as in so many of these divisive plebiscites, the minority abstained: but here's the difference—this minority consisted of Albanians *and* Serbs: "the political parties representing ethnic Albanians and Serbs declared a boycott" (Woodward 1995: 179). Meanwhile, over the border, these same two peoples were preparing for war: Kosovo held its referendum on 22nd October and voted for independence: the Albanians voted and the Serbs abstained (Emerson 1999: 62). Another difference occurred in that the Macedonian outcome was recognised but the Kosovar one was not... until Rambouillet (Sect. 5.6.3).

The war in Kosovo came to an end in June 1999. A demilitarised zone was established around the eastern and northern borders, which the Kosovar Liberation Army then occupied. But at least the violence had now stopped...

5.6.7.1 The Non-break-up of Macedonia

... until February, 2012, when the Albanian National Liberation Army started a campaign of violence in Macedonia. This one was settled fairly quickly, however, and on 13.8.2001, the Ohrid Agreement introduced an element of power-sharing and decentralisation—two of Lijphart's basic criteria for consociationalism (Sect. 3.3). Another, of course, is PR.

Macedonia has a mixture of a multi-party within a two-and-a-bit-party structure. In a country of just a little over two million, the biggest bloc is a coalition of 21 political parties, which might explain its very long name: the Internal Macedonian Revolutionary Organisation—Democratic Party for Macedonian Unity, VMRO-DPMNE, *Внатрешна македонска револуционера организација—Деморкратска партија за македонско национално единство*, ВМРО-ДПМНЕ; the main opposition, the Social Democratic Union of Macedonia, SDSM, *Социјалдемократски сојуз на Македонија–СДСМ*, is a bloc of only nine; and there is a small Albanian party as well. One of the 21 parties in the big coalition was the Socialist Party of Macedonia; the smaller opposition bloc included the SDSM and the New Social Democratic Party. So maybe some of Macedonia's pre-election coalitions are as 'flexible' as some other post-election coalitions in other countries—not least the UK's union of the Labour Party and Ulster's Unionists in 1978, of that of the Tories and the DUP in 2017.

Initially, after the first 1990 elections, the VMRO-DPMNE refused to join in a coalition with the Albanian party but in 1998 they did do so, and since Ohrid, they have worked with the mainly Albanian Democratic Union for Integration, *Bashkimi Demokratik për Integrim*, BDI or, in Macedonian, DUI, ДУИ. In the wake of their 2016 election, the government is again a coalition of VMRO-DPMNE on 51 of the 120 seats, DUI with 10, and a new Albanian party with 5.

And just to finish where this section started, on 30.9.2018, Macedonia had a non-binding referendum on a name change: from 'the former Yugoslav Republic of Macedonia' to 'Republic of North Macedonia'. A massive majority of 94.2% voted 'yes' but the turnout at 36.9% failed to pass the 50% threshold.

So far, just, Macedonia has managed to survive, just. If the power-sharing arrangements agreed at Ohrid can be at least maintained if not indeed enhanced, then maybe all will be well.

5.6.8 A Balkan Conclusion

The 1990 introduction of an adversarial democratic structure—majoritarianism—was (not *the* but) *a* cause of the Balkan conflagrations of 1991–1995. That introduction was facilitated by the EU, not least via the misguided advice of the Badinter Commission. Sadly, few if any lessons were learnt and, as was noted earlier but is worth repeating, the West's collective obsession with majority voting is now a cause of the war in Ukraine (Sects. 5.9.3 and 5.9.4).

Thus the consequences of this obsession cause problems not only in the Balkans. After all, if Kosova could not be an independent state in 1991, but could in 1999, then why not Abkhazia and South Ossetia? (See below). Or anywhere else for that matter, e.g., Hong Kong or Xīnjiāng? At the very least, the contradictions of the Helsinki Final Act should be sorted out... at most, the methodology of majority voting must be questioned. As this journey approached the Bosphorus, the problem was seemingly universal. And worse was yet to come.

5.7   Turkey

> In the sixth century, the "Türks were playing an increasingly dominant trade [on the Central Asian steppe], much to the annoyance of the Chinese..."
>
> (Peter Frankopan 2015: 64).

5.7.1   Turkish Politics

For obvious reasons of self-interest, President Recep Tayyip Erdoğan believes in majority rule. It is worth emphasising (Sect. 3.2.1), that for the Kurds in today's Turkey, the situation is exactly the same as it was in NI where, prior to the Belfast Agreement, the Catholics knew they would never be in government. And this form of permanent exclusion is called democracy?[20]

The Turkish electoral system, a single preference form of PR-list, has a 10% threshold (Sect. 2.4). So if six parties stand, and five of them get 9% each, the winning party with 55% of the vote will get all 100% of the seats. As it were automatically, then, a threshold benefits all those which pass it, and the bigger the party the bigger the benefit.

In 2015, The Peoples' Democratic Party, *Halkların Demokratik Partisi*, HDP, a pro-minority party which has the support of the Kurds, surprised itself let alone everybody else when it got 13.1% of the vote, up 51 to 80 seats. In the same contest, Erdoğan's party, the ruling Justice and Development Party, *Adalet ve Kalkınma Partisi*, AKP, was down to 258, below the 276 requirement for a majority in the 550-member parliament. He himself was not a candidate; he had decided, democratically of course, that he wanted to become an executive president, with powers which were only huge in a palace which was even bigger. So this result was a bit of a blow.

---

[20]The same is true in Israel of course, where the Arab List can get into parliament, but no further. Instead, as in the wake of the 2015 elections, there emerged another pretty horrible majority coalition, with Jewish Home giving the ruling party a majority of just one.

Forming a government should have been fairly easy; after all, there was one big party and only three smaller ones. So either the three little ones could get together, or the one big party could join up with any one of the three. In other words, there were four 'totally democratic' possibilities. The AKP started to talk to all of them, but quickly tired of any link with the HDP. Negotiations with the other two continued but again there were problems and eventually, new elections were called for November.

Meanwhile, in July, the Turkish Government initiated Operation Martyr Yalçin as it was called, a double military attack, one on ISIL in Syria—ISIL is the Islamic State of Iraq and the Levant—and this quickly came to an end; as well as a further onslaught on the Kurdistan Workers' Party, PKK, which continued not only in Iraqi Kurdistan but also in Turkey itself. This was a factor in the next election where, sure enough, the AKP now regained its majority but not at the expense of the HDP; the latter lost a number of seats, down from 80 to 59, but still managed to clear the 10% threshold. Erdoğan was still unhappy. He—oh by the way, the president is meant to be neutral and non-partisan—he wanted his AKP to have a two-thirds majority, so that he could change the constitution and become the all-powerful executive president.

On 15.7.2016, some of the armed forces attempted a coup d'état but, 24 hours later, it was all over. Erdoğan initiated a state of emergency and commenced a purge of countless persons whom he regarded as related to the attempt. Little surprise, then, that by the time the author was in Istanbul—October 2017—people were reluctant to talk about politics.

5.7.2 A Little Conclusion

On 16.4.2017, Turkey had held a referendum. This was not a 'yes-or-no?' question of the **A?** variety; it was 18 of them, all subject to just one 'yes' or 'no'.[21] The argument in favour of the package, apparently, was that this would get rid of unstable coalition governments. Well, so would a dictator. Nevertheless, 18 of the 21 proposals were allowed, and thus the president was to get extra powers, the post of PM would be eliminated, and all ministerial appointments would be subject to the presidential whim. 51.4% said 'yes'—a clear case of democrats voting to be undemocratic. In all, therefore, simple majority rule was the problem.

---

[21]On 2.12.2007, the people of Venezuela were asked 36 questions in this way, and 50.7% said only one 'no'.

5.8   The Caucasus

Caucasian volunteers [and some Russians]... gave significant backing to the Abkhaz forces [against Georgia] in 1992–1993, and there were a few Abkhaz and Georgian... volunteers fighting against the Russians in the [1994–1996] Chechen war.

(Herzig 1999: 57).

5.8.1   The Historical Context

People in the Caucasus believe in simple majority rule... sometimes. In 1991, a majority of Georgians opted out of the USSR, but a 'majority of Abkhazians' then opted out of Georgia; something similar took place in South Ossetia and almost in a third Georgian province, Adjara. In like manner, Azerbaijan also left the USSR, and Nagorno-Karabakh left Azerbaijan. For similar historical reasons, the third country in the Caucasus, Armenia, had but no longer has three enclaves.

The two countries visited in this book are both ancient kingdoms, each with its own language and script. But, like the Balkans, and so unlike Ireland, the Caucasus has been a crossroads of history for thousands of years. The Persians were first; next, Alexander the Great was here, on his way eastwards, followed by the Romans; and then the Persians returned. Armenia had its hey day, over 2000 years ago, when it went all the way to the Mediterranean. Georgia was at its height in the twelfth century under Queen Tamara and her successor, David the Builder, when it stretched from the Black to the Caspian Sea.

One day, with the fifth Crusade in full swing, Europe's Christians heard that "a new and mighty protector of Christianity has arisen." Ha! Fake news. In 1220, Genghis Khan's army of 20,000 came "with whirlwind speed... cut the flower of Georgian knighthood to bits... and moved on through the Caucasus, leaving the Georgians unaware that the Mongols were merely on a reconnaissance mission" (Man 2011: 215–6). They returned and conquered in 1257. When the Mongolian Empire was divided into four, each with one of his descendants in charge, he who was to rule a vast amount of the Middle East which included Armenia, most of Georgia and all of today's Iran, the Ilkhanate Empire (Sect. 6.7.1), somewhat scuppered Genghiz Khan's original idea of world conquest... by converting to Islam.

Later on, it was the Persians again who ruled the Caucasus, and then came the Russians, initially as protectors, shortly afterwards as conquerors (and hence all the lovely literature of Lev Tolstoy and others). Then, after the events of 1917, the Soviet authorities established The Transcaucasian Socialist Federative Soviet Republic, and the three Caucasian countries—Georgia, Armenia and Azerbaijan— were as one. In 1936, however, a Georgian called Josef Dzugashvili—Stalin— decided to divide them up again. Given the complex history of the region, and the fact that the peoples were all mixed up, the task was not easy. So when drawing the border(s) between Armenia and Azerbaijan, if a cluster of Armenians was 'here', or another of Azeris was 'over there', his cartographers made little—or not so little—enclaves. There were three in Armenia, little circles in which the locals were of a different religion and with different surnames to those of their neighbours, while the much bigger 'enclave', Nakhichevan, was treated as a separate but nevertheless integral part of Azerbaijan. Meanwhile, in Azerbaijan itself, there was a large enclave of (some Azeris and) many Armenians called Nagorno-Karabakh.

At that time, 1936, there was no problem; after all, Stalin was in charge. In 1985, however, with Gorbachev now the General Secretary of the Communist Party of the Soviet Union CPSU, in Moscow, with freedom of expression returned, and with the principle of self-determination by majority vote clearly (or ambiguously, Sect. 5.6.2) laid down in international law, the problems were legion. The first clashes were in Nagorno-Karabakh in 1988. The headline in Russia's main newspaper of those days, *Pravda, Правда*, was "Вот, наш Ольстер,[22] *Vot, nash Olster*, This is our Northern Ireland." It is probably fair to say that, at the time, no one in NI knew what Nagorno-Karabakh was, let alone where and so on—and that includes this author.[23]

5.8.2 *Georgia*

As in the Balkans, so too in the Caucasus, the democratic device called the referendum has often served to exacerbate problems, especially any internal ones: in Abkhazia, South Ossetia and Nagorno-Karabakh. There is perhaps one small difference: in the Balkans, they provoked wars; in the Caucasus, they tended to be used retrospectively, to 'justify' crimes of violence if not actual wars, the results of which were often coldly regarded as 'facts on the ground'—to use that horrible war-zone expression.

Georgia was a multi-multi society: not only were there local Armenians, Azeris and Russians; there were also the mainly Muslim Abkhazians and mainly Orthodox South Ossetians; there were the Muslim Georgians in Adjara as well, whereas most of the other Georgians were Orthodox; and amongst the Georgians, there were the various different types—the Megrelians, the Svans and so on. As always, such demarcations are too simplistic: in and around South Ossetia especially, there were lots of mixed marriages. One conclusion to all this was obvious: binary majority rule was a non-starter—or should have been. What's more, there had already been some Abkhaz-Georgian violence in Sukhumi and, partly as a consequence, on 9.4.1989, there was an anti-Soviet pro-Georgian protest in Tbilisi, with more needless loss of life: Soviet troops attacked the demonstrators with spades (Sect. 5.9.2.1).

Just a couple of weeks earlier, on 26.3.1989, the USSR had held its first post-*perestroika* elections, and while lots of contestants were due to compete, it was still a

---

[22]For some unknown linguistic reason, the Russians translate the word Ulster with a capital O.

[23]The Russians, however, knew about NI (Biryukov, 1985). In Marxist theory, the Troubles were a sign of the impending demise of capitalism.

one-party state. Georgia, still Soviet Georgia of course, was scheduled to follow suit in 1990. For those who were interested in Green (or maybe just small 'g' green) politics, there was a Soviet organization called the Экологический Союз, *Ekologichesky Soyuz,* Ecological Union, and in late 1989, lots of environmentalists from across the USSR gathered in Moscow... and there the author met a party activist from Tbilisi, Zurab Zhvania. A few years later, after Georgia had become independent, Zhvania founded the Georgian GP, and quickly became an MP and later PM. History was moving fast.

5.8.2.1 Abkhazia

But first—slow down—troubles were brewing. Accordingly, having compared the complex problems of the Caucasus with the much simpler ones of NI, and having discussed the possibility of power-sharing in both, Zurab invited the author to address a press conference on inclusive governance in Tbilisi on 8.2.1990. The talk was well reported in both the Georgian- and the Russian-language media.[24] The author also gave a second lecture to a number of party activists from several parties, for Zurab was already crossing what would soon become the party divide.

One year later on 17.3.1991, Gorbachev held his supposedly all-Soviet referendum, in which he asked everyone to support the maintenance of the USSR (Sect. 5.9.2.2). Georgia boycotted the poll. Abkhazia joined in enthusiastically, with 98% voting *'da'*. Two weeks later, Georgia followed the three Baltic States and held its own independence referendum, which Abkhazia boycotted. Of course. So too did South Ossetia.

The first President of Georgia, Zviad Gamsakhurdia, was very much the majoritarian centralist. Within two years, the re-born state suffered two ethnic wars and one civil war. He was deposed in January 1992 and died in rather mysterious circumstances shortly afterwards, by which time, Eduard Shevardnadze had taken over, endorsed as was deemed necessary by a 'yes-or-no' election (Sect. 2.1.2).

As with most conflicts, the causes of the Georgian-Abkhaz war were complex, but one of them stands out. For some crazy reason, Gamsakhurdia gave Abkhazia an electoral system which was distinctly disproportional, as shown in Table 5.1 (Gahrton 2009: 83).

In effect, the Abkhazians, who comprised only 18% of the regional population, were not far short of a majority in the local parliament. So the story of the war may be summarised as follows:

- the Georgians give the Abkhazian minority some positive discrimination;
- next, and as a result, the minority can and does pretend it is now the majority;
- so it then takes a majority vote to declare war against its Georgian benefactors!

God, how mad can you get? And do they all still believe in majority rule?

---

[24]For what can only be assumed to be selfish reasons, the *Irish Times* correspondent in Moscow was not interested at all.

Table 5.1 Allocation of seats in the Abkhazian Supreme Soviet

	Abkhazia	Georgians	Russians and others	Totals
Population (%)	18	46	36	100
Parliament (%)	43	40	17	100
Parliament Seats	28	26	11	65

5.8.2.2   South Ossetia

As in Abkhazia, so too in South Ossetia, tensions started to rise in 1989. The situation worsened in the following year when Gamsakhurdia declared the South Ossetian elections to be illegitimate and then, on 5.1.1991, he sent Georgian troops in to Tskhinvali, the local capital. Gorbachev brokered a cease-fire, but Gamsakhurdia accused the Russians of opposing Georgian independence. Eventually, but only with Shevardnadze now in power in Tbilisi (see below), a settlement was reached.

Having had two referendums earlier, there were another pair of them in 2006: the local (South Ossetian) Georgians boycotted a South Ossetian referendum for independence, and the local (Georgian) South Ossetians boycotted an opposite poll in Akhalgori, in which the local Georgians sought closer ties with Tbilisi. This was yet another madness in which the majority votes 'for' and the minority abstains, similar to the NI nonsense of the border poll (Sect. 4.2.2), similar too to the Yugoslav nonsense of two opposing referendums held in Croatia and the *Krajina* (Sect. 5.6.2). Will the world ever learn?

5.8.2.3   Tbilisi

A pause is required, to review events in Georgia proper where in 1992, Zhvania became an MP. "The election of 1992 was technically unique because it was based on the preference principle (after the Irish model). This system was advocated by Zhvania, who even invited an Irish expert[25] on consensus and preference voting systems to Georgia. The success of the Greens in 1992 was partly due to this election system, as they got most of the second and third-choice votes. Maybe the Green success was one reason that the system was later abolished"[26] (*Ibid*: 137–8).

Given the circumstances at the time, it was hardly surprising for the GP to join the opposition to Gamsakhurdia and team up with Shevardnadze. The problems were indeed huge, so in 1992, Zhvania went one step further and joined Shevardnadze's party, the Union of Citizens of Georgia. His participation in the Shevardnadze

---

[25]Me.

[26]The chosen system was not, however, PR-STV, let alone QBS. It was a parallel system, with 75 members elected in single-seat constituencies—the GP won none of these, of course—and 150 elected by PR, in which the Greens won 11 seats.

administration lasted until January 2001, when Zurab resigned because of a corruption scandal. After the next elections in 2004—some Georgians call it the Rose Revolution[27]—he became PM, Mikhail Saakashvili was the new President, and the third member, Nino Burjanadze was the Speaker.

In 2005, Zurab was dead. Supposedly, he was the victim of a gas leak, but many people suspect that he was murdered on the orders of Saakashvili.[28]

On 8.8.2008, Georgian troops were sent in to Tskinvali, and Russian forces entered South Ossetia from the North. As in so many conflicts, both sides were at fault, both Saakashvili in Tbilisi and Putin in Moscow. What is also probably true is the theory that if Zurab had still been alive and in post, the war would probably not have happened. There are countless Georgians who believe this to be correct.

5.8.3 Armenia

In 1915, Armenia was victim to an act of genocide, the consequences of which are still very strong. Today the capital Yerevan looks out at Mount Ararat, but it is in Turkey, and the border is closed.

During the 1991 all- (or not quite all-) Soviet referendum, Armenia actually broke a world record. Officially, like Georgia, the Republic chose to boycott the poll, but the vote went ahead anyway... and a few lonely souls cast their ballots. The turnout was 0.02%; but the majority therein, 72%, was still recognized as valid.

Regardless, Armenia declared its independence on 21.9.1991, and was soon immersed in a war with Azerbaijan. This led to a rail and air blockade, which seriously disrupted the economy. The borders with Azerbaijan on the one side, with Turkey and Nakhichevan on the other, remain closed; only the crossing to Georgia in the North and a little one to Iran in the South remained open. Armenia, however, had and still has a huge diaspora.

5.8.3.1 Nagorno-Karabakh

During the war in Nagorno-Karabakh, on 10.12.1991, the enclave held a referendum, a 'yes-or-no?' '*da-ili-nyet?*' question on independence. As in NI and the Balkans, the majority participated, the minority did not. Furthermore, many members of the minority were now IDPs or worse, dead. So the result was even more silly

---

[27]The overthrow of Gamsakhurdia was revolutionary. In the Rose Revolution, in contrast, Shevardnadze was in his *dacha* or home in Tbilisi and, as far as is known, he participated in the election of his own downfall; so maybe the word 'revolution' is a little too strong.

[28]In addition to four other visits to the Caucasus, in 1990, 1993, and two in 1999, the author was an OSCE election observer in Georgia in 2004 and 2012, (and the same in Azerbaijan in 2003 and 2005). He was also deployed to the region in 2008–2009, just after the Russo-Georgian war, in the EU Monitoring Mission in Georgia, EUMM, near the boundary line with South Ossetia.

than that of the 1973 NI border poll: 99.9% voted in favour, and only 24 individuals said '*nyet*'.

Since then, nobody has recognized the enclave's independence, not even Armenia itself. Initially, Nagorno-Karabakh was not contiguous with its 'kin', but when serious violence broke out in 1988, a corridor was quickly established; at the same time, one of the Azeri enclaves in Armenia, which happened to be on the main road to Karabakh, was 'ethnically cleansed'. Later, in 2017, there was a much larger land grab, and Nagorno-Karabakh, which has been re-named as the Republic of Artsakh, is now contiguous with a large part of Armenia. But it is still unrecognized.[29]

5.8.3.2 The Politics of Armenia

Like so many other new democracies, Armenia got off to a rather bumpy start. The first President, Levon Ter-Petrosyan, was forced to step down by opponents of a peace plan for Karabakh, and they included some of his own ministers like Robert Kocharyan, who was elected as the second President in 1998. The latter, however, was suspected of being involved in a terrorist attack on the parliament on 27.10.1999, when eight persons including Vazgen Sargsyan, the PM, were shot dead.

In 2008, Ter-Petrosyan returned to the fray, but the next president was Serzh Sargsyan (no relation to Vazgen) and Serzh decided it would be nice to be even more powerful. Now for some reason, many Armenians believe in simple majority rule, well sort of. A new constitution was proposed: parliament is to be elected by PR, and quite right too; as a basis of government, however, 50% plus one can be a little unstable, so the party or coalition which aspired to rule is now required to get a slightly bigger majority, 54%; if the winning party did not have such a majority, it would get a few 'bonus seats' to bring it up to this threshold; on the other hand, if it had too big a majority, over two thirds, then the opposition would get a few extras; all very democratic, perhaps, although it would mean that the electoral system was no long exactly proportional, but never mind; it continues, and if the parties concerned still could not manage to form a 54% majority coalition, a second election would be called between just the two leading parties. Now this, of course, would mean that PR was 'out the window', so whether this structure would still qualify as democratic should be highly debatable.

---

[29]In 1999, the author met the Karabakh Minister of Foreign Affairs, a lonely figure who sat behind his desk on which sat just a telephone and a couple of sheets of paper.

5.8.4 A Caucasian Conclusion

Despite the existence of three scripts let alone three languages, and despite the local existence of two religions and two denominations within one of these, there is nevertheless a very distinctive Caucasian culture which extends to all three countries, as evident in the amazing hospitality which the author has enjoyed throughout, with toasts of vodka and wine for Azeri- or Armenian- or Georgian-Irish friendship—but never *Caucasian*-Irish. There is, therefore, a huge potential for peaceful co-existence. The first requirement is a regional political institution, a Caucasian 'Benelux' or some such, something like the Transcaucasian Socialist Federative Soviet Republic with which this section started, but a little less 'sovietski'.

In relation to more immediate problems, it is probably true to say that Georgia will not be able to solve what it calls the territorial problem—sovereignty over Abkhazia and South Ossetia—for as long as it retains a majoritarian mindset. Sure, there have been talks but so far, suggestions have only included ideas similar to those associated with consociationalism, namely, that in each of the bilateral disputes, both sides should have a veto. That, of course, as has been seen in NI and Bosnia, is a formula for impasse. A plural society cannot best be based on a form of decision-making which is dualist and therefore 'duelist'.

Armenia, meanwhile, has already changed. Three months after the current author's visit in January 2018, there were protests on the streets, with people accusing Sargsyan of a power-grab. . . but he was elected PM. . . yet the marches continued and suddenly, on 23.4.2018, after just six days in power, he resigned. People power. So maybe the future is bright, and a former journalist, Nikol Pashinyan, one of the leaders of these demonstrations, was elected PM on 8th May. A post-majoritarian constitution would help. The other immediate problem, of course, is Nagorno-Karabakh; and here too, as in the territorial question in Georgia, if not indeed as in the Balkans, majoritarianism is still, and as always, problematic.

5.9 Russia

The influence of Russia is expressed only in an unfavourable light: by intimidation at elections. . .

Lev Tolstoy, writing in 1863 (Tolstoy 2016: 22).

5.9.1 Russia, a History

The Bolsheviks believed in majoritarianism; after all, the very word 'bolshevik' means 'member of the majority'.

Russia's first tentative moves towards a more democratic future started with the *Zemsky Sobor,* 'Assembly of the Land', which, like the British House of Commons, was "based on custom, not written constitutions" (Riasanovsky 1977: 209). As elsewhere in Europe, it consisted of at least the three estates—the clergy, the boyars and the gentry, and the peasantry were included at a later date. The first gathering was in 1549, under Ivan the Terrible (whom the people regarded not so much as awful but rather full of awe), and some of these gatherings actually elected the Tzar, as was the case with Boris Godunov in 1598 when he was "implored by the patriarch, the clergy, and the people to accept the crown" (*ibid*: 176). Supposedly with modest reluctance, he accepted.

By 1905, however, moves were afoot and these "culminated in a mammoth strike which... has been described as the greatest... most successful strike in history" (*Ibid*: 452). The Tzar Nicholas II capitulated: Russia became a constitutional monarchy, and a parliament, the *Duma*, met for the first time the following year, on 10.5.1906. The Tzar was none too pleased with this democracy stuff, however—too many lefties if not outright revolutionaries for his liking. Accordingly, in 1907, he changed the electoral law so that "the vote of a landlord counted roughly as much as the votes of four... bourgeoisie... 65 middle-class... 260 peasants, or of 540 workers" (*Ibid*: 457). Ah, that was better: the government now had the support of three quarters of the deputies. Then came 1917.

The story of the so-called October Revolution started in London in 1903, with a meeting of the All-Russian Congress of Social Democrats. Their original intention had been to meet in Brussels, but the Tsar's secret police had caught up with them, so those involved chose London instead. For some revolutionary reason, or maybe it was just because everybody else did it this way, they took decisions by majority vote.

In the first vote, the main loser was Vladimir Ilyich Lenin. Oh never mind comrades, "I do not think our differences are so important..." (Deutscher 1966: 71), and he abided his time. Sure enough, he won the next ballot: 19 in favour, 17 against, and 3 abstentions. Oh but this is important. They split. The majority—большинство, bolshinstvo—were called just that, the Bolsheviks; and the minority—меньшинство, menshinstvo—became the Mensheviks. Thus, "by the accidental arithmetic of a single ballot" (*ibid*), among many other consequences, some 24 million were to die in the gulags.

But back to 1917. The real revolution was in February, after which Alexander Kerensky and others formed the Russian Provisional Government. Then came the autumn *coup d'état*, sometimes called the October Revolution, and Lenin took over. Once in charge, he felt obliged to keep his promises, and "The immediate calling of the Constituent Assembly had been one of [his] main slogans..." (Shub 1969: 314). The elections were duly held on 25.11.1917 and, oh dear, the majority wasn't: the Bolsheviks were a minority, they came only second with 175 seats; the Mensheviks were much less popular, a mere 16; and the real winners, the Social Revolutionaries, Kerensky's old colleagues, were the outright winners with 370 of the 707 seats, an absolute majority of 52%.

So Lenin planned his second *coup*. The Assembly was due to open on 18.1.1918, and he "ordered a detachment of. . . sharpshooters to Petrograd" (*Ibid*: 320). "When [Irakli] Tsereteli [a Menshevik] rose to speak, rifles were pointed at his head and sailors brandished pistols in front of his face. The chairman's appeals for order brought more hooting, catcalls, obscene oaths, and fierce howls." On the morrow, "the Assembly was surrounded by. . . troops with rifles, machine-guns and two field pieces" (*ibid*: 326), and it was abolished.

That was the first and last time the Soviet Union had a proper election. . . until 1989; they never did have a referendum, until Gorbachev's nonsense of 1991 (Sect. 5.9.2.2); but decisions continued to be taken in the Politbureau in a binary manner. The first one to lose such a contest was Leon Trotsky, who faced the opposition of Stalin who had aligned himself with Grigory Zinoviev and Lev Kamenev; he, Trotsky, was then murdered. Next the Georgian teamed up with Nikolai Bukharin, and the two former colleagues were executed. Later still, Bukharin was also subjected to a show trial and shot. Stalin won every contest and he was in total charge: "Significantly, no Party congress was called between 1939 and 1952. [This was] 'democratic centralism' within the Party" (Riasanovsky 1977: 560).

Stalin died in 1953. Three years later, Nikita Khrushchev gave his secret speech and denounced him. There was opposition, of course, and another classic case of binary politics: the new Secretary General called it the Anti-Party Group, but their 1957 attempt to depose Khrushchev was unsuccessful; he stayed in power until 1964. The parallel with China's 'gang of four' is remarkable (Sect. 6.3.6).

Despite all the goings-on in the Kremlin, the Soviet Union still had elections of course, of a sort. What's more, they had a written constitution. Firstly, on decision-making: "A law in the USSR shall be deemed adopted when it has been passed in each chamber of the Supreme Soviet of the USSR by a majority of the total number of its Deputies" (USSR Constitution 1985: Article 114). Well, being Bolsheviks, they were bound to support majority voting, were they not? There was also provision for a referendum, Article 108. While on elections, the theory was again as sound as it is in many another such document: "Deputies to all Soviets shall be elected on the basis of universal, equal and direct suffrage by secret ballot" (*Ibid*: Article 95). As usual in so many countries, the document does not specify the electoral system; it just says they shall "be conducted by electoral commissions" (*ibid*: Article 101), and yet, as was seen in Chaps. 1 and 2, so much depends upon the choice of voting procedure. Admittedly, when Stalin said, "It's not the people who vote that count, it's the people who count the votes" he was referring more to blatant cheating; nevertheless, in a rather more subtle way, that is also what happens with FPTP.

Certainly the practice in the Soviet Union was pretty appalling. One polling station in Kiev in the early 1980s, for example, was a sports hall, inside of which there were 12 polling booths. 11 of these were in a line over to one side, near the exit door, and they were all labelled *'DA'*; so anyone wishing to vote *'da'* for the party candidate listed on the ballot paper could do just that, and then go to the door and say bye-bye. In contrast, those who wanted to vote *'nyet'*, had to go over to the one and only polling booth labelled *'NYET'*, which was all by itself in another corner of the room, along way from the door, and the few who did so would immediately be surrounded by various officials, 'Oh what's wrong comrade? Are you not feeling well today?'

As the name suggests, the Soviet Union was a coming together—or maybe they were just brought together—of 15 republics, each according to the original ideals of the revolution with the right to secede, and each an autonomous, soviet, socialist republic. Then, as was the case in Georgia, Armenia and every republic, there were further divisions: all were very autonomous and terribly soviet and absolutely socialist, and they were known as *oblasts* (counties) or *krai* (regions) or whatever. There were of course lots of different peoples in Russia, from the Buryats who live on the shores of Lake Baikal to the Chukchis of the far Far East; the official figure was somewhere between 60 and 120. Even in European Russia, on the western side of the Ural Mountains, there were the Udmurts and the Maris, for example.[30] If these peoples started to demand the right of self-determination, the politics of nationalism would remind the observer of those famous Russian dolls—*matrioshki*—where, inside each, there is another smaller one, and then another tiny one, and then... In other words, inside every majority, there is another minority, and inside the latter. . . Some Russians call the right of self-determination, "*matrioshka* nationalism" (Reid 2002: 136).

5.9.2 The End—or Maybe Not—of Bolshevism

Western diplomacy works on the basis that we in the West know. . . well everything actually (Sect. 7.1). *Ergo*, nobody else knows very much, if anything. So when Gorbachev came to power in 1985 to announce the new policy of *perestroika*—and this of course marked the end of the Cold War (Sect. 4.2.3)—Russia had to change, well, everything. They had to dismantle the Soviet Empire, to liberalise the economy, to introduce democracy, to cater for habeas corpus, to allow for a free press, and so on. But, in the opinion of many western diplomats, while Gorbachev might know *what* to do, he did not and could not possibly know *how*. Damn it, he was a communist. So lots of experts went over to Moscow, to tell him what and how to do, well, everything.[31]

On the subject of democratisation, the advice ran like this: hold elections to a new parliament, which may indeed be called a *Duma*; the Executive, which is yourself the President, should next propose new pieces of legislation; each of these shall then be debated in the *Duma* and voted on, and if a majority vote is in favour—which it almost certainly will be, because you have the majority (all the more so because the

---

[30]To describe the River Volga, therefore, as Russian, is a bit like describing the Danube as Serbian.

[31]One of the economics experts was Sir Robert Maxwell MP, a Czech originally and a crook latterly, so hence his nickname: 'the bouncing Czech'. He was first elected to the House of Commons in 1961 for Buckingham, the author's then home constituency, but everyone that evening in the local pub, The Swan, knew of his nefarious activities. He was nevertheless fêted in the Kremlin in the 1980s, where doubtless he was telling his interlocutors how best to cook the books.

USSR was still a one-party state)—the new law can then be enacted. This, in a word, is majoritarianism or, to use the other term, majority rule. In effect, therefore, the advice could be summed up in the sentence, "Mr Gorbachev, you need majoritarianism." But he doesn't speak English. Accordingly, the phrase was translated. "Микайл Сергеевич, Вам нужен... *Mikhail Sergeyevich, Vam nuzhen, you need...*" and the word for majoritarianism is "... большевизм ...*bolshevism.*"

In other words, as often as not, western political leaders are 'западные большевики, *western Bolsheviks*'.

The Russians nevertheless decided that they would adopt a western polity: the elections to what was still called the Supreme Soviet would be by the French TRS method; decisions in chamber would be taken by majority vote[32]; and "the transition to a multi-party system was 'planned' as the next stage of reform" (Gorbachev 1997: 409[33]).

5.9.2.1   Elections

Accordingly, in 1989, the Soviet Union as it still was held its first post-*perestroika* elections, using TRS. It was fascinating to watch: in the first round, when quite a few constituencies had up to ten candidates contesting the one seat, many public meetings were held in which all the candidates were on stage under an impartial chair, ready to face the public who could ask questions of any or all of them. Generally speaking, everyone was terribly polite to everyone else, and not least the candidates; after all, there were votes to be gained by being nice.

In those constituencies in which the contest went to a second round, however, it all then turned nasty. This was no longer a plurality vote, or rather an FPTP contest; this was a binary battle, win or lose, an **AB?** contest in which, even if by only one vote, the winner would win everything and get elected while the loser would get nothing. It was adversarial politics, plain and simple, and Russian politics now became adversarial—good manners were replaced by bad.[34]

The other fascinating aspect of this election was everything that preceded it, not just the campaign, but the entire process of democratization: all the little *samizdats*[35] which people produced and distributed on the streets, all the little public meetings which took place, as often as not in private homes. In a nutshell, many Russians and not just Moscovites knew perfectly well that the 'experiment' of the previous 70 years had been a disaster, and many were very excited about the prospect of

---

[32]When talking to the leader of Kirov's local council in 1989, the author tried to explain the advantages of an MBC in decision-making. "No, I don't like it," his host concluded. "Now why not?" was the obvious rejoinder. "Because you cannot predict the results."

[33]Reproduced by permission of The Random House Group Ltd. ©1996.

[34]The author lived in Moscow for two years from August 1988.

[35]'Я сам издаю, *ya sam izdayu*, I publish myself'. A *samizdat* can be anything from a one-page hand-out to a complete book.

change. Discussions were numerous, and so too were ideas and disagreements. For these fascinating reasons, Russian journalists were also interested in new and different democratic structures. As a result, the author's own ideas on decision-making were published in an interview in *Pravda*,[36] and in co-operation with his co-author Irina Bazileva, in an article in *Moscow News*, (No. 6/89), in a complete essay in Russia's leading literary journal, *Novy Mir, Новыйч Мир, New World* (No. 3/90)[37] (Emerson and Bazileva 1990: 217–225) and, as a consequence of all this, in a number of other journals and newspapers.

The Parliament met, to debate; but then, just like their western counterparts, the members divided into two, to argue. On one side was the Nobel laureate, Mikhail Gorbachev; on the other the Nobel laureate, Andrei Sakharov. They argued. They all argued. And people, the voters, those who immediately after the elections had been so intrigued by the late night showings of so many parliamentary debates, got bored, switched off, and went to bed. Three months, and the excitement was all over.

The problems, of course, were huge, and Gorbachev's headaches were exacerbated when many in several Republics wanted out: such was certainly the case in the Baltic States, and so too as noted earlier in the Caucasus. Nevertheless, even though his popularity at home was beginning to fade, he still enjoyed the support of the West, and not only because of the Helsinki Final Act (Sect. 5.6.2); he was, after all, a very popular figure... initially. But then matters started to get out of control. On 9.4.1989 in Tbilisi, 21 demonstrators were killed by Soviet troops; most of the deceased were women, one a girl of just 16 (Sect. 5.9.2.1). On 19.1.1990, there were at least 100 casualties in Azerbaijan, again at the hands of Soviet troops. The final straw came in Lithuania where, on 11.1.1991, the tanks were sent in and 11 people died.

5.9.2.2 Put in Yeltsin

In a near desperate attempt to keep the Soviet Union together, on 17.3.1991, Gorbachev organized that all-Union referendum to keep the USSR as one. One Republic changed the question, and six of them actually boycotted the poll—including, as noted earlier, Armenia and Georgia. There was nevertheless a huge majority in favour—more than 113 million or 77.9% of an 80.0% turnout. It meant nothing: the Soviet Union was dead by the end of the year.

As a direct consequence of the violence in Vilnius, the West withdrew its support to Gorbachev and chose instead to uphold Boris Yeltsin; at the same time, as mentioned, the West swopped Milošević for Tudjman (Sect. 5.6.2). First and foremost, Yeltsin was ambitious, and he took advantage of his mentor's problems to satisfy that ambition. Initially, he was the absolutely committed communist, a

---

[36]'Да' и 'нет' не говорите, *'Da' i 'nyet' ne govoritye*, Never say 'yes' or 'no'. 3.2.1989.

[37]The *Irish Times* and other western media took absolutely no interest in any of this.

candidate for the post of chair of the newly elected Russian Congress, which he won[38]; he also wanted to be head of the Russian Communist Party, but this election he lost. Whereupon he tore up his party card. Initially, he had been the absolute atheist, but now, suddenly, a Damascene conversion perhaps, he became very holy and Orthodox. Initially, he had been but now he was still the Russian imperialist, as he was to show in his disastrous wars in Chechnya—the first was 1994–1996, the second started in '99—but he now supported the dissolution of the USSR and the emergence of the new Russian Federation, in order to satisfy his ambition. Initially, he was the darling of the West, especially when he stood on top of a tank in response to the attempted coup of 18.8.1991. And so it came to pass: on 24.12.1991, the Soviet Union was formally dissolved.

As soon became very apparent, his commitment to democracy was not the best, especially when he called up the tanks to fire on the Russian parliament in October 1993—all in a struggle as to whether or not Russia's new 'democracy' was parliamentary or presidential. He won. Russia became presidential. Very. And he ran an economic policy which saw the yet further rise of the oligarchy.

5.9.2.3   Put in Putin

Yeltsin resigned in 13.12.1999. Enter, stage right, Putin, whose policy could be described as Trumpian: make Russia great again. So from "the 'late democratic' period of Gorbachev and under Yeltsin. . . a KGB[39] officer with a 20-year service record became President. . . and the [Russian] power structure was filled by. . . more than 6000 members of the KGB" (Politkovskaya 2004: 96). Yeltsin was one retrograde step; Putin was another. The latter was formally elected President in 2000 and, at the time of writing, 2018, he is still there, a Tzar in all but name, an 'elected dictator' (Sect. 3.2) if ever there was one. For a brief spell, in order to overcome the constitutional rule which restricts anyone from holding the presidency for more than two terms, he swapped positions with his puppet PM, Dmitry Medvedev, but Putin put himself back into the presidency again in 2012.

The author was an OSCE election observer when Putin stood for re-election in 2004—an election best described as a "charade," (*ibid*: 271). There were six other candidates, but he was not going to give them any credibility by debating with them on the TV or anything like that. So what was the point of having an election if he knew he was going to win? Yes, good question. Accordingly, Putin issued a decree explaining his motives. The goal, he wrote, was to get a minimum of 70% turnout in every constituency, and a minimum of 70% support from each turnout. 70 of 70 is, of course, 49, as near as damn it a majority; he was, yes, a good bolshevik. And in any

---

[38]In the first round of the election to chair, 535 voted against Yeltsin, (*Pravda*, 27.5.90); so the contest went into round two, in which 535 cast their votes in favour of him, and so he took the chair.
[39]Committee of State Security, Комитет Государственной Безопасности, Komityet Gosudarstvennoi Bezopastnosti.

constituency where he did not get such a result, according to a report in the newspaper Известия *Isvestiya*: "Тот кто отвесственный будет наказаным. *Tot kto otvestvenny budet nakazenim*; those responsible will be punished." Those responsible? Are they not the voters? No no, not in Russia: they are the local mayors, the schoolmasters, the factory managers, whoever are in charge of the polling stations.

Sure enough, Putin won, gaining 71.3% in the first round (so no second round was necessary). And equally sure enough, there were many constituencies where the results were indeed 70 of 70; moreover, there were some "exceptionally high figures... particularly in the North Caucasus."[40] Appendix 1 of the OSCE report—*Sample of Implausible Turnout and Result Figures*—listed the percentages of turnout and support for five republics; they were all in the 90s. In Chechnya, for example, the highest turnout was 98.3%, and the highest level of support, 98.6. In neighbouring Ingushetia, where the overall figures were 96.2 and 98.2%, the highest in the constituency of Dzeirahskaya were again astronomical: 98.4 and 97.6%.

These figures were indeed "implausible". Furthermore, their fraudulence was confirmed by anecdotal evidence: there was a web-site in Chechnya called "Я не голосовал, *Ya ne golosoval, I didn't vote*," but it was closed down almost immediately. There were also quite a few stories about persons from South Ossetia being bribed to take North Ossetian ID, in return for a vote. Unfortunately, the OSCE did not send any observers into the North Caucasus, even though the likelihood of fraud had been strongly suspected.

Elections for the *Duma* were not much better. After the 1989 TRS elections, the system was changed to a parallel one, part PR and part FPTP; sure enough, there were several candidates, but voters also had the option to vote 'against all'. In the 1993 FPTP part of the election, "the vote against all parties, 14.8%, was greater than for any named party" (Rose and Munro 2003: 56). Two years later, the election result "was among the most disproportionate in the history of proportional representation: 44.8% voted for parties not receiving any seats" (*Ibid*: 274). Sadly, Russia had become a one-party dominant state.

5.9.3 Crimes in Crimea

One of the worst aspects of Russia's activities since Gorbachev has been the murder of some of the world's most courageous journalists like Anna Politkovskaya, 7.10.2006, along with its treatment of those whom it regards as political opponents: some have been sent to prison, like Alexei Navalny whose recent internment was in May 2018; others, most notably Boris Nemstov on 27.2.2015, have been killed.

Another event of notoriety was the annexation of Crimea, a story which goes back to the early days of *perestroika*. "Today we will vote for Ukrainian independence, because if we don't we're in the shit," said Stanyslav Hurenko, the then First Party

---

[40]https://www.osce.org/odihr/elections/russia/33101?download=true

Secretary of the Ukrainian Communist Party in August 1991 (Reid 2000: 216). Thus Ukraine followed all the other former Soviet republics and became a sovereign state, whereupon the West—западные большевики or western bolsheviks—advised Kiev to adopt a form of majority rule—majority voting and power-dividing. This they did, and like Russia, Ukraine became a presidential democracy with elections held under TRS and decisions based on dichotomies.

Most of the people in this huge country are Slavs, most are (at least nominal) Christians, and most speak a Slavic language. But TRS is divisive; if the election goes to two rounds, the final is a contest between just two candidates. So that which was one—the country—becomes two, divided into East and West; those who follow Christianity are divided into Orthodox in the East and Catholic or Uniate in the West; those who speak the one tongue are divided into Russian- and Ukrainian-speakers. Policies, everything, becomes binary.

The 2004 final was between Viktor Yanukovich versus Viktor Yushchenko, the former was pro-Russia, the latter pro-West. Meanwhile, the West was playing the not very wise game of trying to persuade Ukraine to be not only a member of the EU, which might have been OK in Moscow's opinion, but also to join NATO, which was definitely seen as a provocation. After a re-run of the second round, Yushchenko was the victor.

In 2010, the contest was re-joined, and it was now the first Viktor, Yanukovich, versus Yulia Timoshenko, whereupon the former now lived up to his first name. The pre-election campaign was all horribly divisive. What was even more shocking was the fact that, not only those like Putin and friends were observing if not meddling in everything, but so too the supposedly impartial OSCE started to talk about ethnic-Russians and ethnic-Ukrainians. This was dangerous nonsense. They are siblings. As noted above, there are ethnic differences in Siberia and even in European Russia. But in Ukraine? Admittedly, there are the Tatars in Crimea, for example, who could claim to belong to a different category. But in Kiev, no. In most of Ukraine, no. As in the Balkans, the electoral system was a cause of war.

Having won the presidency in 2010—majority rule and all that—Yanukovich pursued a more pro-Russian policy, in response to which there were protests in Kiev. Only in February 2014, after violence had broken out on the barricades in the capital, did the West change its mind about majority rule. The EU rushed over to Kiev and suggested power-sharing, a 180-degree opposite of its previous advice; too late; they arrived on the very day that Yanukovich ran into exile.

5.9.4 Referendums

Before the Scottish referendum of 2014, the two governments in London and Edinburgh agreed to the ground rules (Sect. 4.4.3.2). There was no such agreement between Kiev and Sevastopol. Crimea nevertheless held a referendum, and yet again—as in NI, the Balkans, and the Caucasus—the minority, the unfortunate Tatars, abstained. The West was quick to criticize some of the Russian shenanigans—the presence of 'Russian troops' and so on—but the binary vote? No no, not a word.

There followed two further referendums on 11.5.2014, one in Donetsk and the other in Luhansk. In fact, there was a third as well. To summarise the story in Ukraine (and Ireland): Ukraine (Ireland) opted out of the USSR (UK); so Donetsk (NI) opted out of Ukraine (Ireland); so Dnipropetrovsk Oblast, a region in the western part of Donetsk (West Belfast) tried to opt out of Donetsk (NI). The *matrioshki* dolls had gone mad. The right of self-determination by majority vote referendum can indeed be a cause of war.

The separatists in Crimea and Donetsk do not quote the Edinburgh Agreement; people use only those facts which are useful to them; accordingly, the rebels quoted the word *"Shotlandiya. Scotland."* Like it or not, the binary nature of the Scottish referendum was a (small) cause of war in Eastern Ukraine (Emerson 2016: 51 et seq). Russia's next conflict was the 2008 war in Georgia (Sect. 5.8.2.3).

5.9.5   A Russian Conclusion

When the Cold War came to an end, with the collapse of the Soviet Union and so on, there was huge ground for optimism in regard to both the economy and democracy. But, as the old saying goes, 'Would that we do not live in exciting times.' The changes have seen the poor become poorer, at the expense of a handful of oligarchs who now possess obscene levels of wealth. While on the democratic front, the consequences have been dreadful: the Balkans and the Caucasus both exploded, and war too has raged in Moldova, Ukraine and Tajikistan. If the West had practiced and preached a more inclusive politics, maybe the history of the years since 1985 would have been a little more peaceful.

5.10   An Overall Conclusion

The use of adversarial voting procedures has served the interests of populists. Hitler came to power by first focusing on a minority—any one will do—and along with gays and gypsies, he chose the Jews. Trump did the same, 'Make America great again'—Mexicans, immigrants, etc. Brexit was similar—a desire by some 'little Englanders' to see a return to a position of dominance last seen in the days of Empire. And Russia under Putin is also of this ilk.

In 2018, western democracy has reached a critical stage: if it continues to believe in a binary form of majority rule, then there is the prospect that a right-wing party will take over in one or more countries in western Europe as well. In coalition, this has already happened in Austria and Italy. There is a strong possibility that some-where soon, such a party may win 50% plus one. . . and take over, completely, as in

Russia. For some extraordinary reason, however, many frightfully intelligent people still believe in majoritarianism.

References

Biryukov, I. D. (1985). *Ольстер. Кризис Британской Империалистической Политики [Ulster. The Crisis of British Imperial Politics]*. Moscow: Издательство Мысль, Izdatelstvo Mysel.
Deutscher, I. (1966). *Stalin*. London: Penguin.
Djilas, M. (2000). *Tito*. London: Phoenix Press.
Emerson, P. (1999). *From Belfast to the Balkans*. Belfast: Samizdat.
Emerson, P. (2016). *From majority rule to inclusive politics*. Heidelberg: Springer.
Emerson, P., & Bazileva, I. (1990). *Консенсус. Consensus*. Новый Мир, *Novy Mir,* New World. Известия, *Izvestiya*, Moscow.
Federal Government, Federal Republic of Germany. (1949). *Basic law*. Berlin: Press and Information Office.
Frankopan, P. (2015). *The silk roads*. London: Bloomsbury.
Fulbrook, M. (1991). *The Fontana history of Germany, 1918–90*. London: Fontana.
Fulbrook, M. (2002). *A concise history of Germany*. Cambridge: Cambridge University Press.
Gahrton, P. (2009). *Georgia, Pawn in the new Great Game*. London: Pluto.
Glenny, G. (1996). *The fall of Yugoslavia*. London: Penguin.
Glenny, G. (1999). *The Balkans, 1804–1999*. London: Granta Books.
Gorbachev, M. S. (1997). *Memoirs*. London: Bantam Books.
Herzig, E. (1999). *The new Caucasus*. London: The Royal Institute for International Affairs, Chatham House. Reproduced by permission of The Random House Group Ltd. © 1996.
Holbrooke, R. (1998). *To end a war*. New York: Random House.
Holsteyn, J. (1996). The Netherlands: National debates and local experience. In M. Gallagher & P. V. Uleri (Eds.), *The referendum experience in Europe*. Hampshire: Macmillan Press.
Huntington, S. P. (1996). *The clash of civilisations*. London: Touchstone Books.
Lijphart, A. (2011). *Patterns of democracy*. New Haven: Yale University Press.
Malcolm, N. (1996). *Bosnia, a short history*. London: Papermac.
Malcolm, N. (1998). *Kosovo, a short history*. London: Papermac.
Man, J. (2011). *Genghis Khan*. London: Bantam Books.
McLean, F. (2009). *Eastern approaches*. London: Penguin.
Netherlands, Ministry. (2000). *The Netherlands in brief*. Den of Foreign Affairs, Haag: Ministry of Foreign Affairs.
Office of the High Representative, OHR. (1998). *Bosnia and Herzegovina – essential texts*. Sarajevo: OHR.
Pales, Z. (2011). *Belgium as a crucial test of consociationalism: The 2007–2011 political crisis*. http://www.etd.ceu.hu/2011/pales_zsofia.pdf
Politkovskaya, A. (2004). *Putin's Russia*. London: Harvill Press.
Reid, A. (2000). *Borderland. A journey through the history of Ukraine*. London: Phoenix.
Reid, A. (2002). *The Shaman's coat, a native history of Siberia*. London: Phoenix.
Riasanovsky, N. V. (1977). *A history of Russia*. Oxford: OUP.
Rose, R., & Munro, N. (2003). *Elections and parties in new European democracies*. Washington, DC: CQ Press.
Shub, D. (1969). *Lenin*. London: Pelican.
Silber, L., & Little, A. (1995). *The death of Yugoslavia*. London: Penguin Books.
Thompson, M. (1992). *A paper house*. London: Vintage. Reproduced by permission of The Random House Group Ltd. © 1996.
Tolstoy, L. N. (2016). *The Cossacks*. London: Penguin Books.

USSR. (1985). *Constitution (fundamental law) of the Union of Soviet socialist republics*. Moscow: Novosti Press.

White, S., & Hill, R. J. (1996). Russia, former Soviet Union and Eastern Europe. In M. Gallagher & P. V. Uleri (Eds.), *The referendum experience in Europe*. Hampshire: Macmillan Press.

Wiskemann, E. (1966). *Europe of the dictators* (pp. 1919–1945). London: Fontana Press.

Woodward, S. L. (1995). *Balkan tragedy*. Washington, DC: Brookings Institute.

Chapter 6
Asia, Where Voting Was Invented

> The Mandate of Heaven (or a democratic principle): *"When a ruler becomes unjust or tyrannical, then the people have the right to replace the evil ruler with a new, good one."*
>
> (John and Nagai Berthrong 2000: 49).

Abstract China invented a vast array of devices and gadgets and, for a long time, led the world in pretty well everything. It had the biggest cities, the largest economy, the mightiest armies, and its influence among its immediate neighbours and even further afield was enormous. But China was also influenced by external factors, not least that of Buddhism from India in the first century and, later on in the seventh, Islam via Persia, which explains why both the Iranians and the Uighurs now use the Arabic script. This chapter concentrates on mainland China, but also refers to those other lands visited on this journey: Iran, Taiwan, North Korea and Mongolia.

6.1 Introduction

Ancient China dates back to 1000 BCE and earlier. The first Persian Empire came a little later, in about 500 BCE. And they met, as it were, in lands which were not very hospitable, difficult to conquer and even more problematic to retain, for here were the Himalayas, the Pamirs and the Tiānshān mountains, while to the east and west were seemingly endless expanses of lands, some fertile and some less so. The three main deserts were the Gobi in Mongolia, the Taklamakan[1] in Xīnjiāng, and the Karakum in today's Uzbekistan and Turkmenistan; elsewhere were the open steppes, stretching for hundreds of miles through today's Mongolia, Kazakhstan and Russia. Over the years, the nomads of these lands traded, migrated, fought and conquered.

---

[1]This old Uighur word means 'those who go in do not come out'. The author went round.

© Springer Nature Switzerland AG 2020

P. Emerson, *Majority Voting as a Catalyst of Populism*,

https://doi.org/10.1007/978-3-030-20219-4_6

At one stage, "around 665, [a] new Tibetan Empire overran Khotan . . . and Kashgar, [Kāshí, 喀什]" (Holcombe 2017: 108) while in the eighth century, the Chinese army was in the Ferghana Valley, where today's Kirghizia meets Uzbekistan and Tajikistan (Sect. 6.3.10). Then came the Empire of Genghiz Khan, 1162–1227, which stretched all the way from China to Iran and the Caucasus. All in all, while Europe languished in the Dark Ages, the history of humankind developed more in the East along what came to be called the Old Silk Road. If only in its own mind, China was the centre of the world—*zhōngguó*, 中国, the Middle Kingdom.[2]

In the Míng dynasty (Míngcháo, 明朝) (1368–1644), China was not only an Empire on land; it developed a huge fleet of enormous ships, and sailed all over the Indian Ocean under the command of the famous Admiral Zhèng Hé (郑和), 1371–1435. In the wake of this mariner's death, however, the Emperor curtailed such voyages, and with much smaller vessels, Europe then took over. Initially, the Portuguese, and later the Dutch and the English sailed into Asian waters. To summarise the history of the world in just a line or two, that which had been the world's major trading links, overland journeys by camel, were replaced by voyages under sail; and imperial powers on land, like the British Empire, were founded on maritime ports such as Calcutta.

Europe's renaissance was underway, and later on in the nineteenth century, where earlier the Persians had met the Chinese, the British and the Russians joined in the scramble for control of Central Asia; it was called 'The Great Game'. When they were not contemplating war between themselves, they were not necessarily thinking of peace, however. The Viceroy of India, Sir John Lawrence, "proposed that Central Asia should be divided into British and Russian spheres of influence, the details of which should be worked out between the two governments" (Hopkirk 2006: 318).

After a 'century of humiliation' from the British and other imperial powers, and then the traumatic events of the twentieth century, China again aspires to lead the world. This book relates to voting and governance, but here too Beijing sees a role for itself. "The main plank of American soft power is the stress placed on the importance of democracy *within* nation-states; China, by way of contrast, emphasises democracy *between* nation-states—most notably in terms of respect for sovereignty—and democracy *in* the world system" (Jacques 2012: 470). And while many decisions in the Chinese Communist Party, CCP, and elsewhere were and are taken by majority vote, "the Confucian ethos pervading many Asian societies stressed the

---

[2]A little later on, Britain also wanted to be the centre of the world (and so did Germany but they lost) and hence the Greenwich (rather than the Berlin) Meridian. Later still, New York was chosen as home for the UN General Assembly.

... importance of consensus [which] contrasted with the primacy in American beliefs of... democracy..." (Huntington 1998: 225).[3] "Western cultures can tolerate individualism," one Chinese authority noted, "but in Eastern cultures the emphasis is on collective authority and consensus" (Brown 2011: 100).

Today, China's 'Belt and Road' initiative is bringing China once more into prominence in Central Asia, and reasserting China's pre-eminence in the world's trading relationships. There is even talk of a maritime 'Silk Road' via the Bering Straits and the Arctic Ocean, a 'benefit' from, or should it be called an exacerbation of, global warming. The question of which countries will dominate the world has always been key to human history. During the Cold War, it was a bi-polar world; what followed was uni-polar; and today, China is returning to a position of dominance. With the rise of populism in the West, the question of which structures of governance will come to be the most widespread is becoming more and more relevant.

6.2 Iran

> Ruhollah Khomeini... [soon to be the first Supreme Leader] considered religion and politics as two sides of the same coin.
>
> (Hiro 2009: 363).

6.2.1 Decision-making

For some unknown reason, Iran believes in and uses majority voting. The Shia do anyway; maybe the Sunni are not so keen. It was noted earlier that the Persian Empire of old stretched all the way from the Mediterranean to the Caucasus and the Pamirs, but for this little book, the story starts at the turn of the twentieth century. As in Russia and China at that time, so too in Iran, the people were demanding a greater say in life and, on 10.6.1906, the regime changed from an autocracy into a constitutional monarchy: Iran now had a parliament or *Majlis*. But then something happened which, in theory, had nothing to do with governance, democratic or otherwise, but in fact changed everything. The British discovered oil. Well, that was OK. But then the Brits sort of decided that the oil was British and not Iranian, which was not OK.

---

[3]An extraordinary statement: so consensus is the opposite of democracy? How strange it is that 'consensus' and 'democracy' should be juxtaposed. It can happen, of course, if the former involves vetoes, and when the latter is assumed to be majoritarian.

The Great Game was in full swing, and the two imperials powers, Russia and Britain, signed a convention in 1907 giving themselves spheres of influence in what was, in theory only, a sovereign and independent Iran, one of just two countries in that whole area not to have been directly colonised; the other was Afghanistan.[4] That said, both British and Russian forces were in Iran during WWI, the latter only until 1917. The former then tried to turn Iran into a British Protectorate but it did not work, and in 1925, the Pahlavi dynasty was established, a constitutional monarchy with a parliament and elections and so on.

In WWII, the British and the now Soviet forces returned, forced the king to abdicate in favour of his son, and Iran became the corridor via which the Allies were able to supply their Russian/Soviet allies in the Lend-Lease programme. There was even the Tehran Conference in 1943, but that, of course, was a meeting of "the big three"—Churchill, Roosevelt and Stalin—to discuss the war... though they also had time to write the Tehran Declaration to guarantee Iran's post-war independence.

But—and it was a huge 'but'—the supposedly independent Iran made the 'mistake' of electing a socialist; not only that, Mohammed Mosaddeq wanted to nationalise the oil industry, so he held a referendum, and 99.9% voted in favour. Only 99.9? Only four out of over 20,00,000 ballots invalid? Not democratic enough! So there followed Operation Ajax, a joint CIA-MI6 operation, a "US-UK coup that overthrew the parliamentary regime in 1953" (Chomsky 2017: 107).

Not wishing to be any less democratic, the Shah then held his own referendum, and in a 91.8% turnout, 99.9% voted in favour of his 'White Revolution'. Unfortunately for him, another revolution was in the air, and on 1.2.1979, Ayatollah Khomeini returned from his exile in Paris, the Shah flew away, and the Ayatollah then had *his* referendum. In effect, in 1953, the Iranian people had voted by 99%, to be socialist; then, in 1963, they changed their minds totally and voted by the same margin to be the complete opposite, capitalist; and now, in December 1979— heavens, how fickle can you get?—they voted in similar numbers to be neither, and to be another opposite, an Islamic Republic (Sect. 1.1.2). The one big difference between the second and the third referendum was the fact that the turnout figures were down from over 90 to just 71.6%. The Turkmen Muslims are Sunni so, like the Catholics in NI in 1973, or the Serbs in Croatia or the Georgians in South Ossetia or the Tatars in Crimea etc. etc., they abstained.

---

[4]The British fought two nineteenth century wars in Afghanistan, from 1839–1842, and 1878–1880.

The author giving a lecture in the Allameh Aimin Library, Tehran, where he focussed on the inadequacies of binary referendums, not only in the Balkans and Caucasus, but also in yesterday's and today's Iran. Umm, there were no questions. Photo courtesy of Ali Chaboki.

6.2.2 Elections

In many countries, not least England and Russia, the centre of power temporal has often been closely aligned with its spiritual equivalent, its own form of heavenly mandate. The same is true in Iran where, in 1921, the first King, Reza Khan, "cultivated the clerical leadership" (Hiro 2009: 362), but then, once in power, he reversed the policy. In "the sixth Majlis (1926–8), 40% of the deputies were clerics; in the eleventh. . . there was not a single well-known mullah" (*Ibid*).

In post revolutionary Iran, Islam is once again the established religion... not unlike the Church of England in Westminster. There is the Supreme Leader (as there is in North Korea). He—and it's always a he—appoints six experts in Islamic Law, while the Majlis elects a further half-dozen, all Muslim jurists, to serve on the Guardian Council. The latter supervises elections and vets all candidates for an Assembly of Experts and the Majlis, both of which are elected.

This Assembly of Experts may appoint or dismiss the Supreme Leader. But, as noted, the Supreme Leader and the Guardian Council vet all the candidates. Apart from that rather large theocratic element, Iranian democracy is as good as many another. The electoral system is part TRS in single-member constituencies, and part SNTV in multi-member ones; in the first round of both, the successful candidate needs to get at least 25% of the votes.

6.2.3   A Little Conclusion

Such an ancient civilisation deserves to be regarded with rather more respect than it currently enjoys in some spheres. Given, what's more, the role of the West in the post-war years, the international community—which is often a euphemism for 'the West'—has little justification in pontificating how things should be done, especially when its own ways are so dysfunctional in its own bailiwicks let alone abroad. This is even more true today, of course, in the wake of the West's invasion of Iraq in 2003.

6.3   China, Zhōngguó, 中国

> ...the act of voting is actually a familiar part of life in modern China at almost every level from rural villages to the Central Committee of the [Party].
>
> Charles Holcombe (2017: 394).

6.3.1   Introduction

Western diplomats are currently trying to persuade China to adopt majority voting. Have they forgotten that China actually invented this voting procedure (as too did the Greeks of course)? Do they not realise that, if Xīnjiāng for example were to hold a majority vote referendum on self-determination, there would probably be a bloodbath, as bad if not worse than that which was endured in the Balkans? Worse still: do they not know that, in one of the worst abuses in the history of majority voting, this procedure was used in village assemblies during the Great Leap Forward as a means of sentencing people to death?

6.3.2 An Ancient History

Majority voting was used in ". . . the Court Conference of the Former Hàn Dynasty (Hàncháo, 汉朝) (202 BCE–23 CE), and decisions were based on the opinion of the majority regardless of the position or rank of the individuals on either side. As a rule, [these decisions] were accepted by the Emperor" (Wang 1968: 176).[5]

In addition and every once in a while throughout Chinese history, there were other definite moves towards a democratic society, even if, as happened quite frequently, the Chinese persons referred to had not necessarily been Chinese initially; unlike some other empires, China has managed to assimilate its conquerors, not least in later years the Mongols and the Manchus—(in like manner, the English absorbed the Normans fairly successfully). An earlier set of conquerors had been the Jurchens, who went on to set up the Jìn Dynasty (Jìncháo 晋朝) (1115–1234), but "all peoples who conquered parts or the whole of China. . . had a strong tradition of deliberation and joint decision-making. . . The Jurchens [for example]. . . had the custom before a campaign of convoking a military assembly at which the action to be taken was discussed by all those present, including common soldiers" (Franke and Twitchett 1994: 24). Then, when "the army returns after a great victory. . . another great reunion is held and it is asked who has won merits. According to the degree of merit, gold is handed out; it is raised and shown to the multitude. If they think the reward too small, it is increased" (Fenby 2015: 145). An early citizens' assembly perhaps; the Cambridge History of China uses the term, "a military democracy."

At this time too came what may well be China's first instance of a multi-option vote. In 1197, on the question of whether or not the Mongols should be attacked, "A vote was taken among the highest officials. Out of 84, only five favoured an attack; 46 were for a defensive strategy, and the rest preferred alternating between attack and defence" (Franke and Twitchett 1994: 266). It sounds like a plurality vote.

The Mongols, too, had a tradition by which a "great assembly of the princes and clan leaders, the *kuriltai*, would elect the next khan" (Man 2007: 124). For Kublai Khan, because of various rivalries amongst the other descendants of his grandfather, Genghiz Khan, "the [1259] election would not take place until the following spring" (*ibid*), and even then, it did not quite work out according to plan, so a rather limited

---

[5]Unlike so many other devices which were invented by the Chinese, it was not really an invention for by this time, the Greek City States had been using majority voting for more than a century or two.

ceremony took place instead. He ruled long enough, though; too long some might have said, 1260–1294; the empire included all of Korea, part of Viet-nam and, but for a storm which sank much of his fleet, Japan.

Unfortunately, however, on being assimilated into the Empire, "Consensual institutions like [these] Jurchen chiefs' periodic councils [were] abolished as incompatible with the dignity of a emperor" (Keay 2009: 335).

There may be much more to be learnt about China's work on voting in particular and its contributions, if any, if many, to the science of social choice. The western expert on all Chinese science was of course the late Joseph Needham. Needless to say, the Institute in Cambridge University which is named after him houses his complete works, and so too does the National Library in Beijing. His first of many bound volumes is just an introduction to all the others, and the last heading to be covered in the contents was "Individualism and Democracy" (Needham 1954: 49). Alas, it remained unwritten and in large measure, as far as this author knows, the subject is still largely un-researched.

6.3.3   The End of the Dynasties

In Chinese eyes, the nineteenth century was indeed horrible. From 1839–1842 (while also fighting in Afghanistan—Sect. 6.2.1, fn. 4), Britain used its superior military power in its 'war for drugs'—the first Opium War—and in one of several unequal treaties, dictated many trading conditions and acquired Hong Kong (Xiānggǎng, 香港).

The bullying was even worse in the second war, 1856–1860. "By early February 1857 (again, as with the first Opium War, weeks before the question was actually debated in the House of Commons or Lords), the Cabinet had already sent instructions east" (Lovell 2011: 257). Three years later, the battle now won, "Everyone was wild for plunder. You can scarcely imagine the beauty and magnificence of the places we burnt… these palaces were so large, and we were so pressed for time, that we could not plunder them carefully" (Kraus 2010: 201–2).

In the wake of these two wars, there were eventually 48 treaty ports and a total of "92 cities open to direct foreign trade… about half were foreign concessions… where foreigners had the right to reside, to trade and to own property" (Westad 2012: 173). They were taxed, not by the Chinese, but by the foreign administrations. They were subject, not to Chinese laws, but to foreign statutes. In effect, these were all little trading empires, with lots of missionaries thrown in as well. It could have been even worse: in 1859, "Lord Elgin, the British commander…writing to the then Foreign Secretary [suggested], 'We might annex the Chinese Empire if we were in the humour to take a second India in hand" (Hopkirk 2006: 299).

At about this time, a huge domestic problem emerged, the Tàipíng Rebellion, 1850–1864. Some of the southern Chinese were none too pleased with their northern

Manchu rulers, and the leader of this religious cult, who described himself as the Son of God, a second but more modern Jesus, whipped up the crowds to fight for righteousness. . . while he himself lived a life of debauchery. It caused the loss of 20 million lives. It was very much an internal problem—a Chinese revolt against a Chinese regime—but the influence of Christianity, perceived to be a largely 'European' religion, was huge.

The next humiliation was the Sino-Japanese War of 1894–1895. The *casus belli* was Korea; but the reason was the Meiji Restoration which had transformed Japan into a modern industrialised nation, while China still floundered in a system of governance which was thoroughly old-fashioned. Many were China's home-grown calls for reform, and the most realistic goal was a constitutional monarchy. . . not least because he who was promoting this reform was the Emperor Guāngxù, 光绪. "A Chinese Republic," argued one of his advisers, "would quickly degenerate into mob rule with corrupt elections and incompetent politicians like those [which had been] observed in America" (Nathan 1986: 61). In all, the so-called 'Hundred Days of Reform' was somewhat watered down, a "vast range of educational, military, administrative and economic innovations. . . [but] constitutional reform was notably absent" (Keay 2009: 492). What's more, the Dowager Empress Cíxǐ, 慈禧 was having none of this constitutional stuff, so she locked up the Emperor and took back control herself.

The people, however, wanted change: more reform, more development and far fewer foreign traders and missionaries. Hence, in 1899, the Militia United in Righteousness as they called themselves—the West called them the Boxers—started an uprising. . . which Cíxǐ supported. The western imperial powers responded in the only way they knew how, i.e., militarily, and the revolt was suppressed. In its wake, Cíxǐ nevertheless started to introduce some modernisations. As in Japan, as now in Russia in 1905 (Sect. 5.9.1), and Iran, 1906 (Sect. 6.2.1), the world was changing: some old regimes were being forced to give their peoples some powers, and this she did too. So China sent a mission or two abroad, and one went to the UK, to see how things were done elsewhere: "Just what was British democracy?" they asked. It was a good question. (It still is). In the end, however, "Promises of a parliament were delayed. But provisional assemblies, which did come into being, provided a convenient forum for anti-dynasty gentry" (Fenby 2015: 255).

6.3.4   The Chinese Revolution

So, as happens so often, the reform was piecemeal and inadequate. Hence, in 1911, although almost by accident, the revolution took place: the reformers took over and the Nationalist Party, the Guómíndǎng or Kuomintang, KMT, was set up by Sun Yat-sen, Sūn Zhōngshān,[6] 孙中山. In the first presidential elections, he won

---

[6]A Chinese (Mandarin) transliteration may sometimes be very different, especially when the original word is Cantonese or whatever.

16 votes out of 17—each province had one vote—so that was a huge majority albeit of a miniscule electorate. Parliamentary elections were also indirect, with a larger (though still tiny) electorate of 30,000. The winner was again the KMT, with 269 of the 596 seats in one house, and 123 out of 274 in the other. Alas, the new PM, a very keen advocate of government by cabinet, was assassinated, and a suspect, Yuán Shìkǎi, 袁世凯, was now in charge. The latter wanted to become the next emperor, so he banned the KMT and dissolved parliament. Sun Yat-sen fled to Japan. Mr. Yuan then convened a sort of assembly which voted, unanimously, to invite him to be emperor, and with all due (i.e. no) modesty, he accepted. In China as a whole, however, this move was not liked, some rebelled, he died, and China descended into warlordism.

Meanwhile, it was WWI. In 1914, Japan took over the German-held port of Qīngdǎo and sought yet another humiliation. Understandably therefore, China was very upset when the post-war Paris Peace Conference decided to give Tokyo some concessions in Shāndōng, so thousands of students marched to Tiān'ānmén Square to protest. This May Fourth Movement of 1919 is regarded by many as the beginning of what became the Chinese Revolution of 1949… but it also has an obvious link with June 4th and the massacre in that square, another 40 years later.

The CCP held its first Congress on 23.7.1923, a gathering of only a dozen individuals. Three years later, Chiang Kai-shek (Jiǎng Jièshí, 蒋介石), was the new ruler of the KMT—Sun Yat-sen had died in 1925—and Chiang led the Northern Expedition all the way to Beijing, so to unite the country and bring an end to the dreadful lawlessness of the warlords. There was now just one big struggle as two political parties, the KMT and the CCP, both of which believed in a one-party state, competed with each other, even though the Soviets were supporting the KMT and trying to get both to co-operate. Indeed, at one stage, Máo Zédōng, 毛泽东, "was very active in the [KMT], and became one of sixteen members to its top body, the Central Executive Committee" (Chang and Halliday 2006: 40).

6.3.5 The Chinese Communist Party

Like pretty well every political party everywhere, the CCP was majoritarian. In its statutes, Article III stated, "A member of the CCP must… (ii) seek to promote the interests of the majority of the people of China and of the world… (iii) be able to unite with the majority…" Article V goes on to say, "The whole Party must obey a uniform discipline; the individual must obey the organization, the minority must obey the majority…" (Schram 1969: 329). Similar sentiments may be found in Máo's own teachings: in 1964, for example, he declared, "we must win over the majority, oppose and smash the minority…" (*ibid*: 325).

The theory is compounded by the Marxist-Leninist principle of democratic centralism "in which the minority is subordinate to the majority, the lower level to the higher level, the part to the whole, and the entire membership to the Central Committee..." (*ibid*: 313), a structure which is often spoken of today by Xí Jìnpíng, 习近平 (Xí 2014: 154).

That was the theory. The practice was worse. In Máo's time, "issues were frequently debated, and voted on" (Chang and Halliday 2006: 81), but he did not like to lose and actually "loathed the convention of voting" (*ibid*: 90). In practice, then, and by the time he was the elected Chairman in 1943, "Opinions within the CCP were resolved through discussion in which the minority ultimately submitted to the majority. Under normal circumstances, Mao had the final say. Disputes over major issues were resolved through 'line struggle', in which the proponents of different viewpoints battled it out until one emerged victorious. Those who executed the 'erroneous line' then stepped down, while those who had persisted in the 'correct line' consolidated power. Considered a 'manifestation of class struggle within the party', line struggle tended toward a fight to the death. Once Mao achieved absolute power, line struggle became his tool for striking down dissenters" (Yang 2008: 488).

The KMT was not much better, and its first major act of violence against the CCP was in 1928 when Chiang initiated a massacre of hundreds if not thousands of CCP members in Shanghai in what was called the 'White Terror'. There followed the Long March, as Máo led his CCP to a camp in the far northwest of the country, but the Soviets still wanted the two to work together, especially after the Japanese invaded Manchuria in 1933 and then China proper in 1937. Co-operation, however, remained minimal, and the end of the Second World War marked the beginning of the Civil War, which only ended in 1949 when Chiang fled to Taiwan.

6.3.6   The People's Republic of China

After so much destruction and violence, the country was confronted by huge problems, everywhere, not only domestically but also, in 1950, abroad, when the Korean War started (Sect. 6.6.2). At home, the idealism of communism soon gave way to dictatorship. The Hundred Flowers movement of 1956–1957 was meant to allow Chinese society to express their viewpoints in an open and free manner, but Mao was taken aback somewhat when the praises he had expected were few and far between; instead, quite a lot of criticisms were heard. Meanwhile, in the Soviet Union, Stalin's death in 1953 had been followed by Nikita Khrushchev's 'secret speech' in which the Generalissimo was denounced. Mao worried that maybe a "Chinese Khrushchev would denounce him after his death and launch a campaign of deMaoification" (Dikötter 2016: 17).

So his dictatorship was notched up a gear. In July 1955, he decided to accelerate collectivisation, "apparently against the wishes of a majority of the Party leadership" (Schram 1969: 80), and there followed a classic binary form of politics: the anti-rightist campaign. It was part of the inappropriately named Great Leap Forward, 1958–1962, in which China was going to overtake the UK in terms of its GDP, but there now followed the worst instances of 'the tyranny of the majority'. "At every level. . . ferocious purges were carried out... In 1959–1960 some 3.6 million party members were labelled or purged as rightists" (Dikötter 2011: 102). In many rural assemblies, "which all [the] villagers had to attend" (Chang and Halliday 2006: 385), ". . .the violence was carefully orchestrated as the poor tallied their votes to decide who should die. When names were called out people voted[7] by raising their hands or by casting a soybean" (Dikötter 2017: 73–4). In one account, "participants voted to decide who would be killed; one by one, potential victims' names were read and votes were tallied. The process lasted for hours" (Su 2011: 65). "The moral values and social bonds that had long regulated village life were to be destroyed by pitting a majority against a minority. Only by implicating the people in murder could they become permanently linked to the party"[8] (Dikötter 2017: 75). As it had been in the Soviet Union of the Bolsheviks, so too now in Mao's China, nothing is more pernicious than the violence of the state. Some 24 millions died in the gulags; in what was the biggest man-made tragedy of all time, maybe as many as 40 million died in China's famine. The arguments used in both the USSR and in China, in both the Great Leap Forward and the subsequent Cultural Revolution, 1966–1969, were all horribly bolshevik and majoritarian.

Mao died in 1976. Having endured the anti-rightist campaign, the party now proceeded to work against the Chinese equivalent of Russia's Anti-Party Group (Sect. 5.9.1), the leftist 'gang of four'—another binary contest, this time against the other side—before starting very quickly on a programme of reform.

6.3.7   A Little Contemporary History

Volumes have been written about China's economic miracle, and there certainly have been some fantastic changes. This book however looks only at matters relating to voting, democracy and governance; suffice to start with the observation that, "In recent decades non-democratic China has made greater progress in reducing poverty and raising life expectancy than democratic India" (Runciman 2018: 172).

The first leader after Mao was Huá Guófēng, 华国锋, but he only lasted for a couple of years before the re-habilitated Dèng Xiǎopíng, 邓小平, took over. Again, as in the USSR after Stalin, so too in China after Mao, reform was essential but disagreements

---

[7]Needless to say, the vote was far from free; indeed, those who chose to vote 'against' ran the risk of being themselves denounced.

[8]'Bloodied' was the term used in the 1990s Balkans.

were inevitable and plentiful, often from within the ruling clique: "If whatever is being done now is all correct, then was the past work all wrong?" (Zhao 2010: 92).

Many reforms were discussed, some were rejected, several were initiated. As a result of it all, "Elections in both State and Party organisations [still] remain indirect and their results are mainly determined in advance. The only reform has been to allow rural villages to choose their own leaders by direct ballot; attempts to extend this process to the next administrative level—the rural township—have been consistently blocked" (Gittings 2005: 7).

So this author went to live on a farm in the village of Wǔjiāzhuāng, 武家庄, 50 kms south of the city of Zhāngyè, 张掖, in Gānsù 甘肃 Province. "The combination of lawlessness and economic mismanagement from 1949 onwards in rural China were the driving factors behind the introduction of elections after 1978" (Brown 2011: 18–19). After all, Chinese rulers have always been worried about a potential peasants' revolt, especially something as horrific as the Tàipíng Rebellion, so the best way to reduce any local complaints about a local problem affecting the locals' lives is to let the locals themselves sort it out.

Every few years, then, this village elects a team of three to look after matters of local concern. Everyone gathers in the village hall and, based on a short list of five persons, they cast their ballots and elect the three-person team. If during their term of office, there is general dissatisfaction with the team's conduct, a re-election can be held.[9]

> The village election process has in effect been a massive act of education that has taught over 800 million people, over two decades, the principles of Party and non-Party members running for power, of secret ballots, and of one person, one vote. Village elections were not meant to be the seed of anything else. But perhaps one day their introduction may be seen as a hugely significant moment when ideas of government being accountable to people who had the power to vote them in or out of power started to take root (*Ibid*: 69).

6.3.8   Tiān'ānmén, 天安门

In 1957 during the Hundred Flowers movement, there was a 'Democracy Square' in Beijing University, with hundreds of posters anticipating "by two decades the analysis of China put forward in the democracy movement of the late 1970s..." (Gittings 2005: 66), so no wonder Mao was displeased (Sect. 6.3.6).

---

[9]As it happened, the author's host had been elected some years earlier but had been de-selected by this very process; a fact, it seems, of which he was quite proud. In this village, then, the elections seemed to be functioning as they should; in another village on the outskirts of Beijing, however, there was talk of candidates buying votes.

The author does not know which electoral system was used; voting is 投票, tóupiào, but the correct translation for technical details can be difficult; not least in China, the term 'alternative vote' could be ambiguous.

As part of the anti-rightist campaign in 1952, Huáng Chǐn Chí is tried before a "People's Tribunal" in Fúkāng, in the province of Guǎngdōng. He is found guilty, and then executed. His crime? He owned one quarter of a hectare or two-thirds of an acre.

Whether or not this tribunal actually took a majority vote in not known.
© Getty Images

Sure enough, in 1978, the posters re-appeared on what was now the Democracy Wall, where lots of students "made contact with other dissenters. . . and some talked with foreign journalists (just as Dèng himself had done in order to send a positive message [to the] Wall, when the posters were beginning to attack his leftist opponents). [Unfortunately, however,] Deng's tolerance was short-lived. . ." (*ibid*: 155) and the Wall was closed down in September 1980.

Nevertheless, reforms were happening, slowly, and in doing this work, a rather reluctant Mr. Dèng was supported by two enthusiasts, Hú Yàobāng, 胡耀邦, and Zhào Zǐyáng, 赵紫阳. A "new election law. . . insisted that contests for local People's Congresses should not be unopposed" (*ibid*: 160). Deng, however, did not want to change the main structure of leadership because "it enables us to make quick decisions, while if we place too much emphasis upon checks and balances, problems may arise." He went on to say, "we should neither copy western democracy nor introduce the system of a balance of three powers" (*Ibid*: 179).

In the wake of Gorbachev's *perestroika* policy of 1985, changes were taking place in the USSR and throughout Eastern Europe; many students in China wanted the same. In 1986, some of them started yet another protest, and got support from Mr. Hú who, as a result, was forced to resign. So now Zhào took over as General Secretary. Hú's death three years later, on 15.4.1989, led to a massive protest as 50,000 students descended on Tiananmen Square. . . on the very day that Gorbachev arrived for a four-day official visit to mark the end of 30 years of estrangement between the two super-powers.

The protest grew from there and, at its height, up to 1 million people were involved. On May 20th martial law was declared. "According to [Zhào] there was no vote and the decision [to use force] was illegal—because under Party procedure he should have chaired the session rather than stumbling into it unawares. Another version has it that the Standing Committee did vote and split two-two, and that the elders were then called in to make the decision. Whatever the truth, the die was cast" (Fenby 2012: 180).[10] Zhào is emphatic: "There has been public hearsay that the Politburo Standing Committee meeting resulted in a vote of three against two, but there was no 'three versus two' vote. There were only a few people in attendance.[11] Among the members of the Standing Committee, it was two against two. . ." (Zhao 2010: 29). "Of course, if the opinions of Deng and Yáng [Shàngkūn], who were not members of the Standing Committee, were added. . . they were certainly a majority" (*Ibid*: 30).

Deng supported the crackdown. On 4th June, the tanks were sent in: hundreds maybe thousands died. Zhao was put under house arrest, and Jiāng Zémín, 江泽民, became the new General Secretary, to be followed in 2003 by Hú Jǐntāo, 胡锦涛—(no relation to Hú Yàobāng)—who often spoke of harmony and consensus. What

---

[10]Reproduced by kind permission of Simon & Schuster UK Ltd Copyright © 2012 Jonathan Fenby. First published in Great Britain by Simon & Schuster UK Ltd, 2012.

[11]For unknown reasons, he does not say how many.

else could he say? Then, on 14.3.2013, Xi was elected to the post: 2952 votes in favour, 1 against and 3 abstentions.

For the moment at least, democratisation is going no further. If anything, it is going backwards. The idea of extending elections to the towns was mooted under Hú Jǐntāo, but Xi has put an end to all that. Instead, he is consolidating his power. In September 2017, 'Xi Jinping Thought' was inserted into the CCP Constitution, and there has been a relaxation in the rule which was introduced after Mao, that the post of General Secretary should be limited to two terms.[12]

The author giving a lecture on decision-making in Luòyáng Normal University, 洛阳师范大学, in October 2014.

---

[12]As it happens, in March 2018, the author was in Ānyáng, 安阳, where he was scheduled to give a talk on decision-making in the local university. On Monday 12th, he met the Dean and everything was fixed for the Friday. Perfect. But the 13th National People's Congress was meeting in Beijing from 5th to 20th. The effect was palpable. On the Wednesday, the author's talk was cancelled.

Talks on the same theme in Beijing and Tiānjīn, 天津, Universities went ahead as planned, however, but maybe that was because those in charge were a little older and therefore less concerned about their futures.

6.3.9   The Chinese Dream

For the moment, there are considerable levels of satisfaction in China generally, especially among the middle and upper classes, and as long as the economy keeps growing at its current astronomical levels, maybe today's political structure will continue; but no growth can continue for ever without becoming obese. Furthermore, there are ethnic-minority problems in Xinjiang and Tibet, Xīzàng (see below), and these are replicated though to a lesser extent in Inner Mongolia, Nèiměnggǔ; there are huge concerns over food safety and other environmental issues, as when corners are cut for the sake of production targets; and the shadow of ecological catastrophe is overlooking everything.

Democratic protests are fairly frequent as well and, as the years go by, they are increasing. So far, however, and especially in the wake of Tiān'ānmén, reform of the democratic structure is not a priority. As in any country, the most important task for the powers that be, in their opinion, is to retain that power. To this end, the underlying ethos of the CCP is "the often stated desire... to aim for consensus before implementing a solution, rather than imposing one before this consensus has been reached, which might cause disharmony and conflict" (Brown 2011: 77). The latter can happen so easily, of course, when a decision is taken by a small majority... (as in the UK with Brexit). That said, the consensus found is usually more the party's own suggestion rather than everybody's agreement. But if 'democracy' produces Trump, who in their right mind would want to be 'democratic'?

As one commentator noted, "Some comrades feel we can sort all our problems out with multi-party democracy. Is that really so? Look at Taiwan. Mainland China is vastly more complex compared to Taiwan. If China was to become a multi-party democracy it would end up as a political battleground, a place where ambitious people run riot for their own power interests, and separatists can carve up the place" (Brown 2014: 164).

6.3.10   Xīnjiāng, 新疆

"The Uighur... as ferocious horsemen, were sidetracked into contention for supremacy on the Mongolian steppe. Their presence attracted overtures from [the first female Emperor] Wǔ Zétiān [武则天, 690–705] in her tussle with the revived Eastern Turk Khaghanate and began the long association between the Uighur and the Táng. As allies the Uighur would be of special assistance to [Emperor] Táng Xuánzōng [唐玄宗, 713–756] in his own tortuous dealings with the Eastern Turk Khaghanate; and in 745... it was the Uighurs who would succeed it in Mongolia with an essentially Uighur 'Third Turk Khaghanate'." "[It] lasted nearly a century (745–840) before the Uighurs were finally dispersed, many of them resuming their westward drift to Xinjiang, where they would remain" (Keay 2009: 266–7). Indeed, in that year of 840, they "were scattered by yet another steppe tribe, the Kirghiz, and the centre of Uighur power relocated west to Xinjiang" (Holcombe 2017: 111).

So the Uighur and the Chinese had been allies. Times change. Indeed, long before the British and Russians were thinking about carving up Central Asia, others had played their own 'great games', and borders across these lands have ebbed and flowed with the fortunes and foibles of history, with new frontiers appearing while old ones have disappeared. In all, that which is perceived today as a nice peaceful minority might well have been anything but in years gone by. And those who today see themselves as rivals may well have been allies. In more recent history, where change seems to be more and more rapid, some live to realise their mistakes. "In steps that it... has come to regret, China also encouraged, recruited and trained Uighur Muslims in Xinjiang, before helping them make contact with and joining the Mujahidin" in neighbouring Afghanistan (Frankopan 2015: 479).

The situation in Xīnjiāng, therefore, is complex. There is the Uighur minority, some of whom want independence. But if as some people think there should be a binary referendum on just such a policy, one has to ask about the other minorities: the Tajik, the Kazakh, the Huí , 回,[13] and so on. The problem is again one of 'matrioshka nationalism' (Sect. 5.9.1). Little wonder, China regards the policy of self-determination by majority vote as an absolute no-no, although its main reason for so doing lies in its desire to avoid a Soviet or any other style of break-up.

If only because of what could happen in Xinjiang, those in Hong Kong and Taiwan who campaign for a referendum on independence in their own bailiwicks should also desist (see below). The people of Scotland should do the same, if but for the sake of Ukraine (Sect. 5.9.4) and likewise, Catalonia should first think of the Balkans (Sect. 5.6.5). Multi-option ballots might be acceptable. But a binary one in Xinjiang could be horrible.

6.3.11 A Little Conclusion

There is one huge reason why China prefers to stay the way it is. In the 1990s, the USSR fell apart and the Balkans exploded (Sects. 5.9.2 and 5.6.2 respectively), in part because of the introduction of the western adversarial form of democracy. China is not going to repeat that sort of mistake. Therefore, for as long as Beijing is in charge, there will be no referendum in Hong Kong or Taiwan, let alone in the western provinces. A Chinese expert on China's village elections explained: "...if democracy inflamed separatism in places like Tibet or Xinjiang, then it was too dangerous" (Brown 2011: 100).

Secondly, there will be no moves towards a multi-party democracy and all the factionalism which such would possibly if not probably create, for reasons which are similar to those used in the USA against the introduction of PR (Sect. 2.7). "If China

---

[13]The Huí are Muslim Han Chinese.

imitates the West's multi-party parliamentary democratic system, it could repeat the chaotic and turbulent history of the Cultural Revolution when factions sprung up everywhere." This was Xīnhuá, 新华, the state news agency in 2011 (Fenby 2012: 163). They certainly discuss these matters, however; they debate them; and not only that, they publish articles on democracy by foreign authors, even those which mention Tiān'ānmén[14] (Emerson 2014).

For all the disagreements that arise from time to time in any country, democratic and non-democratic alike, there is a common acceptance among China's ruling classes of a "dialectic that has been embedded in elite Chinese political discourse since the era of Mao." But this dialectic is international. Beijing also sees "a world that is split between alternatives, one where things are 'either-or'; where there are enemies and friends, good and bad, and where the choices they make are between stability or chaos. . ." (Brown 2014: 190). So maybe China's one party state will evolve into what will also, one day post Trump, be the metamorphosis of America's primitive and dysfunctional two-party structure.[15]

6.4   Hong Kong, Xiānggǎng, 香港

> There are few, if any, other such free, undemocratic societies.
>
> (Rana Mitter 2008: 91).

6.4.1   A Very Little History

For as long as the British were the colonial masters in Hong Kong, they did not believe in majority rule. When change became the order of the day, however, they suddenly became terribly interested in democracy. . . and it was binary majority rule, of a sort, from then on.

The area of Hong Kong was incorporated into China in 214 BCE. This text now fast-forwards a little. . . and a British fleet arrived off Hong Kong in June 1840, on its way via a blockade and the occupation of Zhōushān, 舟山, a port in Zhèjiāng, 浙江, to deliver a letter from Lord Palmerston to the emperor. The British Foreign

---

[14]The *Open Journal of Political Science, OJPS*, is based in Wuhan. It has published five of the author's articles, albeit with rather lax levels of scrutiny.

[15]In 2018, the author spent a month in Xinjiang, mainly in Urumqi, (Wūlǔmùqí, 乌鲁木齐) Kashgar (Kāshí, 喀什) and Turpan (Tǔlǔfān, 吐鲁番). Most especially in Kashgar, security measures included numerous police stations or lookout posts in many urban areas, a lot of stop-and-search foot patrols in random arrests, and countless police vehicles seemingly forever driving up and down the main streets with sirens blaring. It was all very reminiscent of Belfast in the 1970s. One huge difference lies in the existence of labour camps, many of which have been reported in the western press of late; there again, albeit on a much smaller scale, NI's H-block prison was often the focus of criticism.

Secretary (and future PM) conceded that "Beijing has every right to ban [opium], but contended that. . . since Chinese officials were often complicit in breaking [that ban], it was unfair to expect foreign suppliers to respect it" (Keay 2009: 464). Hardly a *casus belli* but hence the first Opium War, as a result of which Hong Kong was ceded to the British, in perpetuity, in 1842, and Zhōushān was returned. The peninsula of Kowloon, Jiŭlóng, 九龙, was added after the second Opium War, 1856–1860, and the colony was more than doubled in size by the addition of the 'new territories' in 1898.

The island became "a Crown Colony, governed by a Charter, on 26.6.1843. [The Governor] was to appoint a Legislative Council, which was to have no effective powers, even though his appointees were dismissible by [him] at any time" (Welsh 1997: 147). These officials were all British. The first Chinese members were only invited to join in the 1880s, when it was decided that the Legislative Council, LegCo as it is now called, would have Chinese members "as of right" (*ibid*: 297), and a form of indirect elections was introduced, the same format as was to be subsequently used in 1985 (see below).

There was still some reluctance, however, to do anything more. In the 1950s, for example, the then Colonial Secretary, Viscount Lennox-Boyd, was "satisfied that there was no general demand or need for the introduction of an elected element into the [LegCo]" (*Ibid*: 458). But a shadow loomed large, and was getting larger. The 1898 treaty with China had only 'leased' the new territories for 99 years; the area was due to be handed back in 1997. "Beijing felt that a system which had suited London for the best part of 150 years without any change, and which contained no hint of democracy, would also suit them very well indeed" (*Ibid*: 520). As noted, however, the British authorities had suddenly become frightfully democratic.

6.4.2   One Country, Two Systems

Lord Patten—the same who was to be involved in the NI Peace Process (Sect. 4.2.4.4)—was the last governor, 1992–1997, and on 1.7.1997, Hong Kong became China's first Special Administrative Region, SAR. In an agreement which is due to remain in force for just 50 years, the LegCo is indeed to be elected. It is to be an indirect election, with 35 members coming from geographical constituencies by a form of PR-list, while a second 35 are to be elected in functional constituencies, mainly by first-past-the-post FPTP, or the alternative vote AV. Inevitably, the reader may conclude, it was resolved that decisions in the LegCo were to be taken by majority vote: either a simple majority or, in some instances in a sort of consociational vote, by a majority of both groups of members, those elected in the geographical and those from the functional constituencies.

Given the use of PR in the elections, Hong Kong now has many parties. Given the use of majority voting in the LegCo, these parties have divided, or have been divided, into two: a pro-Beijing and a pro-democracy bloc. Everyone knows what 'Beijing' means, but not everyone is agreed on the interpretation of the second term.

Amongst some of their other goals, however, many pro-democracy members want universal suffrage, especially for the election of the LegCo's Chief Executive or President. At the moment, candidates have to be approved by Beijing.[16] Hence, from 26.9 to 15.12.2014, the streets of Hong Kong were covered in 'yellow umbrellas'. At its height, some 100,000 protesters were involved, many of them camped out in little tents, blocking some of Hong Kong's main roads.

6.4.3   A Little Conclusion

The protests were eventually dispersed and, on the face of it, not a lot has changed. The subject, however, has been raised and remains. What's more, other ideas have been mooted, not least that of independence. As implied earlier, however (Sect. 6.3.11), any referendum in Hong Kong (or Taiwan—see below) would suggest that a referendum could also be conducted in Xinjiang. In all probability, such a poll would be bloody.[17]

Hong Kong is now divided. There was some violence associated with the protests of 2014, but nothing in comparison to the much more serious instances of violence which took place in Xinjiang in 2009, for example. Nevertheless, to base the future of Hong Kong on a decision-making process that was binary, either in a referendum or even if only in the LegCo, would be unwise. To continue to use majority voting is not the best way of promoting harmony.

6.5   Táiwān, 台湾

Taiwan's "free politics can be rumbustious—fist fights break out in the legislature, and are shown on mainland television as evidence of the dangers of democracy."

(Fenby 2012: 123).

---

[16]Meanwhile, in effect, presidential candidates in the US have to be 'approved' by their bank manager: millionaires only need apply.

[17]The author was in Hong Kong in 2014, and met with many of the demonstrators both on the island of Hong Kong and in Kowloon. At the invitation of Professor Benny Tai, one of the leaders in the 2014 protests, the author gave a talk in Hong Kong University in 2018 on the subject of decision-making. The purpose of the lecture was to suggest that, not least because Xinjiang is also part of China, to campaign for a binary referendum in Hong Kong (or Taiwan) would be not a little irresponsible. To ask instead for some regional autonomy, as Benny himself was suggesting, would however be utterly reasonable. . . but that option would only be on a ballot paper if the vote, and the debate which preceded it, were multi-optional.

6.5.1 Another Little History

When the island of Formosa was formally annexed into the Chinese Empire in 1683, the local population consisted of some aboriginals, whose descendants are still there, and some Chinese. As a result of the 1895 Sino-Japanese War, however, in a further nineteenth century humiliation, the island was ceded to Japan. And it was under Japanese rule that Taiwan held its first elections, but only for half of the Assembly; the others were appointed from Tokyo.

After WWII, Taiwan was returned to China which by then, of course, was fighting its Civil War. When Máo Zédōng proclaimed the People's Republic of China in Tiān'ānmén Square in 1949, some two million more Chinese, the KMT of Chiang Kai-shek, came and took over from the local population of about six million, while still claiming to rule the Republic of China.

There had been elections of a sort in the KMT when it was still on the mainland, and both Chiang and those elected representatives were re-elected, every four years... but by the 1960s, quite a few were dead. Its rule, however, was still that of a one-party state; furthermore, the 'White Terror' continued against any opponents of the KMT (Sect. 6.3.5).

By the time of Chiang's death in 1975, whereupon his son took the reins, the Republic of China (Taiwan) had lost its seat in the UN to the People's Republic of China—all the result of some 'ping-pong diplomacy' and President Richard Nixon's visit to China in 1972. Taiwan was feeling a bit isolated, but now the son started to introduce some changes. In 1986, Taiwan had a second political party, the Democratic Progressive Party, DPP, and in 1992, the regime held its first multi-party elections. A few years later, the KMT lost its majority.

6.5.2 Taiwan Today

Despite the abuses to which majority voting has been put on the mainland, and probably because of the influence of Japan and the US, Taiwan believes in majority rule, which could be good if it were based on preferential voting. They hold free elections which is fine, although the electoral system could be better; they have adopted a two-party structure, which is definitely not the best; and decisions are taken by majority vote.

The 2000 presidential election "was a true milestone: the first peaceful democratic transfer of power from one politician to another in Chinese history" (Holcombe 2017: 389). But it is all very binary: the island is either blue, which means KMT, or green, DPP. The KMT tends to be pro-Beijing, even though, of course, the KMT and the CCP were arch enemies not that long ago; while the DPP talks of independence, not for the aboriginals of course, but for everyone which includes the large majority of Chinese descent.

6.5.3   A Little Conclusion

The island has its own President—the first woman was elected to the post in 2016, Tsai Ing-wen, (Cài Yīngwén, 蔡英文)—its own currency, its own police, its own army, its own parliament, its own flag, its own everything. . . except its own name. So there is constant talk of a referendum, even though, "It is. . . incumbent upon us to oppose and contain any rhetoric or move for 'Taiwan independence'" (Xi 2014: 258).[18]

Given that Hong Kong is now an SAR (Sect. 6.4.2), it might be possible for Taiwan to operate under a similar sort of arrangement. There are certainly a lot of links between the two jurisdictions, but unfortunately, many of these conversations concern the possibilities of a referendum in one and/or the other, while few, if any, refer to the possible consequences such a plebiscite could have in other parts of China.

6.6   North Korea

> Kim Il-sung's death [is] referred to as the Celebration of Kim Il-sung's Eternal Life.
> (Jang Jin-sung 2014: 19).

6.6.1   A Tiny History

Many people in the Democratic People's Republic of Korea, DPRK, believe in Kim Il-sung, the Supreme Leader; in his son, Kim Jong-il, the equally Supreme and Dear Leader; and in his grandson, Kim Jong-un, the third Supreme Leader and Great Successor. If decisions are taken by a majority, it is usually a majority of one.

It was not always like this. In 503, for example, "a distinctive feature of Sillan society[19] [was] a degree of collective decision-making [admittedly involving only] the top aristocracy," but it was a "Council of Nobles [which] decided such crucial issues as the royal succession" (Holcombe 2017: 117). Later on, however, Korea was subjugated by the Chinese and in 1910, it became a colony of the Japanese.

---

[18]The CCP General Secretary is not here mentioning the two jurisdictions to which the current author refers.

[19]Silla was one of three kingdoms in what later became the one state of Korea in 676.

6.6.2   The Korean War

In 1945, Germany was divided where the 'allies', the Red Army and its US counterpart, met; the line was drawn, and shortly afterwards, it became the Iron Curtain. When the Pacific War ended a little later on, the future of Korea was less certain. Soviet troops came into the north of the peninsula, and US soldiers landed in the south. There was some talk of a united Korea but it did not work out, so in 1948, two guys in Washington drew a line on the 38th parallel. In May, a puppet regime was set up in the South under Rhee Syngeman—he had spent most of the war in the US—so September saw the establishment of North Korea under Kim Il-sung, and he had been in the Soviet Union or Manchuria for much of the time.

On 29.8.1949, the USSR exploded its first atomic bomb. On 1st October, Mao declared the foundation of the People's Republic of China. So US Senators like Joseph McCarthy started to worry about "reds under the beds." Accordingly, when North Korea invaded the South in 1950, the US responded with gusto. It was all done in the name of the UN, of course, which was possible only because the Soviet Union—a veto power—was boycotting the world body in protest at China's seat in the Security Council being held by Taiwan. The US forces quickly regained the South. . . and then just kept going all the way to the Chinese border; whereupon an army of 200,000 Chinese entered the fray and pushed them back to the 38th, which then became the De-militarised Zone, DMZ. An armistice was signed on 27.7.1953. The war had killed a million people. . . and had changed nothing but mind-sets.

6.6.3   South Korea

Initially, post-war, the North did rather well, if but economically. While the South, politically, did not. Indeed, on "one occasion, [the Seoul president] literally locked up members of the National Assembly until they voted as he desired" (*Ibid*: 339). So he was not very popular, and there was a military coup in 1961. This was followed by an assassination and another coup, 18 years later. Enough. On 18.5.1980, hundreds of students rose up in a protest which rapidly turned into a gun battle— the Gwangju massacre—and hundreds were killed. Unlike the events of China's Tiān'ānmén nine years later, however, this Korean tragedy led to a democratic transformation, and Seoul is now the capital of a stable two-party democracy—if the first adjective can rightly sit alongside the second. Despite all these political upheavals, the economy nevertheless became one of Asia's 'tigers'.

South Korea uses a parallel electoral system in which 253 MPs are elected in FPTP elections, and 47 come from a PR contest; the total, then, is 300. Because of such a high proportion of FPTP seats, it has a mainly two-party system. In the last general election in 2016, the biggest party won 123 seats, and the other big one got 122—a majority of just one. For some reason, however, some bills in parliament require not just a 50% majority, but a 60% weighting, and this can cause problems.

6.6.4   North Korea

In stark contrast to the political events in Seoul, Pyongyang opted for a personality cult, first with Kim Il-sung, who died in 1994, next with Kim Jong-il, and he was succeeded by Kim Jong-un in 2011. The statues are everywhere, over 35,000 of them it is said, and people are expected to stand in silent homage to the Eternal Supreme Leader and his first successor. . .just the two of them for the moment, and doubtless the grandson will also be built in stone when his time comes to pass.

In 1972, Kim Il-sung introduced his policy of *Juche*, which means self-reliance. The people are masters of their own destiny, it declared. But it did not work. In the 1990s, the collapse of the Soviet Union led to a cessation of aid from that source, and this, combined with many mistakes which cannot be blamed on outsiders, not least the huge amount of money spent on the security forces, resulted in a terrible famine; on a per capita scale, it was comparable to the great famine in Mao's China during the Great Leap Forward. Eventually, and unlike the regime in Beijing, Pyongyang asked for international aid.

The theory of *Juche*, however, continued. Accordingly, in what after all is called the *Democratic* People's Republic of Korea, the people have the Supreme People's Assembly, a huge building for all of 675 elected MPs. South Korea may have the larger population—50 as opposed to just 25 million—but Pyongyang certainly has the bigger parliament. Every four years or so, the people may choose their representatives from a choice of one: a list of candidates chosen by the Workers' Party, which stands alongside its allies, two other much smaller parties, and there is no opposition. Alas the Party is not the best either, for "there was not a single General Meeting of the Workers' Party for over 20 years between. . . 1980 and. . . 2004" (Jang 2014: 137).

Sure enough, in the last election in 2014, in what was reputed to be a 100% turnout, the Workers' Party won 606 seats, its two sister parties won 72 between them, and there were three independents. Democracy in action? Well according to Article 92 of the 'Socialist Constitution', "Regular sessions are convened [only] once or twice a year" (Juche 2017: 21). The reader will be pleased to know, however, that if something does happen, "Laws, ordinances and decisions of the Supreme People's Assembly are adopted when more than half of the deputies attending signify approval by a show of hands" (*Ibid*: Article 97). So they too believe in and use majority voting. The same document goes on to say, "The Constitution is amended or supplemented with the approval of more than two-thirds of the total number of deputies." So sometimes it is just a simple majority vote, and sometimes it's weighted. Maybe the DPRK is indeed sort of democratic. On a more serious note, its human rights record is appalling, albeit not quite as bad today as it has been.

6.6.5   A Nation Re-united?

Germany was re-united in 1990. By the look of things, Korea may well come together again. . . fairly soon (Ireland will probably have to wait a little longer, unless Brexit. . .).

For a long time, despite being in theory still at war, the two 'halves' of the peninsula lived relatively peacefully, although there have been some fairly serious incidents from time to time. On 29.1.2001, however, President George Bush spoke about "the axis of evil," so to link Iran and North Korea as supposed supporters of terrorism. Given what the West has done to smaller states like Iraq and Libya, one can understand that North Korea might well have feared for its own future. The DPRK exploded its first nuclear device on 9.10.2006.

However, on 12.6.2017, Kim met Trump in Singapore.[20] Change was in the air. And since that meeting, the South has been meeting the North more regularly than before. Suffice here to say that if Korea is to be re-united, it would be better if it were not done under a policy of majority rule; instead, perhaps a joint presidency and an all-party power-sharing arrangement should be considered.

6.7   Mongolia

> . . .in 1228, scribes and sources were present together. . . a perfect opportunity to capture legend and recent events, with particular reference to. . . the rise of Genghis [Khan]. And so it was that Mongolia's first written book was commissioned: *The Secret History of the Mongols.*
>
> (Man 2011: 34).

6.7.1   A Little Background

As mentioned earlier, this part of the world has seen empires come and go, and one of them, from 744–840, was indeed the Uighur Khaganate (Sect. 6.3.10). A few others followed until a certain Temujin, 1162–1227, a Mongol, won a number of battles and thus unified what had been a disparate collection of rulers. Accordingly, in 1206, "a national assembly [or] *khural*. . . proclaimed him leader of the newly united nation, and confirmed the investiture of his title, Genghis Khan" (*Ibid*: 128).

These rulers tended to have quite a few wives and concubines, so the question of succession could be problematic. Accordingly, what had been the Mongolian Empire was divided into four, one for each of four grandsons: the Golden Horde

---

[20]The author spent ten days in North Korea, crossing the border from Tumen in the northeast to spend a few days in that part of the country, before going to Pynongyang and the DMZ. His visit coincided with this historic meeting in Singapore.

in a huge swathe of today's Russia; the Chagatai in Central Asia; the Ilkhanate in the Middle East, from Iran to the Caucasus; and lastly, China, where the new leader was Kublai Khan, 1260–1294. His *khural,* however, was not in Karakorum, the then capital of Mongolia, but in Xanadu, just outside today's Beijing, where the Mongol barons gathered "to select their next leader. The results of the vote were mixed; each rival had his devoted supporters, setting the scene for years of conflict" (Bergreen 2009: 127).

For many, however, the main question, then and now, was/is as follows: was China part of Mongolia (past tense)? or is Mongolia part of China (present tense)? Initially, it was the former, and Kublai Khan founded the Yuán Dynasty (*Yuán Cháo,* 元朝), in 1271.

In 1368, China fell to the Míng Dynasty, 1368–1644, who were definitely Chinese; and this gave way to the Manchus of the Qīng Dynasty (Qīngcháo, 清朝), and they weren't Chinese either... originally. So when the Chinese revolution happened in 1911, Mongolia decided to be independent and, on 29th December that year, gave themselves a royal coronation and a King. Yuán Shìkǎi, the new ruler in Beijing, disagreed, and died, but China regained control until 18.3.1921, when the Mongolian Revolution and the Mongolian People's Revolutionary Party, MPRP, with the Soviet Red Army in support, defeated the Chinese and the White Russians, so to declare a Mongolian People's Republic on 26.11.1924.

It was all very 'sovietski', with a Mongolian version of Stalin's collectivisation in 1928 and purges against the Buddhist clergy in 1937. Up to 10% of a population of just under one million was to suffer. After WWII, China agreed to recognise the independence of Mongolia, subject to a referendum, which duly took place on 20.10.1945; and on a 98.5% turnout, 100% said 'yes'. Ah, at last—for this book anyway—an independence referendum that actually solved a problem without bloodshed.

In 1951, there were elections, but Mongolia was still a one-party state, and the MPRP won 176 seats, with 118 going to non-party candidates. Thus it continued, more or less—with rather more MPRP and rather fewer independents—every three years until, in the wake of Gorbachev's *perestroika* and the Soviet Union's first proper (though still one-party) elections in 1989, there were demonstrations in Ulaanbaatar, asking for change. Sure enough, Mongolia is now a multi-party democracy with the MPRP now renamed the Mongolian People's Party, MPP; a Democratic Party, DP; and just to confuse everyone, a different MPRP, established in 2010.

6.7.2 Mongolian Elections

There is a festival in Mongolia called *Naadam*. In winter, with temperatures down to -40C, there's not an awful lot one can do. So in summer, it's time to celebrate, and every year, in every district, there are games, which all culminate in a huge event in the capital where champions are crowned. The games involve horse-riding, of course, as well as archery and wrestling. And unlike the western so-called sports of wrestling and boxing, in Mongolia, nobody hurts anybody. Two great big fellers grapple with each other, and the one who brings the other to the ground is the winner; the loser, at worst, a little bruised.

For some lovely reason, the people in Mongolia believe in a democracy which is like a *naadam*. You win today, I win tomorrow, and everybody enjoys themselves. Accordingly, and just as Russia's first post-*perestroika* elections in 1989 were conducted, at least initially, in a remarkably civilised way (Sect. 5.9.2.1), so too here in Mongolia, the democratic contest is very well organised. The local authorities sought outside help—"In 1990 members of the Mongolian legislature asked the president of the Public Choice Society for advice on a new constitution. . ." (McLean and Urken 1995: 13)—but much of the electoral law has a distinctly Mongolian stamp on it.

In every constituency, every contesting party regardless of size is allowed only so many posters, and all must be in just one part of town. Likewise, each party shall be allowed to spend only so much money. Thirdly, each must have only so many campaigners. In other words, everything was to be frightfully fair, in theory. . . and was reasonably fair in practice. The party campaigners were out in (limited) force, but all three groups would pitch their stalls—or rather their *gers* or yurts—at the same roundabout. There were flags and bunting a'plenty, and voters could go to any or all of the parties, there to ask questions or whatever. The main feature of the entire election which was totally inappropriate was the western electoral system—TRS.

But first, the campaign. At one rally in the 2017 presidential election contest, a possible future president spoke to the assembled masses with policies for education, the economy, the environment, and, oh yes—Mongolia was suffering from a rather severe drought at the time—a promise for rain. (As happens quite often in politics everywhere, the politician talks of the 'what' and not necessarily of the 'how'). In another regional capital, a second presidential candidate gave his address; again there was mention of education, the economy, the environment. . . and rain. Shortly afterwards, the author was in a regional centre, meeting some of the local officials, after which he saw some activity on a local mountaintop: the shamans were busy, praying for rain. And the rains came. . . *before* the election, so it must have been the shamans!

Out on the steppe, then, campaigners and punters alike were all enjoying the fun. But TRS is divisive, and in Ulaanbaatar there was all the usual 'mud' that is associated with adversarial politics, from accusations over money laundering to insults about parentage, and so on.

TRS is indeed a crazy system (Sect. 2.1.3). In the first round, the three candidates—DP, MPP and MPRP—got 38.6, 30.8 and 30.6% respectively. It was just like the scenario painted in Table 1.2! So if only by a whisker, the 30.6 MPRP candidate was eliminated, and he then campaigned for a boycott of the second round in the hope that the percentage of abstainers would be bigger than either of the other two percentages. Meanwhile—and this was the first time that a Mongolian contest had gone to the second round—the Electoral Commission had to print another load of ballot papers and get everything else ready, quickly, because the law says it has all to be done within a fortnight. They therefore gave themselves the maximum 14 days and announced the second round would be on July 9th. But that's *Naadam*! The final championships of the 2017 festival could not take place if there wasn't a president to open the games! The protest was HUGE! Social media went viral. Right oh; the elections were brought forward by two days, the outcome was DP 55.1 and MPP 44.9, so well beyond dispute, and the sun then shone on *Naadam*.

For reasons of international diplomacy or intrigue, international election observation missions like this one, which was run by the Organisation for Security and Co-operation in Europe, OSCE, do not comment on the electoral system (see also 4.2.4.7). In the words of the Head of Mission, it was "taboo," mainly because the French would get upset if the OSCE spoke negatively about TRS, just as the British would go ballistic if an international organisation of which it is a major member criticised their beloved FPTP. If, however, the electoral system had been preferential, it could all have been completed in one round; and if the count had been conducted according to a Borda methodology, maybe some of the inter-party mudslinging could have been avoided.[21]

6.7.3 Electronic Voting

Mongolia is huge. The population is sparse. In quite a few of the rural areas, a voter might live up to 100 km away from the polling station. Furthermore, 30% of poling stations were without electricity.

No problem. There was a generator out the back. The voter—many of whom were dressed in their national costume for the day—arrived, put her finger onto the little pad provided, and her biometric identity was immediately confirmed by the computer. If all was in order, she was then issued with a ballot paper, and the automatic display showed an additional 'one' on the official turnout figures. She then marked the ballot, in secret of course, before feeding it into the counting machine. That was it, her democratic duty to her country was complete, and off she went.

Come ten o'clock in the evening, the polling finished, the door was locked, and someone then pressed the button so that—zap—the data was fed automatically to the capital where, after a nanosecond or few, the nationwide results were declared. Well, that was the theory. In some of the rather more remote locations, the machine had to be dismantled and loaded onto the back of a truck, along with the generator. Then off they all went to a local mountain top, there to see if they could get a modem connection.

---

[21]The author, a long-term OSCE observer in Arkhangai and Khovsgul Aimags (or provinces), suggested a better methodology to the Mongolian authorities, the OSCE and his own Irish government. The first addressee replied. The OSCE did not respond. And nor did the Irish; instead they terminated the author's participation in any future observation missions.

Meanwhile, after a draw at the local electoral commission offices, 50% of the polling stations were required to do a paper count, just to make sure that all this electronic stuff was working properly. If there had been any discrepancies, a paper recount would have been ordered in all polling stations, but everything was fine. Would that Mongolian observers came to our NI elections.

6.7.4 A Little Conclusion

As in Russia, so too in Mongolia, so too everywhere, people have a natural understanding of what a democracy should be. Unfortunately, and not least because people often accept western advice—some of which is excellent but much is distinctly majoritarian—many democratic structures are then based on single-preference electoral systems and binary decision-making. If more traditional methodologies had been adopted, maybe the resulting polities might have been rather more inclusive.

6.8 The Main Conclusion

With the exception of mainland China and, for the moment at least, North Korea, many countries in Asia are enjoying the fruits and/or suffering the consequences of exclusive, win-or-lose forms of governance. In many villages in China, open democratic elections within a one-party structure are working fairly well. The simple two-party structure in the jurisdictions of Hong Kong and Taiwan is certainly much more democratic than what they had had before, although a more pluralist polity might be advisable for both. Most importantly, however, is the third conclusion: because of the fragile situations which exist in Tibet and Xinjiang, what must be avoided at all costs is any thought of a binary referendum on independence, anywhere, not only in Hong Kong and/or Taiwan, but also in Scotland and Catalonia, and so on. A more inclusive, win-win polity is required.

References

Bergreen, L. (2009). *Marco Polo – From Venice to Xanadu*. London: Quercus.
Berthrong, J. H., & Berthrong, E. N. (2000). *Confucianism. A short introduction*. Oxford: One World.
Brown, K. (2011). *Ballot box China*. London: Zed Books.
Brown, K. (2014). *The new emperors*. I. B. Tauris, used by permission of Bloomsbury Publishing, London.
Chang, J., & Halliday, J. (2006). *Mao, The unknown story*. London: Vintage Books.
Chomsky, N. (2017). *Who rules the world*. London: Penguin Books.

Dikötter, F. (2011). *Mao's Great Famine*. London: Bloomsbury Publishing.

Dikötter, F. (2016). *The cultural revolution*. London: Bloomsbury Publishing.

Dikötter, F. (2017). *The tragedy of liberation*. London: Bloomsbury Publishing.

Emerson, P. (2014). A democratic China? *Open Journal of Political Science, 4*(3). http://file.scirp. org/Html/4-1670125_48302.htm.

Fenby, J. (2012). *Tiger head snake tails*. London: Simon and Shuster.

Fenby, J. (2015). *The dragon throne*. London: Quercus.

Franke, H., & Twitchett, D. (1994). *Cambridge history of China* (Vol. 6). Cambridge: CUP.

Frankopan, P. (2015). *The silk roads*. London: Bloomsbury Publishing.

Gittings, J. (2005). *The changing face of China*. Oxford: OUP.

Hiro, D. (2009). *Inside Central Asia*. New York: Overlook Duckworth.

Holcombe, C. (2017). *A history of East Asia* (2nd ed.). Cambridge: CUP.

Hopkirk, P. (2006). *The great game*. London: John Murray.

Huntington, S. P. (1998). *The clash of civilizations and the remaking of world order*. London: Touchstone Books.

Jacques, M. (2012). *When China rules the world*. London: Penguin Books.

Jang, J. (2014). *Dear leader*. London: Rider.

Juche, 106. (2017). *The socialist constitution of the Democratic People's Republic of Korea*. Pyongyang: Foreign Languages Publishing House.

Keay, J. (2009). *China, a history*. London: Harper Press.

Kraus, R. (2010). The politics of art repatriation. In P. Gries & S. Rosen (Eds.), *Chinese politics. State, society and the market*. London: Routledge.

Lovell, J. (2011). *The Opium War*. London: Picador.

Man, J. (2007). *Kublai Khan*. London: Bantam Books. Reproduced by permission of The Random House Group Ltd. © 1996.

Man, J. (2011). *Genghis Khan*. London: Bantam Books. Reproduced by permission of The Random House Group Ltd. © 1996.

McLean, I., & Urken, A. (1995). *Classics of social choice*. Ann Arbor: University of Michigan Press.

Nathan, A. J. (1986). *Chinese democracy*. Berkeley: University of California Press.

Needham, J. (1954). *Science and civilisation in China, Vol I, Introductory orientations*. Cambridge: CUP.

Runciman, D. (2018). *How democracy ends*. London: Profile Books.

Schram, S. R. (1969). *The political thought of Mao Tse-tung*. New York: Frederick A Praeger.

Su, Y. (2011). *Collective killings in rural China during the cultural revolution*. Cambridge: CUP.

Wang, Y.-C. (1968). An outline of the central government of the former Han dynasty. In J. L. Bishop (Ed.), *Studies of government institutions in Chinese history* (Harvard-Yenching Institute Studies XXIII). Cambridge, MA: Harvard University Press.

Welsh, F. (1997). *A history of Hong Kong*. London: Harper Collins.

Westad, O. A. (2012). *Restless empire. China and the world since 1750*. London: The Bodley Head. Reproduced by permission of The Random House Group Ltd. © 1996.

Xí, J. (2014). *The governance of China*. Beijing: Foreign Languages Press.

Yang, J. (2008). *Tombstone*. London: Allen Lane.

Zhao, Z. (2010). *Prisoner of the state*. London: Pocket Books.

Chapter 7
Majoritarian Democracy: The Catalyst of Populism

All reforms owe their origin to the initiation of minorities in opposition to majorities.
Mohandas Gandhi (Sigmund 1966: 81).

Abstract Things get changed for the better if first things go wrong. Things—votes for Brexit, Trump and so on—are now going wrong, not only because some people voted in favour thereof, but partly and maybe even largely because of the primitive voting procedures which were and still are used in these sorts of decisions and elections. It is not beyond our collective human wit, however, to realise the weaknesses of our current structures and to implement change, one of the most significant of which could be a more detailed definition in Charters of Human Rights of what is democracy, and a more comprehensive description of how decisions should be made.

7.1 The Science of Social Choice

Democracy is still so young. Maybe the human race is still quite immature as well; we are, after all, only a few hundred thousand years old. At this stage of our evolution, the main success story of democracy is that its introduction has facilitated bloodless hand-overs of power. Compared to many of the violent events of earlier centuries, that is no mean achievement. On the downside, however, voting processes—both referendums and/or elections—have often been provocations to violence, and not only in those countries discussed in this book.

One fact stands clear above all others: as noted in the text, many people in politics do not have a sound understanding of voting theory; secondly, there is a general antipathy towards anything even vaguely mathematical. Instead there is just the general assumption that, if the people have voted, *ergo*, the social choice from that

© Springer Nature Switzerland AG 2020
P. Emerson, *Majority Voting as a Catalyst of Populism*,
https://doi.org/10.1007/978-3-030-20219-4_7

ballot, be it a decision or an election, is democratic, regardless of the counting methodology used.

Now as was noted in Chap. 3 (Sect. 3.3.1), Kenneth Arrow's 'impossibility theorem' (Arrow 1963) states that 'nothing is perfect', that no vote counting formula can always be 100% accurate... which is perhaps true. In responding to any arguments in favour of change, however, some politicians refer directly or by implication to this theorem, thereby to suggest that one voting procedure is as good as another, which is just nonsense. Both in decision-making and in elections, some voting systems are good while others are poor and a few are downright hopeless—(dividing phenomena into three or more is often wiser than any simple binary split).

7.2   A Western Dissident

To many people, majority voting seems to be so obviously correct. After all, or so it seems, the world is binary: night follows day, tides ebb and flow, electrons are positive or negative, and so it goes on. In a similar fashion, human values fall into two categories: fair or foul, right or wrong, guilty or innocent, with eventual consequences for everybody, we are told, in the ultimate pair of opposites, heaven and hell. Furthermore, few would dispute that minority rule was often wrong, and our ancestors certainly suffered more than enough at the hands of the monarchs of old and the dictators of more recent years. It is all too easy to conclude, therefore, that its supposed opposite, majority rule, is not only right but is a right, that this is an indisputable fact, an unquestionable truism.

Partly as a consequence, the term 'majority rule' is used ubiquitously. But the question, "What is majority rule?"—according to the dictionary definition—"is a deep and still unresolved question," (McLean and McMillan 2003: 329), and its authors advise their readers to refer to other sections of their dictionary such as "Borda" and "Condorcet" (*ibid*). Maybe this complexity is the reason why human rights lawyers are so reluctant to get involved, so when writing charters on democratic rights,[1] they talk of elections without discussing the detail of various electoral systems, and they rarely if ever even mention the various methodologies of decision-making. But they should.

---

[1] According to Article 21 of the UN Declaration of Human Rights:

1. Everyone has the right to take part in the government of his country, directly or through freely chosen representatives.
2. Everyone has the right to equal access to public service in his country.
3. The will of the people shall be the basis of the authority of government; this will shall be expressed in periodic and genuine elections which shall be by universal and equal suffrage and shall be held by secret vote or by equivalent free voting procedures.

Meanwhile, in society at large, many people refer to the "right of a majority to rule" and "the right of self-determination" (Sect. 1.4) as if such definitions as do exist were water-proof. They are not. Indeed, as was seen in the Balkans (Sect. 5.6.2) and elsewhere, relevant documents like the Helsinki Final Act have sometimes been a source of conflict rather than a guideline to facilitate resolution let alone reconciliation.

Despite our collective inability to be more specific on these matters, Euro-centricity has tended to produce diplomats and others who are convinced that the West knows best. We applaud those who dissent in regimes which we consider are so obviously wrong—yesterday's Soviet Union and today's China and the even more authoritarian North Korea—but we tend to ignore those of our own dissidents who dare to question the basic tenet that majority rule is founded on decisions taken by the primitive and divisive methodology of majority voting.

Paradoxical though it may sound, however, majority rule should not be based on majority votes. Nor should so many objects be divided into pairs of opposites, and not least because some couples are complements. The most obvious example is male and female, and a human of one gender cannot (pro)create without the other. In like manner, democracy is for everybody, and not just for one (social, let alone religious or ethnic) group in society. In divided societies, therefore, phrases like 'democratic Unionists' or 'democratic Serbs' are oxymorons (Sects. 4.2.3 and 5.2.2). And in all societies, any binary political structure is at best inappropriate; it implies a win-or-lose polity which, by definition, is for the victors and not the vanquished; so it too is not for everybody, and is not, therefore, in its ideal sense, democratic.

Democracy should be based on win–win voting procedures. A democratic deci-sion should not be the will of just one faction in society let alone that of just one individual party leader; rather, it should be the product of a confluence of ideas, the distillation of numerous opinions, a collective wisdom. The identification of such cannot best be facilitated by means of a decision-making process which is only binary; but it can be done by means of a preferential vote. Majority rule should be based on pluralism.

7.3   Evolution

In some histories, if there are any hidden fault-lines in regimes or institutions when they are established, the effects of these weaknesses gradually get worse and worse until at last people come to the realisation that change is an imperative. A simple example relates to the demise of FPTP in New Zealand where, as a consequence of some ridiculously unfair election results, public pressure built up to such an extent that a Royal Commission was established and, as a consequence, the people were able to choose a better system, MMP (Sect. 4.4.3.1).

Some fault-lines are more serious. Democracy, it seems, is becoming less and less relevant to the most powerful in the world, the major corporations. Or maybe it's worse: the corporations are taking over. In the US at least, "the costs of electoral campaigns [have] skyrocketed, driving the parties into the pockets of concentrated capital," (Chomsky 2017: 52), and the various aspects of a democratic way of life—elections and parliaments, etc.—are little more than an inconvenience, like a rainy day. But "how can you convince politicians to vote for reforms designed to free them from the binds of corporate influence when those binds are still tightly in place?" (Klein 2014: 152). It is indeed a huge problem.

The bigger fault-lines, however, may be even more calamitous. If a country uses divisive voting procedures, it may well divide. If a society is not already divided when majority voting and/or a two-party political structure are introduced, it may then split; if it is already divided, such an event may well exacerbate that division. The first was Brexit; the second happened in the Balkans. Indeed, as a result of the Brexit referendum, England is now more divided and more racist than ever, with arguments on immigration a huge contributory factor. Likewise in the US, the divisive electoral system has now reached—to use George Washington's words (Sect. 3.2)—its "frightful and despotic" *denouement*—Trump. It surely cannot, but probably will, get worse.

If they were not apparent before, the fault lines are now, therefore, blindingly obvious. The success of Trump in the USA was a fake result, largely the result of the US electoral system of FPTP (Sect. 2.1.3). Brexit in the UK was another distorted outcome, the product of a binary poll, an "*A*, yes or no?" choice disguised as an "*A* or *B*?" question. And, as may well be seen in the forthcoming Euro-elections of May 2019, the rise of the right in continental Europe is worse than it should be, partly as a result of single-preference electoral procedures. In a nutshell, these disasters are all, in part, the products of inaccurate voting procedures. These are the fault lines.

Despite everything, I remain the optimist. And the hope of this book is that these recent events—the growth of populism in Western Europe, the nonsense of the Brexit referendum, and the election of two extremists in the Americas, Trump in 2016 and now Jair Bolsonaro in Brazil—will make people come to the conclusion that binary voting in decision-making, that single-preference electoral systems like FPTP and most varieties of PR-list, along with power-dividing systems of governance, are not only inadequate, inappropriate and inaccurate; it's worse than that; they are downright dangerous.

The fear is that populism will grow; that right-wing parties may well take over; that with rising sea levels in the Bay of Bengal, for example, the next refugee crisis will show that European civilisation simply cannot cope. And authoritarianism of a Chinese hue could well take over.

The hope however, which can overcome this fear, is that our democratic structures will evolve from their current divisive nature into a more inclusive, compassionate and consensual polity; that the advent of computers into the debating chambers of this world will facilitate a more sophisticated political dialogue (or rather 'polylogue') and thereby cause the collapse of the party whip system and the whole system of party political patronage; and finally, to ensure our collective survival, that charters on human rights will be written to stress, not only that consensus is right, but also that collective and all-inclusive decision-making is a universal democratic right, as too is a form of governance based on all-party power-sharing.

References

Arrow, K. (1963). *Social choice and individual values*. London: Yale University Press.

Chomsky, N. (2017). *Who rules the world*. London: Penguin Books.

Gandhi, M. K. (1966). Indian home rule. In P. E. Sigmund (Ed.), *The ideologies of the developing nations*. New York: Frederick A. Praeger.

Klein, N. (2014). *This challenges everything*. London: Allen Lane.

McLean, I., & McMillan, A. (2003). *Oxford concise dictionary of politics*. Oxford: OUP.

Annex A
Another Profile

A.1   A Five-option Profile

The analysis of the two voters' profiles of Tables 1.2 and 1.4 showed how the use of different vote counting methodologies can produce different outcomes. There is one further methodology which deserves an analysis, the Condorcet rule. Hence Table A.1, which is Table 1.4 with the addition of a new possible compromise, option *E*, the proposal of a new single participant. Initially, remember, there was just a dozen people debating the three options of Table 1.2; then two people suggested option *D*, which all twelve voters thought was quite a good idea; and now, another newcomer has proposed option *E*, which is also viewed very positively: it is the 2nd or 3rd preference of all the other 14.

An initial inspection of this voters' profile would suggest option *A* is still extremely divisive; that option *C* is not much better; that *B*'s popularity varies somewhat; that *D* is held in a rather better regard; and that now option *E* best represents everyone's consensus. So perhaps *E* is the new social choice; and maybe *E-D-B-C-A* is the latest social ranking. But what happens in practice?

Table A.1 15 Voters' profile on five options

Preferences	Number of voters				
	5	3	1	2	4
1st	*A*	*B*	*E*	*D*	*C*
2nd	*E*	*D*	*B*	*E*	*E*
3rd	*D*	*E*	*C*	*B*	*D*
4th	*B*	*C*	*D*	*C*	*B*
5th	*C*	*A*	*A*	*A*	*A*

© Springer Nature Switzerland AG 2020
P. Emerson, *Majority Voting as a Catalyst of Populism*,
https://doi.org/10.1007/978-3-030-20219-4

In a plurality vote, the result is *A*-5, *C*-4, *B*-3, *D*-2 and *E*-1; so the winner is still *A*.

A TRS ballot would produce a second round majority vote between *A* and *C*, which doubtless *C* would win, *A*-5, *C*-10.

In AV stage (i), the score is *A*-5, *C*-4, *B*-3, *D*-2, *E*-1, so that's the demise of *E* for a stage (ii) score of *A*-5, *C*-4, *B*-4, *D*-2. Stage (iii) sees *D*'s votes go (not to the eliminated *E* but) to *B*, for a score-line of *A*-5, *C*-4, *B*-6. And hence stage (iv), *A*-5, *B*-10, and the winner is now *B*.

In an MBC (Sect. 1.6.1)—5 points for a 1st preference, 4 for a 2nd, 3 a 3rd etc.—the scores are:

$$A = (5 \times 5) + (0 \times 4) + (0 \times 3) + (0 \times 2) + (10 \times 1) \quad = \quad 25 + 0 + 0 + 0 + 10 \quad = \quad 35$$
$$B = (3 \times 5) + (1 \times 4) + (2 \times 3) + (9 \times 2) + (0 \times 1) \quad = \quad 15 + 4 + 6 + 18 + 0 \quad = \quad 43$$
$$C = (4 \times 5) + (0 \times 4) + (1 \times 3) + \times (5 \times 2) + (5 \times 1) \quad = \quad 20 + 0 + 3 + 10 + 5 \quad = \quad 38$$
$$D = (2 \times 5) + (3 \times 4) + (9 \times 3) + (1 \times 2) + (0 \times 1) \quad = \quad 10 + 12 + 27 + 2 + 0 \quad = \quad 51$$
$$E = (1 \times 5) + (11 \times 4) + (3 \times 3) + (0 \times 2) + (0 \times 1) \quad = \quad 5 + 44 + 9 + 0 + 0 \quad = \quad 58,$$

so the MBC social choice is *E*.

Finally Condorcet, which as was said earlier (Sect. 1.1.5), compares all the options in ten pairings: *A:B*, *A:C*, *A:D* and *A:E*; *B:C*, *B:D* and *D:E*; *C:D* and *C: E*; and *D:E*. They are best shown as in Table A.2.

All the shadings indicate which option has won which pairing, so reading horizontally, the scores are *E*-4, *D*-3, *B*-2, *C*-1, *A*-0, and as shown in Table A.3, the Condorcet winner is option *E*.

Table A.2 The Condorcet count

-	A	B	C	D	E
A	-	5	5	5	5
B	10	-	11	4	3
C	10	4	-	5	4
D	10	11	10	-	5
E	10	12	11	10	-

Table A.3 The Condorcet social ranking

-	A	B	C	D	E	Social Ranking
A	-	5	5	5	5	0
B	10	-	11	4	3	2
C	10	4	-	5	4	1
D	10	11	10	-	5	3
E	10	12	11	10	-	4

Table A.4 Five different options and four different outcomes

Voting procedure	Social choice	Social ranking and scores				
Plurality voting	*A*	*A*-5	*C*-4	*B*-3	*D*-2	*E*-1
TRS	*C*	*C*-10	*A*-5	–	–	–
AV	*B*	*B*-10	*A*-5	–	–	–
MBC	*E*	*E*-58	*D*-51	*B*-43	*C*-38	*A*-35
Condorcet	*E*	*E*-4	*D*-3	*B*-2	*C*-1	*A*-0

A.2   A Comparison

The results of each analysis are displayed in Table A.4.

In this as in so many profiles, the Condorcet social choice is the same as the MBC social choice—{*the champion does indeed have the best goal difference*—(Sect. 1.1.5)}—and even the two social rankings, ***E-D-B-C-A***, are the same. Here too, this correct answer is the exact opposite of the plurality vote social ranking. As said earlier, plurality voting can sometimes be horribly wrong and occasionally, as in Tables 1.2 and 1.4 and here too in this voters' profile, it could not be more wrong!

Annex B
Partial Voting in an MBC

B.1 A Free Vote with Full Ballots

There will undoubtedly be some parliamentary votes or referendums when, for whatever reasons—of principle, religious belief or whatever—some MPs or members of the public may choose to abstain. In like manner, others may decide to submit a partial vote, casting preferences on only some of the options listed. That too is their prerogative. So how should such ballots be counted?

Recall what happened when a dozen voters cast their preferences in Table 1.2, which is here repeated as Table B.1 while the analyses of Table 1.3 are duplicated in Table B.2.

Table B.1 A dozen voters' profile with full ballots

	The 12 voters		
Preferences	5	3	4
1st	*A*	*B*	*C*
2nd	*B*	*C*	*B*
3rd	*C*	*A*	*A*

Table B.2 Three different options and three different outcomes

Voting procedure	Social choice	Social ranking and scores		
Plurality voting	*A*	*A*-5	*C*-4	*B*-3
TRS	*C*	*C*-7	*A*-5	–
AV	*C*	*C*-7	*A*-5	–
BC	*B*	*B*-27	*C*-23	*A*-22

© Springer Nature Switzerland AG 2020
P. Emerson, *Majority Voting as a Catalyst of Populism*,
https://doi.org/10.1007/978-3-030-20219-4

B.2   A Free Vote with Partial Ballots

Consider what happens if, say, the four C supporters submit partial ballots by casting only their 1st preferences; the corresponding voters' profile is shown in Table B.3.

There is no change to a plurality vote analysis of course; it is still A-5, C-4, B-3, so the winner is still A. With TRS and AV, again, there is no change: C-7, A-5. With the Borda rule, however, the difference is significant.

The top shaded row of Table B.4, the full ballots analysis, is taken from Table B.2. But now, with the partial votes of Table B.3, if the $(m, m–1 \ldots 1)$ rule (a) (Sect. 1.6) is used, the outcome is B-19, A-18, C-15. If, however, the preferences are counted according to the BC rule (b) of $(n, n–1 \ldots 1)$, the scores are C-23, B-19, A-18; and while the scores under rule (c) $(n–1, n–2 \ldots 0)$, are smaller than those of rule (b), the social ranking under either rule (b) or rule (c) is, of course, the same.

The conclusion is clear: if the count is conducted according to the rules laid down for an MBC, by submitting only partial votes, the C voters will have shot themselves in the foot: in an MBC with full ballots, C came second (Table B.2), but now, having submitted only partial ballots, it comes last! A simple {rule (b) or (c)} BC, however, would reward the C voters' intransigence.

Table B.3 A dozen voters' profile with some partial ballots

Preferences	The 12 voters		
	5	3	4
1st	A	B	C
2nd	B	C	–
3rd	C	A	–

Table B.4 Three Borda analyses of Table B.3

MBC	B	B-27	C-23	A-22
Voting Procedure	Social Choice	Social Ranking and Scores		
MBC {rule (a)}	B	B-19	A-18	C-15
BC {rule (b)}	C	C-23	B-19	A-18
BC {rule (c)}	C	C-15	B-11	A-10

B.3   Comparing the MBC to the BC

When comparing an MBC to a BC, there is of course no difference at all if every voter has submitted a full ballot. The difference comes only when some or all of the voters submit partial ballots.

Table B.5 compares the two analyses of Tables B.1 and B.3. The two shaded columns show that, when everybody submits full ballots, there is no difference at all in the BC or MBC social choices or social rankings.

Table B.5 A comparison of Tables B.1 and B.3

Voting Procedure	B.1 Social Choice	B.3 Social Choice	B.1 Social Ranking and Scores			B.3 Social Ranking and Scores		
MBC {rule (a)}	*B*	*B*	*B*-27	*C*-23	*A*-22	*B*-19	*A*-18	*C*-15
BC {rule (b)}	*B*	*C*	*B*-27	*C*-23	*A*-22	*C*-23	*B*-19	*A*-18
BC {rule (c)}	*B*	*C*	*B*-15	*C*-13	*A*-10	*C*-15	*B*-11	*A*-10

With partial voting, however, as shown in the two B.3 columns, un-shaded, the differences can be considerable: the MBC winner is not the same as the BC winner! Admittedly, if rule (b) or rule (c) is used in the Table B.3 analysis, then, as shown in the bottom two rows of Table B.5, it is to *C*'s advantage to submit only partial votes, for *C* now wins... which is why de Borda was so much in favour of rule (a).

B.4   Conclusion

If all the voters submit full ballots, the MBC results from Table B.2 are:

$$B\text{-}27, C\text{-}23, A\text{-}22.$$

If the *C* supporters submit only partial ballots, casting only a 1st preference, the MBC results from Table B.4 are:

$$B\text{-}19, A\text{-}18, C\text{-}15.$$

and *C* goes from being second to third.

If instead the 5 *A* supporters truncate their votes while the other 3 + 4 voters hand in the same full ballots from Table B.1, the scores are:

$$C\text{-}18, B\text{-}17, A\text{-}12,$$

so *A*, having been a close third, would now be a very poor third.

Lastly, if the *B* voters had been the only ones to submit partial votes, the final outcome would have been:

$$B\text{-}21, A\text{-}19, C\text{-}17,$$

so instead of winning by four points, it would now win by only two.

And if all three sets of voters submit only their 1st preferences, the whole thing morphs into a plurality vote, which as noted is what M de Borda bitterly opposed. So, to comply with his teachings, the methodology should be that of an MBC.

In a nutshell, with an MBC, it always pays to submit a full set of preferences, that is, to participate in the democratic process and to the full. Furthermore, the experience of the de Borda Institute shows that, on most occasions, most people do indeed cast full or nearly full ballots. An interesting example in this regard was a vote held in Dublin City Council in 2013, even though the count used was a BC.[1]

---

[1] http://static1.1.sqspcdn.com/static/f/220414/24541246/1429003665077/Report+on+Rosie +Hackett+decision-final2.pdf?token=DeQMcqXZNHhxik2Fld9A3eqZDeA%3D

Annex C
Taking an MBC Decision

C.1 The Rules of Debate

If the debate is taking place in a parliamentary setting, it may be assumed that Mr/Ms Speaker has already been appointed to oversee the proceedings. To assist this chair, a team of, say, three 'consensors' may also be elected.

Prior to the debate, a problem may have arisen and maybe a motion has already been promulgated. Any parties wishing to advocate an alternative motion may do so but, instead of proposing an amendment to one or other particular clause, they should re-word the proposal to make it a complete, alternative package {as in a constructive vote of (no) confidence, (Sect. 5.3.1)}. This can be shown by just highlighting that part which has now been changed.

Complete proposals will be accepted only if they comply with an agreed norm like the UN Charter of Human Rights.

The debate starts, therefore, with one or more options already 'on the table', and these the consensors will edit if necessary, to ensure all the proposals are in a similar format; accepted options shall then be displayed in summary on a computer screen and if need be in full on a dedicated web-site.

When the debate starts, with a fixed amount of time allocated to those who are moving a proposal and a smaller number of minutes given to those who wish to contribute to the debate, speakers can criticise, praise or query any part of any proposal, or even suggest something new; obviously, in most settings, any one party can move only one proposal. Then, during the course of the debate, if the original mover agrees, a proposal can be altered; if two movers join together, two proposals may be composited into one; and if all including the original mover are of one mind, a proposal may even be withdrawn. Accordingly, as the debate proceeds, the list of options may change, both in substance and in quantity.

If at the end of the day, everything boils down to just one option, this can be regarded as a verbal consensus and no vote need be taken. If however—and in many parliaments with the obvious exceptions of China and North Korea, this is a more

© Springer Nature Switzerland AG 2020
P. Emerson, *Majority Voting as a Catalyst of Populism*,
https://doi.org/10.1007/978-3-030-20219-4

likely scenario—there may still be some differences in the room, the chair may call for a vote. Accordingly, the consensors shall draw up a (short) list of about 4–6 options. The chair will confirm with all the movers that they accept this list, and then the MPs may cast their preferences as per the rules laid down in Sect. 1.6.

C.2   Analysing the Count

If one option has received a sufficiently high level of support—this measure, called a consensus coefficient, CC, is the option's MBC score divided by the maximum possible score—then that outcome may be declared to be the result. If two proposals are as it were neck-and-neck, the consensors may choose to form a composite of the two, and this too will doubtless have a good CC.

Consider first the theory. If x people participate in a hypothetical ballot of n options, and if all x submit full ballots and give option D, say, their 1st preference—and such a 1st preference means n points, of course—then D will get an MBC score of x.n points, the maximum. So that's a CC of 1.0. If all x give option C their last preference, C will get an MBC score of just x.1 points and a CC of x.1/x.n = 1/n.

Assume 30 people are casting preferences on 5 options: if option D gets 150 points, the maximum, it gets a CC of 1.0. If option C gets an MBC score of 30 points, the minimum, it gets a CC of only 0.2. While option A, for example, if it gets the 3rd preference of all 30, will get a mean MBC score of 90 and a CC of 0.60. In like manner, if 15 people give option B their 2nd preference, and 15 give it their 4th, then it will get a score of $15 \times 4 + 15 \times 2 = 60 + 30 = 90$, which again gives a CC of 0.60.

Now if one proposal gets a very high score, then obviously, some of the other scores will be fairly low. If, however, the 'winning' option gets a CC of 0.61, only just above the mean, then equally obviously, some if not all of the other options will be at about the same level; in which case there is no consensus so no decision should (yet) be taken.

But back to a success story: if the winner's CC is 0.9 or more, then it has near unanimous support. If it is 0.8 or so, then the word consensus might be appropriate. While a CC of just over 0.7 might signify that the winning option is only the best possible compromise. All of these levels, of course, must be laid down in standing orders and should apply to every debate, but they may vary a little, as implied in Table C.1, depending on the number of options to be voted on. Likewise, when the options can be laid out in a spectrum, the significance of different orderings of preferences must also be publicised, (Sect. 1.6.4), prior to the vote, so that when casting their preferences, the voters can know how particular sets of preferences will be interpreted. It is also the consensors' job to display all the various options and their scores, and of course to determine the outcome.

If success proves to be elusive, the chair might choose to resume the debate, not least in a search, as can happen in any negotiation process, for other options. It may

Table C.1 Consensus coefficients (assuming full ballots)

Number of options	Maximum CC	Mean CC	Minimum CC
3	1.0	0.67	0.33
4	1.0	0.63	0.25
5	1.0	0.60	0.20
6	1.0	0.58	0.17
7	1.0	0.57	0.14
8	1.0	0.56	0.13
9	1.0	0.55	0.11
10	1.0	0.55	0.10

be that the inconclusive ballot nevertheless showed that some options were marginally more popular than others, in which case the vote may be regarded as a straw poll, and any further discussions might be concentrated on the former set. No matter what the outcome, a ballot should always be useful.

C.3   Partial Voting

The scenario described above relates to those occasions when all the voters submit full ballots. In a different setting, if all 30 voters gave option B a 1st preference in partial votes of only one preference, then option B would get an MBC score of only $30 \times 1 = 30$ points, and a corresponding CC of 0.2... which would not be enough for that option to then be adopted. For a decision to be taken in consensus voting, (not necessarily all but many) voters must be consensual.

If furthermore all 30 voters gave option E, say, no preferences at all, then E would get the absolute minimum score of 0 points and a CC of 0.

So an option's CC is a measure, not only of that option's support amongst those voting, but also of the degree to which the given electorate has participated in the whole decision-making process. With an MBC, therefore, as noted above, standing orders should state what is the minimum CC required for a decision.

C.4   The Result

No matter what the outcome, the voters' profile and their social ranking may be displayed, as well as the consensors' analysis: the outright winner or the winning composite. In a parliamentary setting, if the debate has involved a spectrum of options, (Sect. 1.1.4), the web-page should also show the curves, single-peaked or otherwise, of all the MPs.

Annex D
Range Voting

D.1 An Analysis

It is often claimed that range voting is easy to understand and use. But is it? After all, in a 3-option vote on options *A, B* and *C*, in which the voter is allowed to distribute only 1 point, there are of course just 3 ways of voting: *A, B* or *C*. If given 2 points to distribute, the choice goes up to 6: either 2 points to *A, B* or *C*, or 1 point to each of the three pairs, *A-B, A-C* or *B-C*.

Next, with 3 points, there are in fact 9 ways of voting:

3-0-0; 2-1-0; 2-0-1; 0-3-0; 1-2-0; 0-2-1; 0-0-3; 0-1-2 and 1-0-2. (There is also the possibility of voting 1-1-1, but that of course would have no effect on the subsequent social ranking.)

With 4 points on 3 options, there are 15 ways of voting; with 5 points to distribute, it goes up to 21; with 6, the total is 28... and so on... and with 10 points to play with, the voter has 55 different ways of voting.

With 3, 4, 5 or 6 points to disperse on 4 options, the choice is of course greater: and there are now, respectively, 20, 34, 52 and 74 possible voting patterns.

With the same 3, 4, 5 or 6 points on 5 options, the degrees of choice increase, again respectively, to 35, 65, 105 and 155.

Now the number of points to be allocated may vary, but a figure which is often suggested is 10 points. In this case, with 3, 4, 5 or 6 options on the ballot paper, the voter will have a choice of 55, 202, 455 and 851 possibilities. In contrast, an MBC on 3, 4, 5 or 6 options offers the voter 6, 24, 120 and 720 ways of voting. Furthermore, an MBC seldom varies, but the choice involved in range voting depends very much on the number of points to be allocated.

On balance, then, the MBC is easier to understand. Its main advantage over range voting is the much more important fact that, while the MBC encourages the voter to acknowledge the validity of his/her neighbours' aspirations—or at least, those which

P. Emerson, *Majority Voting as a Catalyst of Populism*,
https://doi.org/10.1007/978-3-030-20219-4

are listed on the ballot—range voting incentivises selfish behaviour. Indeed, as was noted earlier, (Sect. 1.2), a voter with 10 points to distribute could 'plonk' them all onto just one option... and if everyone does that, the mechanism morphs into a plurality vote which, as shown in Chap. 1, is next to useless.

Annex E
A More Complicated Matrix Vote

E.1   A Second Example: The Ballot

Consider, not the simple example of Chap. 3, (Sect. 3.3.2), but a more complex scenario in which a parliament of 100 MPs, again representing parties **W, X, Y** and **Z,** now with 40, 30, 20 and 10 seats each, seeks to elect an all-party power-sharing administration of 12 members, as listed in Table E.1—the original six ministries of Table 3.2 plus six new posts. Let it now be assumed that parties tend to act, not in a fixed relationship with another party, but more independently; that parties continue to operate without a whip, that or party members defy it, so not every MP does as the party might wish, and some might just vote for themselves.

E.2   The Vote

The reader may recollect that a matrix vote count is conducted in two phases—the QBS election of the new cabinet members, and then the MBC appointment of each of them to a particular portfolio. As in the first simpler example, to facilitate the count in this more complex scenario, all the candidates' 1st preferences are counted; so are their 2nd preferences; and so too are their MBC scores. The QBS election, based on the voters' top preferences, identifies the 12 most popular candidates, and this data is recorded in the left-hand shaded column. Then comes the second phase, an MBC analysis of all the points scored in the matrix, the un-shaded part of the ballot paper, in which ministers are appointed to the corresponding ministry in descending according of the sums received in the matrix.

© Springer Nature Switzerland AG 2020
P. Emerson, *Majority Voting as a Catalyst of Populism,*
https://doi.org/10.1007/978-3-030-20219-4

Table E.1 A 12 × 12 matrix vote ballot paper

Preferences	Names of candidates	Prime Minister	Global Warming	Finance	Foreign Affairs	Home Affairs	Environment	Justice	Education	Defence	Overseas Aid	Health	Transport
1st													
2nd													
3rd													
4th													
5th													
6th													
7th													
8th													
9th													
10th													
11th													
12th													

In the simplest form of QBS election, (Sect. 2.5.1), remember, the analysis elects:

+ in stage (i), all candidates gaining a quota of 1st preferences;
    followed if need be...
+ in stage (ii), all pairs of candidates gaining two quotas of 1st/2nd preferences;
    followed if need be...
+ in stage (iii), one candidate from any pair of candidates (not including any candidates already elected) gaining one quota of 1st/2nd preferences;
    followed if need be...
+ in stage (iv), the candidate(s) with the highest MBC scores.

On completion of the election of the 12 cabinet members, the MBC analysis as in (Sect. 3.3.2.3) is based on the sums gained in the matrix, with each successful candidate being appointed to the appropriate ministry, in descending order of these sums, starting with the highest. There is the added proviso that, when two (or more) sums tie, priority is given to the more (or most) successful candidate(s) as per the QBS results (on the left-hand side of Tables E.3 and E.4); and if the sums still tie, priority is given to the ministry with the higher MBC score (in the bottom row).

Now as before, with 40% of the seats in parliament, party **W** may expect to win 40% of the 12 cabinet seats, which if all goes well would be 5 of them. On 30% of the parliamentary seats, party **X** could expect 3 or 4 cabinet posts; **Y** could hope for 2 or at best 3; and **Z** probably just the 1.

When it comes to the vote, most party members will doubtless vote for their own party nominees. Given, however, that parties are not working in formal coalitions, **W** and **Y** against **X** and **Z**, the party **Y** candidates may not get all the 6th preferences of all 40 **W** members, and the **W** nominees might not get all 20 of the party **Y** 3rd preferences. So the QBS social ranking will probably be a bit more mixed up, as too will the preliminary results.

Let it be assumed that every party is optimistic, that each hopes to get at least its quota of cabinet posts, and that the respective nominees are Wi, Wj, Wk, Wl and Wm; Xi, Xj, Xk and Xl; Yi, Yj and Yk, and finally Zi. Other party members might be Wn and Wo; Xm and Xn, etc. Let is also be assumed that:

- party **W** nominates Wi for the post of PM, Wj for Finance, Wk for Global Warming, Wl for Justice and Wm for Defence;
- party **X** nominates Xi for PM; Xj for Finance and Xk for Global Warming;
- party **Y** wants Yi for Overseas Aid and Yj for Defence; and finally,
- party **Z** hopes Zi will take on Transport.

So, lots of ministerial posts are being contested, not least that of PM. In addition, as stated (Sect. 3.3.2.2), a voter may cast not just one tick, but three: a gold, a silver and a bronze tick. If, then, in the count, the said candidate is not chosen for the ministry the voter has ticked in gold, the tick (points) will be transferred to the voter's silver slot, and if need be to the bronze. Needless to say, for any one candidate, not every gold tick supporter will have identical silver and bronze ticks.

In the average matrix vote count for a dozen representatives, there may be three of four such gold-to-silver transfers, not many more. So the count is not quite as complicated as this initial description might imply.

Now a member of party **W** might well cast her gold ticks as per Table E.2, with her silver ticks shown in brackets—and she would probably cast her silver ticks only for those of her own party. This example does not include any bronze ticks.

Table E.2 A W party MP's 12 × 12 matrix vote ballot paper

Preferences	Names of candidates	Prime Minister	Global Warming	Finance	Foreign Affairs	Home Affairs	Environment	Justice	Education	Defence	Overseas Aid	Health	Transport
1st	Wi	✓		(✓)									
2nd	Wj			✓	(✓)								
3rd	Wk		✓				(✓)						
4th	Wl							✓					
5th	Yi										✓		
6th	Yj								✓				
7th	Wm						✓						
8th	Yk									✓			
9th	Xj				✓								
10th	Zj					✓							
11th	Zi												✓
12th	Xk											✓	

E.3 The Count

The reader will know that in a full ballot in a 12-option/candidate MBC, a 1st preference is worth 12 points, a 2nd preference 11, a 3rd 10, and so on. So by the time all the data are collated, electronically, into Table E.3, the preliminary results might look quite complicated; but nothing will be too complex for the computer, of course.

With 100 persons electing 12 representatives, the quota is 8. Accordingly, with 40 voters, party **W** has 5 quotas, so if whipped, its MPs could give each of its five nominees a quota. Party **X**, with 30 voters, has 3 quotas and a further half-dozen 1st preferences—a possible bargaining chip for inter-party negotiations. Party **Y** has 2 quotas of 1st preferences and 4 'spare' 1st preferences. While **Z** has 1 quota and 2 left-overs. So in theory, parties **X** and **Z** could co-operate to get another candidate a quota. Or maybe **Y** with 4 left-overs would be a more reliable partner. The possible tactics are several.

In effect, as was noted in Sect. 3.3.2.3, the matrix vote allows and actually encourages the MPs, not only to submit a full ballot, but also to vote across the

Table E.3 The consolidated 12 × 12 matrix vote results

Preferences	Successful candidates	Prime Minister	Global Warming	Finance	Defence	Overseas Aid	Justice	Environment	Education	Foreign Affairs	Health	Home Affairs	Transport	MBC scores
1st	**Wi**	**600**	(100)	100 (300)				100		100 (100)				900
2nd	**Wj**			**500**		100			100	(300)	100			800
3rd	**Wk**		**500**			200	(400)							700
4th	**Xi**	400					100			**100** (300)	100			700
5th	**Yi**				100 (200)	300		100	100					600
6th	**Wl**						**400**			100				500
7th	**Wm**				300				100					400
8th	**Xj**			200			100		(250)		100			400
9th	**Xk**		250			50 (200)		100						400
10th	**Yj**				300	(200)								300
11th	**Xl**							50				200	50	300
12th	**Zi**							50	50				100	200
totals for 12		1000	750	800	700	650	600	400	350	300	300	200	150	6200
totals for all		1200	1100	1000	900	800	700	600	500	350	300	200	150	7800

party divide. And this, it is again suggested, is a pre-requisite of a good power-sharing governmental structure.

Let it be assumed, then, that the consolidated results are as shown in Table E.3, with the 12 successful candidates shown in descending order (top to bottom) of QBS popularity in the now un-shaded left-hand column; with the ministries in descending order (left to right) of 'relative importance' named in the top row and scored down below; and with the allocated points sums shown in the matrix, the golden tick sums in regular print, the silver tick sums in brackets.

Assuming each voter casts a full ballot of twelve preferences, each exercises a total of $(12 + 11 + \ldots + 1)$ points $= 78$ points. So for 100 voters, the total exercised is 7800 points. 6200 were cast in support of successful candidates, so the remaining 1600 points went to the unsuccessful ones.

So W_i, for example, has received an MBC score of 900 points from gold ticks; 600 of them for the premiership, and 100 each for the three ministries of Finance, Environment and Foreign Affairs. And of these 900 gold points, 500 of them are also silver ticks, 300 for Finance and 100 each for Global Warming and Foreign Affairs. If and when golden ticks are transferred as silver ticks to a new ministry, they are added to any sum already in this new destination.

As stated, the MBC analysis takes place in descending order, based on the sums in the matrix. The largest sum in Table E.3 is 600, in bold dark tint in the top-left-hand corner of the matrix, which means W_i becomes the PM. All the other data shown in the W_i row of the matrix, shown in an above average tint, is now irrelevant, while any other golden ticks in the PM column, like X_i's 400, can now be transferred as per their silver allocation; in the instance of X_i, 300 golden ticks are transferred as silver ticks to Foreign Affairs, giving X_i a total of 400 for this ministry. But this sum of 400 must wait awhile. . .

. . .for the next highest sum is 500, and there is a tie of two 500 sums, again shown in a dark tint. But there is no contention: the first 500 sum is for W_j to take on Finance, and the second 500 is for W_k to take on Global Warming. So that's three posts filled and a lot more data, shown in a very light tint, are again no longer required.

X_i's 400 is next, for Foreign Affairs, as is W_l's 400 for the Department of Justice. Again, there is no contention, so both are successfully appointed; these sums are also shown tinted in bold.

The next largest sum is 300, of which there are three shown shaded but in regular type: one is for Y_i to take Overseas Aid, so that's done; and two for W_m and Y_j who thus tie for the post of Defence; as per the rules, it therefore goes to the more popular candidate, who is W_m. So far, then, seven ministers have been appointed.

The next highest sum is 250— all silver ticks from Finance and Justice—so X_j gets Education; then with 200, X_l gets Health; while on 100, X_k gets Environment and Z_i gets Transport, leaving Y_j to get Home Affairs by default.

E.4   The Result

The final results are shown in Table E.4: an all-party power-sharing coalition of a dozen cabinet members, five from party **W**, four belonging to **X**, two to **Y** and one to **Z**. The candidates are already in descending order of QBS popularity, which might not quite coincide with the MBC scores in the right-hand column because of the quota. This final matrix probably appears as a rough diagonal.

One possible disadvantage of the matrix vote is that, as in this example, the last appointment(s) may be made by default. In a parliament of hundreds, however, this is highly unlikely. In any case, as noted earlier, this applies to the least important ministries and the least popular ministers, so hardly a serious flaw. It might also be speculated that the chances of a tie for any one appointment are also extremely low; nevertheless, if they do occur, the rules as stated above can cope with any such eventuality.

It should also be pointed out that the bottom row of MBC scores indicates not only the relative importance of the various ministries, for it may be that certain posts are hotly contested, while others are not so contentious. This row of data is therefore, (Sect. 3.3.2.3), only an indication.

Table E.4 The final 12 × 12 matrix vote results

Preferences		Ministers of…												MBC golden scores
Successful candidates		Prime Minister	Global Warming	Finance	Defence	Overseas Aid	Justice	Environment	Education	Foreign Affairs	Health	Home Affairs	Transport	
1st	Wi	600												900
2nd	Wj			500										800
3rd	Wk		500											700
4th	Xi									400				700
5th	Yi					300								600
6th	Wl						400							500
7th	Wm				300									400
8th	Xj								250					400
9th	Xk							100						400
10th	Yj										0			300
11th	Xl											200		300
12th	Zi												100	200
MBC totals for 12		1000	750	800	700	650	600	400	350	300	300	200	150	6200
MBC totals for all		1200	1100	1000	900	800	700	600	500	350	300	200	150	7800

Glossary

NB Items marked § are described elsewhere in this glossary. Proper names are emboldened.

Absolute majority see majority.

AMS The additional member system is a semi-proportional electoral system based on one ballot and two counts, the first under FPTP in small constituencies, the second under PR-list in a few larger regional or one larger national constituency. See also MMP.

Approval voting ...is non-preferential. It can be used in decision-making or in a (non-PR) election. Voters vote for as many options/candidates as they wish; each 'approval' has the same value, and the option/candidate with the most approvals wins. See also range voting.

Arrow's theorem ...suggests a perfect voting mechanism, a perfectly accurate interpretation of any group of voters' preferences, is impossible; see impossibility theorem.§

Autocracy Rule by a minority of one, an autocrat.

AV (IRV, PV or STV) The *alternative vote* can be used in decision-making or in a (non-PR) election. It is a form of preference voting in which the electorate votes 1, 2, 3... for their 1st/2nd/3rd ... preferences, voting for as many or as few options/candidates as they wish. If in the count no option/candidate gets 50% + 1 of the 1st preferences, the least popular is eliminated and its votes are transferred according to its voters' 2nd or subsequent preferences. The process continues until an option/candidate gets or exceeds 50% + 1, or until only one option/candidate remains. See also PR-STV.

BC *Borda count.* This points system can be used in decision-making or in a (non-PR) election, although it is more suitable in the former application; for its use in PR§ electoral systems, see QBS. The BC is a form of preference voting in which the electorate votes 1, 2, 3... as in AV§. Where there is a choice of n-options/candidates, a 1st preference gets n points, a 2nd preference gets $n-1$, a 3rd preference gets $n-2$, and so on; the winner is the option/candidate with the most points. See also MBC.

© Springer Nature Switzerland AG 2020

P. Emerson, *Majority Voting as a Catalyst of Populism*,

https://doi.org/10.1007/978-3-030-20219-4

Binary A binary decision-making process is one in which every decision is a two-option, for-or-against choice, or a series of such majority votes. (See also binary majority rule.)

Block vote This is a (non-PR) electoral system of FPTP§ in multi-member constituencies where voters may support as many candidates as are to be elected. The term is also used to describe the vote of, for example, a trade union delegate, whose single vote may supposedly represent many members.

Borda See BC.

Citizens' Assembly A form of deliberative democracy, usually involving a hundred or more individuals.

Citizens' initiative This is a mechanism whereby a certain number of citizens can demand a referendum§ on a topic of their own choosing.

Coalition

 majority A majority coalition is a union of two or more parliamentary parties in a government which then commands a simple majority§ of seats in that parliament.

 minority A minority coalition is a union of two or more parliamentary parties in a government which fails to command a simple majority§ of seats in that parliament.

 grand A grand coalition involves the two biggest parties and thus enjoys a large majority of seats.

 all-party An all-party coalition is a power-sharing government involving all the main parliamentary parties.

Composite is an amalgam based on two or more compatible options/policies.

Condorcet A Condorcet count can be used in decision-making or in a (non-PR) election. The voters cast their preferences on the options/candidates, voting 1, 2, 3... as in AV§; in the count, pairs of candidates—pairings—are examined separately and in, say, a three-option contest, if A is more popular than B *and* if A is also more popular than C, then A is the Condorcet winner. See also paradox.

Confidence See vote of...

Confidence + supply In a hung parliament§ a big party may choose to rely on a much smaller party to vote with the big party on any important matter, and especially on a vote of confidence.

Consensor In consensus§ decision-making, the chair or facilitator may be assisted by a team of impartial *consensors* who monitor the debate in order to recommend which voting mechanisms if any are to be used, and which options are to be included on any relevant ballot paper.

Consensus See also consensus coefficient.

 verbal A verbal consensus is an agreement, sometimes taken after lengthy discussions and after all concerned have agreed to a compromise, without resort to a vote.

 votal An agreement taken (again, sometimes after lengthy discussions and) after all have agreed to identify their best compromise via an MBC§ vote is a consensus decision, if its CC is sufficiently high.

Consensus Coefficient, CC. If S_a is the MBC§ score of option A, if V is the valid vote§ and if n is the number of options/candidates to be voted on, the CC of option A, C_a, is defined by the formula:

$C_a = S_a/V.n$

That is, an option's CC is its MBC§ score divided by the maximum possible score; and it varies from bad to good, from zero to one.

Consensus voting The term applies to those inclusive methodologies in which the outcome is the most popular amongst everybody, and not necessarily just the majority. See also MBC, QBS and matrix vote.

Consociationalism ...is a form of government where decisions are taken by simultaneous majorities§ from both or all communities, eg. from both unionist and nationalist (Northern Ireland); from both Czech and Slovak (Czechoslovakia); from all three, Bosniak, Bosnian Croat and Bosnian Serb (Bosnia). In effect, every relevant grouping has the power of veto§.

Constituency A constituency is a geographical area represented by one or more elected representative(s). Single-seat constituencies are used in non-PR electoral systems; multi-member constituencies have two or more representatives. The word 'constituency' may also be used in a non-geographical sense, to describe a particular group of people who, *inter alia*, relate to one or more representatives.

Constructive vote ...of confidence. See vote.

Cycle See paradox of voting.

Deliberative democracy relates to a process in which a representative sample of citizens come together to deliberate on one or more topics. Its findings are usually regarded as non-binding. See also focus groups.

Democracy Rule by the people, *demos*. It can be direct as it was initially for certain rich males in ancient Greece and a few ministers in China, and/or indirect via an assembly of elected representatives.

consensual A consensual democracy is an all-party power-sharing§ polity involving representatives of all the main political parties/opinions, and in which decisions are taken in consensus§.

consociational A consociational democracy is rule by a cross-community all-party coalition§, in which dichotomies are resolved if and only if every grouping offers majority support.

majoritarian A majoritarian democracy is rule by a single party or coalition which has the support of a majority§ of elected representatives, and in which decisions are taken and/or ratified by majority vote.

d'Hondt See divisors.

Divisor system Both divisors and quotas§ are rules of thumb for allocating seats in PR-list§ elections according to party strengths. With the former, every party's vote total is divided by a prescribed set of divisors to give a series of descending sums. Seats are awarded to the parties with the highest resulting sums. Different sets of divisors include the following:

d'Hondt	1	2	3	4	....
St. Laguë	1	3	5	7	....
modified St. Laguë	1.4	3	5	7	....

So party **X** with 20 votes will have d'Hondt sums of 20, 10, 6.7, 5...; and party **Y** with 15 votes will have d'Hondt sums of 15, 7.5, 5... So if three seats are to be awarded, the three highest sums are 20, 15 and 10, so **X** gets two seats—20 and 10—while **Y** gets just one—15. In some profiles, different divisors may give marginally different results.

Droop See quota.

Dualism ...is a democratic structure in which decision-making is based on choices of only two options. There are, then, three categories of rule: dictatorship, dualism and pluralism§.

Electorate All those eligible to vote.

Filibuster A long speech, the main purpose of which is to obviate any vote.

FPTP *First-past-the-post* with two candidates is a majority vote§; with three or more candidates, it is a plurality vote§.

Focus groups A form of deliberative democracy, usually involving just a score or so of participants.

Franchise The right to vote in public elections, especially in state or parliamentary elections.

Gerrymander The 'art' of adjusting constituency boundaries so that a particular party benefits.

GNU A government of national unity is the same as an all-party coalition.

Grand coalition See coalition.

Hare See quota.

Hung parliament ...is one in which no one party has an absolute majority§ of seats.

Impossibility theorem *Inter alia*, a voting methodology should (i) not be vulnerable to manipulation by a dictator; (ii) be independent of irrelevant alternatives; and (iii) should allow the voters to cast their preferences as they please.

Irrelevant alternative If in a multi-option ballot, with say options *A, B, C* and *D*, the most popular option is *C*, then if the count is independent of irrelevant alternatives, *C* should still be the most popular option, even when one of the options like *A* is removed, or when another less popular option like *E*, and/or a clone like *B'*, is added to the ballot paper.

IRV (AV, PV or STV) *Instant run-off* is the name used in the Americas for AV.

Majoritarianism The belief in and/or practice of simple or binary majority rule§.

Majority See also coalition.

    absolute An absolute majority is 50% or more.

    consociational a double or triple majority from two or three constituencies.

    qualified A qualified majority is used in the EU where different countries have different numbers of votes depending on their size, and where the result depends on a certain weighting.

relative/simple Somewhat ambiguously, a relative/simple majority may be only the biggest minority.

weighted A weighted majority involves 2/3rds or some such other ratio greater than 1/2.

Majority rule Dualism§. Simple or binary majority rule is a form of democracy based on decision-making by majority vote. Pluralism§. When there are more than two options, however—which *should* be nearly always—the "two best interpretations of majority rule" rely on decision-making by MBC§ or the Condorcet§ rule.

Majority vote A vote with only two options/candidates—"*A* or *B*?"—or maybe only one—"*A*, 'yes-or-no'?"

Matrix vote The matrix vote is a PR§ electoral system by which an electorate can elect a fixed number of persons to be members of a team which may involve very different positions. It is ideally suited (a) for the election of the chairperson, secretary, treasurer, etc. at an association's AGM; and (b) for a power-sharing administration in which the parliament or assembly elects a cabinet or executive. In a parliamentary setting, the matrix vote is best based on a QBS§ election, to choose the most popular candidates, and then an MBC§ count of the same preferences to appoint these successful candidates to the various ministries.

MBC A *modified Borda count* can be used in decision-making or in a (non-PR) election. It allows for partial voting as follows: if someone casts (1st, 2nd... last) preferences for all n options/candidates, points are awarded as in a BC§: $(n, n{-}1, ..., 1)$ or, which is the same mathematically, $(n{-}1, n{-}2 ... 0)$; if, however, an individual votes for only m options/candidates, where $n \geq m \geq 1$, points are awarded according to the rule $(m, m{-}1, ... 1)$.

MMP *Mixed-member proportional* is a PR§ electoral system based on two votes and two counts, the first by FPTP§, the second under PR-list§. In many countries, the ratio of FPTP MPs to PR-list MPs, is 50:50.

Modified St. Laguë See divisors.

Multi-member See constituency.

Pairings See Condorcet.

Parallel Voting ... is a mixture of FPTP§ (or TRS§) plus PR-list§, but the overall result is not affected by the PR element and thus it differs from MMP§. Parallel voting is only semi-proportional.

Paradox of voting A paradox of [binary] voting or a cycle can occur when there are three or more persons taking majority votes on pairs of options from a list of three or more options. If, for example, in a 'society' of three people, Messrs j, k and l, Ms j has 1st-2nd-3rd preferences *A-B-C*, Mr k chooses *B-C-A*, and Ms l prefers *C-A-B*, then in any system of majority voting and if all three vote sincerely, *A* will be more popular than *B*, *B* more popular than *C*, and *C* more popular than *A*. This can be written as:

$A > B, B > C$ and $C > A$, or

$A > B > C > A > ...$

which goes on and on for ever.

Partial vote In a ballot in which the voter may cast (up to) n preferences, a ballot of only m options, where $n > m \geq 1$, is a partial vote. See MBC.

Party structure Depending on various factors, not least a country's electoral system, there are a number of different party structures:

no-party state every MP is an independent, as in Nauru;

one-party as in China, where one large party has a monopoly of power;

two-party as was in the UK, and as is in the USA, where power tends to alternate between two major parties;

one dominant as in Russia and Turkey, where one big party rules the roost from one election to the next;

multi-party as in many European countries, where half-a-dozen or more parties are represented in parliament;

all-party as in Switzerland, in which all the main parliamentary parties are in government; a GNU§.

Plebiscite A referendum§ usually on an important topic such as national sovereignty.

Plural society A society which includes two or more different ethnic and/or religious groups.

Pluralism or pluralist majority rule A democratic structure in which decision-making is based on choices of three or more options. In contrast, see dualism§.

Plurality The largest minority. See FPTP.

Plurality voting This is a decision-making system or a (non-PR) electoral system where the voter casts only one 'x'. If there are only two candidates, it is a majority vote§ and the option/candidate with a majority§ of the votes is the winner. With three or more (a plurality of) options/candidates, the option/candidate with the most votes wins; this may be an absolute majority of the votes, or it may be just the largest minority, a plurality.

Points system See BC/MBC.

Power-dividing Majority rule.

Power-sharing the opposite of power-dividing, and the term usually implies all-party power-sharing. Instead of the parliament dividing itself into two—government and opposition—an all-party power-sharing arrangement distributes the ministries among all the major parties and tries to take decisions in consensus.

PR *Proportional representation* refers to an electoral system which is designed to ensure that the number of party candidates (and sometimes independents) elected is in proportion to the number of votes gained. PR systems are used in multi-member constituencies§.

PR-list In PR-list elections, each party 'lists' its candidates in its own order of priority. Seats are awarded to parties on the basis of a divisor§ or quota§ system and, if party X wins n seats, then in a closed list system, the first n names from the top of the list are deemed elected; in an open system, success goes to the n most popular candidates.

PR-list closed An electoral system in which the voters vote for one party only.

PR-list open In the three main types of open PR-list electoral systems, the voter may choose either:

(i) one party or one candidate of that party, as in Bosnia;

(ii) one or more candidates of one party only, as in Belgium;

(iii) one or more candidates of one or more parties, as in Switzerland.

Profile, voters' A voters' profile is the set of all the 1st and subsequent preferences of all concerned.

PR-STV *Proportional representation—single transferable vote* is based on AV§. Candidates gaining the quota§ are deemed elected. Transfers take place, not only from candidates eliminated, but also from those elected with a surplus over and above the quota. PR-STV constituencies§ usually have from three to six elected representatives.

PV (AV, IRV or STV) *Preferential voting* is the name used for AV in Australasia.

QBS The *quota Borda system* is a PR§ electoral system based on an MBC§. The electorate votes by casting preferences, 1, 2, 3… as in AV§. In a multi-member constituency§ of four representatives, the count consists of two Parts, with two stages in each. If, after any stage, seats are still to be filled, the count proceeds to the next stage.

In Part I stage (i) of the count, any candidate gaining the quota§ of 1st preferences is elected.

In Part I stage (ii), if any pair of candidates gets two quotas of 1st/2nd preferences, both are elected.

In Part II, only those candidates who are still unelected are taken into counted.

In Part II stage (iii), any pair of candidates getting one quota of 1st/2nd preference is 'elected', the seat going to whichever candidate of the pair has the higher MBC§ score.

Finally, in Part II stage (iv), seats go to those candidates with the higher/highest MBC scores.

Qualified majority See majority.

Quorum A minimum number or percentage required for a sitting to be regarded as valid.

Quota In an electoral system, a quota is a specified number of votes which, if attained, ensures the election of the candidate concerned. The most common quotas are the Hare (which is defined as V, the valid vote§ divided by n, the number of seats), V/n; and the Droop {which divides V, the valid vote by $(n+1)$ the number of seats plus one}, $V/(n+1)$. See also divisor systems. Quotas can also apply to a minimum number of persons from a specific gender or ethno-religious group.

Range voting can be used in decision-making or in a (non-PR) election. The voter is given a fixed quantity of points which she can distribute as she wishes, either spreading them over a number of options/candidates or 'plonking' all the points on just one or a few options/candidates. See also approval voting.

Referendum A referendum or plebiscite§ is usually a two-option but sometimes a multi-option vote by which the electorate may decide a matter of policy. A multi-option referendum can be conducted under the rules of any one of a number of methodologies.

St. Laguë See divisors.

Sincere voting A voter is said to vote sincerely when she votes for those options/ candidates in her order of preference, without taking any tactical§ considerations into account. She is likely to act in this way if she thinks her preferred options/ candidates are also society's favourites and probably the winners.

Single-peaked preferences A voter's preferences are said to be single-peaked if, when the options are laid out on, say, a 'left-right' or cheap-expensive axis, his 2nd and subsequent preferences lie in descending order to one side and/or the other of his 1st preference.

SNTV *Single non-transferable vote*. This electoral system is semi-proportional. The voter casts only one preference, but the constituencies§ are multi-member.

Special voting The term used in Belgium for consociational§ voting.

STV (AV, IRV or PV) *Single transferable vote* is another name for AV; the term STV often applies to PR elections as PR-STV; in single-seat constituencies and in decision-making, AV is more generally used.

Suffrage See franchise.

Tactical voting A voter is said to vote tactically (as opposed to sincerely§) if, instead of casting preferences for her preferred option(s) or candidate(s) as she would have wished, she uses her preferences in a way that may result in what she hopes will be, for her, the least unfavourable outcome.

Threshold The threshold of an electoral system is the minimum percentage of votes required for a candidate to be elected; the effective threshold is usually the logical consequence of the mathematics of the specific electoral system concerned, while a legal threshold can be another laid-down minimum of, say, 5% as in Germany or 10% as in Turkey.

Top-up A top-up is the second part of an election count, applicable to some electoral systems in which votes are counted either in a different way and/or in a bigger constituency, usually to ensure a greater degree of overall proportionality.

TRS The *two-round system* of voting can be used in decision-making or in a (non-PR) election. The first round is a plurality vote§, and, if no one option/ candidate gains more than 50% support, the second round is a majority vote between the two leading options/candidates from the first round.

Turnout The number of people who, literally, turn out to vote; it is normally expressed as a percentage of the total electorate§.

Two-tier A two-tier electoral system consists of one election, which may be FPTP§ or PR§ in small constituencies, and a second election, which invariably is PR, in larger regional or national constituencies. Examples include Austria, which has a two-tier system based on closed list PR; the Swedish version is open list PR; while Germany's MMP consists of two votes, one under FPTP and the other under list PR.

Unanimity A decision is said to be unanimous if all concerned vote in favour. It is not to be confused with consensus§ although, on issues which are not contentious, the unanimous and consensus viewpoints, as too the majority and minority opinions, are all one and the same.

Valid vote The number of voters deemed to have filled in their ballot paper correctly, be it in full or only in part.

Veto The ability to prevent a policy being passed.

Vote of confidence or vote of no confidence. Normally a majority vote§ with regard to a government or a premier/chairperson; the vote is usually of the "*A*, yes or no?" variety. A constructive vote of no confidence is one in which an alternative must be offered: so the vote is "*A* or *B*?"

Weighted majority See majority.

Whip A party whip is an instruction from the party's leadership to its elected representatives to vote in a certain way. It may also be used to describe the functionary who issues such orders. Those who disobey may, as a result, lose the party whip and thus put their party membership (and careers) at risk.

Win-win A win-win decision is one in which (nearly) everybody wins something but nobody wins everything. It is the opposite of a zero-sum decision§.

Zero-sum A zero-sum decision places voters in a win-or-lose situation: some win and win everything, while others lose everything.

Index

© Springer Nature Switzerland AG 2020
P. Emerson, *Majority Voting as a Catalyst of Populism*,
https://doi.org/10.1007/978-3-030-20219-4

Printed by Printforce, the Netherlands